Basic Family Therapy

Fifth Edition

Philip Barker
MB, BS, FRCPsych, FRCP(C), DPM, DCH
Professor Emeritus of Psychiatry
University of Calgary

D0913487

Blackwell Publishing

Blackwell Publishing editorial offices:
Blackwell Publishing Ltd, 9600 Garsington Road, Oxford OX4 2DQ, UK
Tel: +44 (0)1865 776868
Blackwell Publishing Professional, 2121 State Avenue, Ames, Iowa 50014–8300, USA
Tel: +1 515 292 0140
Blackwell Publishing Asia Pty Ltd, 550 Swanston Street, Carlton, Victoria 3053, Australia
Tel: +61 (0)3 8359 1011

First published 1981 by Granada Technical Books
Second edition published 1986 by Collins Professional and Technical Books
Third edition published 1992 by Blackwell Scientific Publications
Fourth edition published 1998 by Blackwell Science
Fifth edition published 2007 by Blackwell Publishing

ISBN: 978-1-4051-4436-0

Library of Congress Cataloging-in-Publication Data
Barker, Philip, 1929–
Basic family therapy / Philip Barker. – 5th ed.
p. ; cm.
Includes bibliographical references and index.
ISBN-13: 978-1-4051-4436-0 (pbk. : alk. paper)
1. Family psychotherapy. I. Title.
[DNLM: 1. Family Therapy. WM 430.5.F2 B255b 2006]
RC488.5.B336 2006
616.89′156–dc22
2006020546

A catalogue record for this title is available from the British Library

Set in 10/12 pt Times
by SNP Best-set Typesetter Ltd., Hong Kong
Printed and bound in Singapore
by Markono Print Media Pte Ltd

The publisher's policy is to use permanent paper from mills that operate a sustainable forestry policy, and which has been manufactured from pulp processed using acid-free and elementary chlorine-free practices. Furthermore, the publisher ensures that the text paper and cover board used have met acceptable environmental accreditation standards.

For further information on Blackwell Publishing, visit our website:
www.blackwellpublishing.com

Contents

Dedication

Richard Miles, my publisher for some 25 years, died during the preparation of this book. It was largely because of Richard's enthusiastic support that the first edition of *Basic Family Therapy* saw the light of day in 1981. We worked together on the following three editions and also on five editions of *Basic Child Psychiatry*. Richard was one of the most helpful, supportive, warm and courteous people I have ever met. Knowing and working with him was a privilege and I will always treasure the wonderful memories I have of him.

Introduction

There have been many advances in the field of family therapy since the fourth edition of this book appeared 8 years ago. These have included new ways of working with families and new theoretical underpinnings for the work family therapists do. Previously accepted ideas have been re-examined and, sometimes, questioned. Family therapy is, as it has always been, a field that is in a continuing, but creative, state of flux.

There is no one way of helping families that are confronting problems. Not only do families' problems differ, but so also do the societies and cultures within which they exist. Recent years have seen an increasing acknowledgement by family therapists – reflected in many articles appearing in the family therapy journals – that flexibility and sensitivity to culture are essential to effective work in this field. And it is not only culture and societies' norms to which we must be sensitive. There are also specific problems that require special consideration and, often, special therapy techniques. Examples are families in which there are one or more members with substance abuse problems; those with 'acting out' adolescents; those in whom there are members with attachment disorders; and those attempting to deal with the aftermath of an episode of infidelity on the part of a marital partner. So, one size does not fit all.

Are there, in spite of the above considerations, some basic principles that are widely applicable? I believe there are, and in this edition of *Basic Family Therapy*, as in previous ones, I have tried to set these out as clearly as I can. My aim is to provide a clear, easy-to-read and readily understandable introduction to the subject. As the volume of available information on family therapy increases, I believe there is more need than ever for an eclectic introduction to the subject.

It is not possible to learn family therapy from a book. There can be no substitute for supervised practice. What a textbook such as this can offer is a basic orientation to the field and a guide to further reading. The ever-expanding literature on family therapy can be confusing to the newcomer. Moreover, many books on the subject are written from a particular theoretical viewpoint and/or reflect the work of a particular, often charismatic, therapist. These can be valuable contributions to the field, but they also have the danger of being one-sided.

I have aimed to be eclectic in my discussion of the family therapy field as it is today. There are various views of eclecticism. Some consider it a euphemism for a muddled approach based on unclear theoretical foundations. I do not see it this way. We need to have at our disposal a range of methods of intervening in families with different problems and aims. Families vary in the interventions to which they will respond positively. I have therefore tried to outline some of these. All the schools of therapy have something to contribute to the work we do with families. I have tried to define what each has to contribute. While every therapist must have a theory of change, and a clinical approach, I also offer, in Chapter 13, a method of working with families that the new therapist may find useful. In due course each therapist will develop her or his personal style and way of working.

The book has been extensively rewritten for this edition. Not only are new therapeutic techniques and theories discussed, but there is new material on cultural issues; on special therapeutic challenges; and on research, 'evidence-based' practice and the evaluation of outcomes. But perhaps one of the biggest changes, certainly since the first edition, is the increased emphasis on family therapy as a collaborative activity involving therapist and family as partners in the quest for solutions to the family's problems. No longer is the therapist someone who 'does' something, from a position of authority and as a person with special expertise, to bring about the desired changes; he or she is instead a partner in a joint enterprise, a trend that is occurring in many areas of medicine.

It is an ethical imperative that all of us who practise family therapy keep up to date with advances in the field and the latest research. In view of the quantity of new knowledge that becomes available month by month, this presents a challenge. We must continually examine the available literature so that we can evaluate the evidence for the effectiveness, or otherwise, of various possible clinical approaches. In Chapters 17 and 18 I have outlined ways of approaching what may seem to be a daunting task. A glance on a regular basis through at least a selected few of the many available family therapy journals need not take up a lot of time. You may then choose to read in full those articles that are of particular interest to you. Many journals are available online so you may not have to leave your office or home to do this.

Philip Barker

Chapter 1
The Development of Family Therapy

Family therapy emerged during the second half of the twentieth century, as an often potent means of helping individuals and families with a variety of problems. Until the 1950s the emphasis of psychiatrists and other psychotherapists was on the psychopathology and treatment of individuals. Even group therapy had as its main aim the resolution of the problems of the individuals in the group. While the importance of patients' environments was not denied, the current family environment of those seeking treatment was not looked upon as a possible focus for intervention.

The second half of the twentieth century also saw an increasing interest in larger systems in areas other than family therapy. By way of example let us see how this change affected the science of physics. Gleick (1988, page 6), in his book *Chaos*, wrote:

'The mainstream (of physics) for most of the twentieth century has been particle physics, exploring the building blocks of matter at higher and higher energies, smaller and smaller scales, shorter and shorter times. Out of particle physics have come theories about the fundamental forces of nature and about the origin of the universe. Yet some young physicists have grown dissatisfied with the direction of the most prestigious of sciences. Progress has begun to seem slow, the naming of new particles futile, the body of theory cluttered . . . the field had been dominated long enough, they felt, by the glittering abstractions of high-energy particles and quantum mechanics.'

Gleick (1988, page 7) goes on to say that:

'Understanding nature's laws on the terms of particle physics left unanswered the question of how to apply those laws to any but the simplest of systems. Predictability is one thing in a cloud chamber where two particles collide at the end of a race around an accelerator. It is something else altogether in the simplest tub of roiling fluid, or in the earth's weather, or in the human brain.'

We need only substitute 'psychotherapists' for 'physicists', 'individual psychotherapy' for 'particle physics', and 'family systems' for the various systems mentioned in the last sentence above, to get some idea how it is that family therapy has emerged as a major treatment modality. Working with individuals, and studying individual psychopathology, can carry us only so far. In child psychiatry, for example, it is commonplace to meet children who are perfectly behaved at home and exceedingly difficult at school; or fine with their grandparents but troublesome with their parents; or 'good' with one parent and 'bad' with the other. To explain such discrepancies we must consider not only the individual subject but also the systems of which that person is a part.

Understanding individuals tells us little about how they will behave in social situations of different sorts. Family therapists tend to see human problems in the context of their clients' environments, especially their families, although the wider systems of which families are a part are gaining increasing attention. They concentrate on interpersonal processes, rather than on those occurring within the minds of the individuals in the families they treat. We might think of them as traffic engineers whose job it is to see that vehicles travel smoothly on highways. Therapists with an 'intrapsychic' orientation would correspond to mechanics, whose concern is the internal workings of vehicles.

The fact of the matter, of course, is that good treatment may require both approaches, or at least the taking into account of both sets of factors. While the two types of therapy require different skills and training, and are based on different theoretical systems, the therapist should ideally have skills in both areas.

Among the first to point out the importance of the family in the therapeutic endeavour were Christian Midelfort who, in 1957, published *The Family in Psychotherapy*; and Nathan Ackerman, whose book *The Psychodynamics of Family Life* (1958) marked an important point in the development of family therapy. Ackerman pointed out that while psychiatrists had 'acquired adeptness in the retrospective study of mental illness, in the minute examination of family histories . . . they (had) not yet cultivated an equivalent skill in the study of family process here and now' (Ackerman, 1958, page 89). He went on to say that, by acquiring skills in working with whole family groups, we would come to have 'a new dimension to our insights into mental illness as an ongoing process that changes with time and the conditions of group adaptation'. Prophetic words, indeed!

The early years of family therapy

Prior to the Second World War, the response of psychiatrists to the difficulties their patients appeared to have in adapting to their family and social environments was often to remove patients from their families in order to ensure recovery in a setting away from the possible adverse effects of their family environments. This was often in a psychiatric hospital far away from their families; or if psychoanalysis was to be the treatment used, the transference relationship with the therapist was supposed to replace that with the actual family member(s) with whom the subject was believed to have difficulty.

After the publication of *The Psychodynamics of Family Life*, Ackerman's thinking developed gradually. His second book, *Treating the Troubled Family* (1966), is indeed a book about the treatment of 'the family as an organic whole'.

Other pioneers include John Elderkin Bell who, however, did not publish descriptions of his work until the early 1960s (Bell, 1961, 1962). His book *Family Therapy* did not appear until 1975.

In the 1950s several groups embarked on the investigation and/or treatment of subjects with schizophrenia and their families. In 1952 Gregory Bateson obtained a grant to study communication and its different levels. He was joined in 1953 by Jay Haley and John Weakland and by a psychiatrist, William Fry. In 1954 the group embarked on a 'Project for the Study of Schizophrenia'. Don Jackson joined this group as a consultant and as the supervisor of psychotherapy with patients with schizophrenia. The work of this group had a profound influence on the thinking of many family therapists. Bateson and his colleagues introduced the concept of the 'double-bind', discussed in a later section.

The Mental Research Institute (MRI) was founded by Don Jackson, in Palo Alto, California, in 1959. Although Jackson acted as consultant to the Bateson group, the MRI was a separate entity. It contributed much to the development of family therapy, and continued after Bateson's group disbanded in 1962.

Theodore Lidz (Lidz & Lidz, 1949) began studying the families of patients with schizophrenia at Johns Hopkins Hospital, Baltimore, in 1941, later moving to Yale University. He introduced the concepts of *schism*, the division of the family into two antagonistic and competing groups; and *skew*, whereby one partner in the marriage dominates the family to a striking degree, as a result of serious personality disorder in at least one of the partners.

Lyman Wynne started to study the families of schizophrenics shortly after he joined the staff of the National Institute of Mental Health in 1952. In 1972 he became Professor in the Department of Psychiatry at the University of Rochester, New York, and continued to study schizophrenic families until his retirement. He introduced the concepts of *pseudo-mutuality* and *pseudo-hostility*.

Pseudo-mutuality (Wynne et al., 1958) arises when an individual feels the need for a relationship with someone, perhaps because of painful earlier experiences of separation anxiety. A person in a pseudo-mutual relationship tries to maintain the idea or feeling that he or she is meeting the needs of the other person; in other words that there is a mutually complementary relationship. Those involved in pseudo-mutual relationships are predominantly concerned with fitting together at the expense of their respective identities. Genuine mutuality, by contrast, thrives upon divergence, the partners in the relationship taking pleasure in each other's growth. Each has a real wish that the other achieve fulfilment of desires and expectations. In pseudo-mutuality there is dedication only to the sense of reciprocal fulfilment, not to its actuality. With pseudo-hostility (Wynne, 1981), the apparent emotional relationship, in this case hostility, is a substitute for a true, intimate relationship, which is absent. Wynne and his colleagues concluded that the families of 'potential schizophrenics' are characterized by pseudo-mutuality and consequently have rigid, unchanging role structures which they cling to as essential.

Wynne et al. (1958) also introduced the idea of the 'rubber fence'. He described how the psychological boundary to the family moves, if it has to, to keep the individual family members confined within the system. The boundary itself, though it may move, is quite impervious to outsiders and new information. A consequence is that the children do not have normal and necessary experiences with people outside the family. Instead, there is a continual effort to maintain the family as a self-sufficient social system. The 'rubber fence' prevents members from psychologically leaving, even though the feelings and ideas acceptable within the family may constantly shift (Singer and Wynne, 1965).

Carl Whitaker, a psychoanalytically trained psychiatrist, had started experimenting with the treatment of family groups before he took up the Chair of Psychiatry at Emory University, Atlanta, in 1946. With John Warkentin and Thomas Malone he continued this work, developing his own distinctive approach to family therapy. Nichols (1984) later described Whitaker as 'strong-willed and colorful . . . dynamic and irreverent'. After resigning his university appointment in 1955, he continued in practice in Atlanta until 1965, developing his own, highly personal approach to therapy (Whitaker, 1958).

Ivan Boszormenyi-Nagy, another psychoanalyst turned family therapist, founded the Eastern Pennsylvania Psychiatric Institute in Philadelphia in 1957. With his colleagues, James Framo, David Rubenstein, Geraldine Spark and Gerald Zuk, Boszormenyi-Nagy developed an approach to family therapy that paid particular attention to its multigenerational aspects. He proposed the concept of 'invisible loyalties'. This was the title of a subsequent book of which he was co-author. He was one of a number of therapists who came to feel that work should not be limited to the nuclear family or to current transactions. Multigenerational linkages and the wider family system began to be taken increasingly into account.

Like Whitaker, Boszormenyi-Nagy and his colleagues made extensive use of co-therapy, the practice of having two therapists in the room with the family being treated. Boszormenyi-Nagy, together with Framo, edited the book *Intensive Family Therapy* (1965), the contributions to which surveyed much of the contemporary family therapy scene.

Two other important early pioneers were Murray Bowen and the British psychiatrist Ronald Laing. Bowen (1960) developed the concept of schizophrenia as a process requiring three generations to develop. Typically, he said, the grandparents were 'relatively mature but their combined immaturities were acquired by one child who was most attached to the mother' (Bowen, 1960, page 354). When such a child married an equally immature spouse the same process was repeated in the next generation. The result was one child who was very immature while the others were much more mature. Bowen believed that such a child is liable to develop schizophrenia in an attempt to adapt to the demands of growing up.

Laing also studied the families of schizophrenics. His findings concerning the first 11 patients and their families were reported by Laing and Esterson (1964) and his ideas were also set out in a chapter entitled 'Mystification, confusion and conflict' (Laing, 1965). He placed great emphasis on the concept of *mystification*. The term can be used both to describe the *act* of mystification and the *state* of mystification. The state of mystification is one of being befuddled and clouded. The mystified person feels masked from situations and finds them obscure. The act of mystification is what is done by others to bring about this state in a person. The person may or may not be aware of being befuddled, and so may not *feel* mystified.

Laing believed that some mystification occurs in everyday life. People sometimes deny the experience of others and replace it with their own. A mother may use a 'straight' way of telling her son to go to bed, saying for example that it is bedtime or that it is her function to determine when he should go to bed; or she may use a 'mystifying' way saying, for example, 'I'm sure you feel tired, darling, and want to go to bed, don't you?' Here a command is dressed up as an expression of solicitude and concern. It attributes to the child feelings, such as fatigue, which he may not have.

Mystification is a means whereby one person tries to control another. The person who is trying to achieve control does not use direct means, but instead attributes opinions, feelings or values to the other person. An example is to be found in the following quotation from Laing (1965, pages 349–50):

> '*Mother*: I don't blame you for talking that way. I know you don't really mean it.
> *Daughter*: But I do mean it.
> *Mother*: Now, dear, I know you don't. You can't help yourself.
> *Daughter*: I can help myself.
> *Mother*: No, dear, I know you can't because you're ill. If I thought for a moment you weren't ill, I would be furious with you.'

Laing links his concept of mystification with the ideas of Wynne and Lidz. He considers that it functions to maintain stereotyped roles at the expense of reality, rather as pseudo-mutuality and pseudo-hostility were considered to do. It also serves to fit other people into a set mould as described by Lidz et al. (1958). The imperviousness to children's needs and the masking of disturbing situations in the family, both of which are described by Lidz and his colleagues, are common concomitants of mystification.

Laing (1965) also refers to Searles' (1959) description of six ways 'to drive the other person crazy'. Searles was another early student of the families of schizophrenics, and Laing pointed out that all six of the processes Searles describes are mystifying, involving, as they do, things which undermine the other person's confidence in his or her own emotional reactions and perception of reality. The six ways are:

(1) Repeatedly drawing attention to areas of the subject's personality of which the subject is unaware.
(2) Stimulating the person sexually in situations in which sexual gratification would have disastrous consequences.
(3) Exposing the person to stimulation and frustration, either simultaneously or in a rapidly alternating pattern.
(4) Relating to the person simultaneously at levels which are unrelated, for example sexually and intellectually.
(5) Switching 'emotional wavelengths' while discussing the same topic, for example talking in a humorous way and a serious way about the same thing.
(6) Switching from one topic to another while maintaining the same 'emotional wavelength', for example talking about a matter of life and death in the same vein as a trivial matter.

The 1960s

Most of the pioneers mentioned above continued their work with families in the 1960s, although Bateson's group disbanded in 1962. The pioneers were joined by many new entrants to the family therapy field.

Jackson, at MRI, continued to develop his methods of treating families. Although he had psychoanalytical training, increasingly he concentrated on the study and treatment of interpersonal processes. He introduced the term 'behavioural (or communicational) redundancy', to describe the way family members, and others in ongoing relationships, develop repetitive patterns of interaction – patterns that therapy must sometimes help alter if the changes clients seek are to occur. He also wrote about homeostatic mechanisms (the means whereby families maintain relatively set ways of functioning); complementarity/symmetry; 'quid pro quo' processes; and the double-bind. He distinguished between families' 'norms' – rules that are not overtly acknowledged, but can be observed when the functioning of families is studied; 'values' – rules that are consciously acknowledged; and 'homeostatic mechanisms' – rules about how the family's norms and values are to be applied. These 'rules about rules' he dubbed *metarules*.

Jackson's work appeared in a number of papers, some written with John Weakland (Jackson & Weakland, 1959, 1961; Jackson, 1961, 1965). Jackson was also co-author of *Pragmatics of Human Communication* (Watzlawick et al., 1967), which set out much of what had been discovered at the MRI concerning human communication, especially in families. He died in 1968.

Jay Haley, an original member of Bateson's group, made major contributions to the growth of family therapy during the 1960s. He was much influenced by the work of Milton Erickson, which he later described in the book *Uncommon Therapy: The Psychiatric Techniques of Milton H. Erickson* (Haley, 1973). *Strategies of Psychotherapy* (Haley, 1963) set out Haley's early position, and a series of publications have since traced his development as one of the most continuously creative of the fathers of family therapy (Haley, 1967, 1976, 1980, 1984).

Haley developed a directive approach to therapy with families. He also stressed the importance of the hierarchical structure of the family, seeing many family problems as due to confused or dysfunctional hierarchies. He believed that the therapist must be in charge of the treatment, rather than allowing the family members to take over. He does not hold the attainment of insight by clients in high regard. For him, the main need is to get the family to *do* something – something that will help them change their habitual, but dysfunctional, ways of interacting.

In the 1960s, Murray Bowen expanded the range of his clinical work, so that he treated the families of children with problems other than schizophrenia. In doing so he discovered that many of the processes which he and others had observed in the families of schizophrenics were also to be found in other families. He described what he called the *undifferentiated ego mass*, observing that in many families with problems, members often seemed to lack separate identities (Bowen, 1961).

In the mid-1960s Bowen experienced an emotional crisis. He came to understand this as related to unresolved issues in his own family which, it turned out, were not in his current nuclear family, but in his family of origin. His came to understand his problems as the result of the process of *triangulation*. Triangulation occurs when a third member is drawn into the transactions between two people, often a marital couple. Instead of communicating directly with each other the couple communicate through the 'triangulated' third person, who may be a child. Thus one spouse may voice complaints about the other to a child, who is then faced with the problem of whose side to take, or whether to take either parent's side, and indeed how to react generally. This child may develop undue anxiety, antisocial behaviour or other problems. At the same time, the parents' issues remain unresolved.

Apparently, Bowen believed that such unresolved problems existed in his family of origin. Eventually he returned to his family in Pennsylvania and managed to 'detriangulate' himself, a process which he described in a paper published anonymously (Anonymous, 1972), though its authorship soon became known. This paper is included in the volume *Family Therapy in Clinical Practice* (Bowen, 1978), which includes all Bowen's major publications.

Ackerman continued as a leader of the family therapy movement throughout the 1960s. In 1961, with Jackson, he co-founded *Family Process*, the first journal devoted to family therapy. He made many other contributions to the family therapy literature (Ackerman, 1961, 1966, 1970a, 1970b, 1970c). He died in 1971, and is commemorated in the name of the Ackerman Institute in New York City.

During the 1960s, Wynne and Boszormenyi-Nagy continued to work along lines similar to those they had pursued in the 1950s.

Virginia Satir, a charismatic and enormously talented therapist with a forceful personality and strong views, joined Jackson shortly after he founded MRI. Her book *Conjoint Family Therapy* (1967) influenced many therapists. She emphasized the communication of feelings in families and, more than many family therapists, was interested in the personality and development of the individuals in a family and the psychodynamic processes behind their behaviour.

The second chapter of *Conjoint Family Therapy* is entitled, 'Low self-esteem and mate selection'. It explores how people, whose views of themselves are poor, depend on what others think of them. They present a 'false self' to the world, rather as Winnicott (1960) defines the term. People with low self-esteem are liable to marry other similar people. Each partner is deceived by the psychological defences of the other – that is by the false self the other presents to the world. At the same time each has fears of disappointment and difficulty in trusting others, including, of course, their respective mates. Satir suggests that this can lead to serious marital difficulties.

A major figure to emerge in the United States during the 1960s was that of Salvador Minuchin. A native of Argentina, and a psychoanalytically trained psychiatrist, he went to work with young delinquents at the Wiltwyck School for Boys in New York City. He soon realized the limitations of current methods of treating these young people and their families, mostly urban slum families. Along with a group of colleagues, he developed methods of working with them. His innovative approach, published in *Families of the Slums* (Minuchin et al., 1967), was probably responsible for his being offered the directorship of the Philadelphia Child Guidance Clinic. Under his direction, this became one of the world's foremost family therapy centres.

Minuchin was largely responsible for the development of the 'structural' school of family therapy. Structural therapists are interested in how families are organized in sections, or subsystems, and in the boundaries between these parts; also in the boundaries between the family unit being studied and the wider community. Therapists using this model see family problems as related to their structure. There may be a structure which does not permit satisfactory functioning, for example a lack of an appropriate boundary between the parental and the child subsystems. The structural approach is already evident in *Families of the Slums* (Minuchin et al., 1967), but was set out in perhaps its classic form in *Families and Family Therapy* (Minuchin, 1974).

Minuchin also advocated the use of the one-way observation screen. Until the advent of family therapy, therapists rarely watched each other work. Even therapists in training limited themselves to reporting to their supervisors what they believed had happened during their therapy sessions. Family therapists opened up the process, both by the common practice of having observers watch and listen through one-way observation screens, and by the use of videotapes which enable therapy to be reviewed, if necessary, repeatedly.

Although most of the early family therapists worked in the United States there were important developments elsewhere. A 'family psychiatric unit' was established at the Tavistock Clinic, London, in the late 1940s. Under the direction of Henry Dicks (1963, 1967), the staff of this unit worked mainly with marital couples who were having problems in their relationships. Another British pioneer of family therapy was Robin Skynner, who made two noteworthy contributions to the family therapy literature before the 1970s (Skynner, 1969a, 1969b). In Germany, family therapy had made enough progress that Horst Richter could, by 1970, publish his book *Patient Familie*. This was later translated into English and published as *The Family as Patient* (Richter, 1974). In Montreal, Canada, Nathan Epstein led the 'family research group' at the Department of Psychiatry of the Jewish General Hospital. This developed into one of the earlier systems for describing the functioning of families, the 'Family Categories Schema' (Epstein et al., 1968).

The 1970s

Family therapy came of age in the 1970s. It was increasingly accepted in major psychiatric centres. Family therapists began to address themselves to a wider range of disorders, and there was less emphasis on people suffering from schizophrenia and their families.

Many new centres for the study and development of family therapy were established in the 1970s, and many new books appeared. Peggy Papp (1977) edited *Family Therapy: Full Length Case Studies*, which presented the work of 12 prominent family therapists, including herself. Each contributed an account of the treatment of a family. The book provides a snapshot of family therapy in the 1970s, and illustrates the diversity of approaches used by therapists at that time. Lynn Hoffman's (1981) *Foundations of Family Therapy* surveyed the state of family therapy as the 1970s came to an end.

The Philadelphia Child Guidance Clinic, under Salvador Minuchin's leadership, became one of the world's leading family therapy centres. The child guidance clinic was closely associated with the Children's Hospital of

Philadelphia. This facilitated the joint study of children with psychosomatic disorders and their families and led to the book *Psychosomatic Families: Anorexia Nervosa in Context* (Minuchin et al., 1978).

Haley spent several years at the Philadelphia Child Guidance Clinic before going to Washington, DC, where, with his wife, Cloe Madanes, he founded the Family Institute of Washington, DC. Also established in Washington, DC, by Murray Bowen, was the Georgetown Family Center.

During the 1970s Murray Bowen continued to refine his theory, renaming the 'undifferentiated family ego mass' the 'nuclear family emotional system'. He ceased treating the families of schizophrenics, applying his methods instead to a wider range of problems, not usually involving a psychotic family member. Wynne, on the other hand, continued to study people with schizophrenia and their families and built up a team of researchers at the University of Rochester (Wynne et al., 1978). They also addressed the issue of the relative 'invulnerability' of some children by studying the presence of healthy communication patterns and other aspects of healthy family functioning that may coexist with disturbed family relationships. These might reduce the risk of severe psychopathology and promote healthy or even superior functioning in the offspring.

In Canada, Epstein and his colleagues made the Department of Psychiatry at McMaster University, Hamilton, Ontario, an important centre for the practice and teaching of family therapy. With colleagues he developed, from the Family Categories Schema, the McMaster Model of Family Functioning (Epstein et al., 1978) and, later, the McMaster Model of Family Therapy (Epstein & Bishop, 1981).

The 1970s saw important developments in Europe, especially Italy and Great Britain. In Milan, Italy, Mara Selvini Palazzoli played a major role in setting up the Institute for Family Study. This was founded in 1967 but had its main impact in the 1970s. She was one of four psychoanalytically trained psychiatrists who became the 'Milan Group'. The others were Gianfranco Cecchin, Giulana Prata and Luigi Boscolo. They were much influenced by the work of the Palo Alto therapists, especially Bateson, and by Watzlawick and his colleagues. They found that families often came for help, yet seemed determined to defeat the attempts of their therapists to help them change. They proposed the term 'families in schizophrenic transaction', for such families and described them, and their treatment, in the book *Paradox and Counterparadox* (Palazzoli et al., 1978a; the book was originally published in Italian in 1975).

Among the contributions to family therapy made by the Milan group were: their techniques of 'circular interviewing' and 'triadic questioning', whereby the therapist asks a third family member about what goes on between two others; their concept of developing hypotheses about the functioning of a family in advance of the interview and then devising questions to test the hypotheses; developing a better understanding of how the 'symptom' is connected to the 'system'; and their way of structuring each therapy session. The latter comprised a five-part 'ritual' consisting of a pre-session discussion, the interview, the intersession discussion, the intervention and the postsession discussion.

In Rome, Maurizio Andolphi started working with families early in the 1970s, and in 1974 founded the Italian Society for Family Therapy. By 1979 he was able to publish an excellent systems-based book, *Family Therapy: An Interactional Approach*.

In Britain, Skynner, in 1976, published *One Flesh: Separate Persons* (published in the USA as *Systems of Family and Marital Psychotherapy*). This provided a view of family therapy as seen by a British psychiatrist trained in the Kleinian school of therapy. Important work was also being done at the Family Institute in Cardiff, Wales. The first director of this institute, Sue Walrond-Skinner (1976), published *Family Therapy: The Treatment of Natural Systems*, a book addressed primarily to social workers. Brian Cade and Emilia Dowling were among the other members of the staff of this institute who were responsible for placing it in the forefront of family work in Britain. Walrond-Skinner (1979) also edited the book *Family and Marital Psychotherapy*, with contributions by 11 British family therapists, giving a wide-ranging view of the British family therapy scene at that time.

Another British pioneer of the family approach to psychiatric problems was John Howells, a child psychiatrist turned family therapist, who founded the Institute of Family Psychiatry in Ipswich. He distinguished his approach as 'family psychiatry', rather than 'family therapy'.

Mention must be made here of Milton Erickson. Erickson was not a family therapist. He was an unconventional but creative psychiatrist who made much use of hypnosis in his practice of psychotherapy. He studied hypnotic phenomena throughout his long career and published extensively on hypnotherapy. He greatly influenced Haley who wrote *Uncommon Therapy: The Psychiatric Techniques of Milton H. Erickson* (Haley, 1973), a fascinating description of how Erickson worked.

Erickson's importance in the development of family therapy is due to his interest in the interpersonal processes in which his patients were engaged, and his use of strategic and solution-focused methods of treatment. Traditional psychodynamic psychotherapy explores and aims to resolve the repressed conflicts of individuals. The objective of the family therapist is rather to get the family members to *do* something different, to interact with each other in a different way; this was how Erickson approached many of the clinical problems with which he was confronted. Moreover, he found, as family therapists have too, that telling people what to do does not always work. Instead indirect, or 'strategic', methods, including paradoxical ones, may be needed.

Conversations with Milton H. Erickson, MD, Volumes II and III (Haley, 1985a, 1985b), consist of transcriptions of conversations between Erickson and, in most cases, Jay Haley and John Weakland. These took place in the

1950s and early 1960s and make it clear that Erickson had by that time developed many innovative, strategic ways of helping families change. Erickson's influence on the mainstream of family therapy has mainly been indirect, however. He himself wrote little on the subject and his innovative ideas were spread mainly by those who studied with him, notably Haley and Jackson.

The 1970s also saw an explosive development of the family therapy literature. Books not so far mentioned include *Family Therapy: Theory & Practice* (Guerin, 1976), *The Family Life Cycle* (Carter & McGoldrick, 1980) and the first two editions of this book (Barker, 1981a, 1986). Many new journals joined *Family Process*.

The 1980s

The 1980s saw something of a *rapprochement* between the various schools of family therapy. Many of the pioneers were charismatic characters with strongly held views, and in family therapy's early days it was hard to discern a body of knowledge which all, or even most, family therapists would accept. Increasingly, however, a middle ground was defined, if not precisely, as therapists of the various previously distinct schools began to accept and use the concepts and techniques of others.

New concepts and techniques continued to emerge. These included the 'narrative' approach, and the technique of 'externalizing' problems of the creative Australian therapist, Michael White (White & Epston, 1990); various cognitive approaches to treating family problems (Epstein et al., 1988); and the 'systematic family therapy' of Luciano L'Abate (1986). In *Milan Systemic Family Therapy* (Boscolo et al., 1987), two of the original members of the Milan group, with Lynn Hoffman and Peggy Penn, set out a method of therapy developed from that presented in *Paradox and Counterparadox* (Palazzoli et al., 1978a). Minuchin's contribution in the 1980s was *Family Kaleidoscope* (1984). Beautifully written, it presented this great family therapist's views of the contemporary family and how families may be helped.

The 1980s also saw a great interest in brief, solution-focused therapy. *Patterns of Brief Family Therapy* (de Shazer, 1982) was influential in this. It describes the work of the Brief Family Therapy Centre in Milwaukee, Wisconsin, and is presented as a 'practical integration of Milton Erickson's clinical procedures and Gregory Bateson's theory of change'. It describes a quite stylized approach to therapy, employing a therapy team, one member being the 'conductor', the person who goes into the room with the family, the others being the observers behind the one-way screen. The team, observers and conductor, devise interventions, which are often tasks for the family to perform that may enable the family see their problems in a different light. In other words the problems are 'reframed'.

During the 1980s, books appeared focusing on various particular aspects of family therapy such as 'transgenerational patterns' (Kramer, 1985); 'doing therapy briefly' (Fisch et al., 1982); the use of rituals (Imber-Black et al., 1988); 'families in perpetual crisis' (Kagan & Schlosberg, 1989); and the use of family systems principles in family medicine (Glenn, 1984; Henao & Grose, 1985) and in nursing (Wright & Leahey, 1984, 2005); the families of adolescents (Mirkin & Koman, 1985); and the alcoholic family (Steinglass et al., 1987).

An important contribution was Michael Nichols' book *The Self in the System: Expanding the Limits of Family Therapy* (1987). 'If people were billiard balls,' Nichols says, on page x, 'their interaction could be understood solely on the basis of systemic forces. The difference is that human beings interact on the basis of conscious and unconscious expectations of each other.' In advocating for the inclusion of consideration of family members' personal experience in the family therapist's thinking, Nichols takes further the ideas of Kirschner and Kirschner (1986).

The 1990s and the early years of the new millennium

Family therapy now has a well established place among the psychotherapies. The rather uncritical enthusiasm of some of the pioneers has given way to a more balanced view of its place in the therapeutic scheme of things. There has also been an ongoing re-examination of many of the ideas and assumptions that previously characterized the field.

Steinglass (1996), writing as the journal *Family Process* entered its 35th year of publication, mentioned family therapy's 'ups and downs'. He used its approach to major mental disorders as an example. He pointed out that during the 1960s and 1970s family therapists were 'hot on the trail' of family factors that might cause or contribute to schizophrenia, but they largely abandoned this as evidence of genetic factors emerged. Yet during the 1990s, they were back working with patients with schizophrenia and their families, psychoeducational family therapy now being viewed as important.

Some of the assumptions made, implicitly if not overtly, during the 1960s have been questioned. For example, free and open communication within families was assumed to characterize healthy functioning. But an in-depth examination of the question of secrets in families (Imber-Black, 1993) showed that this is not a simple issue. Some secrets are 'functional' and the borderline between pathological secrecy and appropriate privacy is not always clear.

In the book *Therapy as Social Construction* (McNamee & Gergin, 1992) a series of writers questioned many of the traditional views of the process of therapy. The editors wrote of how they saw that there had been 'a generalized falling-out within the academic world with the traditional conception of scientific knowledge' (page 4). The concept of the scientist, or the therapist, being the 'expert' who will solve people's problems has come to be questioned. The solutions of many of our problems must come from within, so many came to contend.

But family therapy theories come and go. Thus the concept of the 'functionality' of symptoms and the behaviour of family members was popular in the early days of family therapy, but later fell into disrepute. But now it is being suggested that it may have a place and needs to be revisited (Roffman, 2005). New approaches to therapy have continued to be developed. The use of the 'reflecting team' (see Hoffman, 2002, pages 149–168) is but one example.

During the 1990s interest increased in the application of cognitive behavioural methods in family therapy. In *Understanding and Helping Families: A Cognitive-Behavioral Approach* Schwebel and Fine (1994) described and discussed the 'cognitive-behavioral family model' (CBF). The basis of this approach is the assumption that the 'experiences, thoughts, emotions and behaviours (of individuals) are heavily shaped by the manner in which they cognitively structure their world' (page 30). Therapy aims 'to help participants become aware of and correct' their unhealthy cognitions.

In Chapter 3 (pages 36–55) of their book Schwebel and Fine describe the *family schema*. In CBF this term describes 'all the cognitions that individuals hold about their own family life and about family life in general' (page 50). These cognitions are 'the guidance system that directs the individual's family related behaviour' (page 55). Since that was written the application of cognitive-behavioural techniques in family therapy has received increasing attention (Dattilio, 2005; Dattilio & Epstein, 2005).

Another development has been increased attention to spiritual issues. These have come to be seen by many as an important consideration when working with families (Hodge, 2005).

Family therapy is also being applied to an ever-widening range of family types and ethnic groups. For example, the September 2005 issue of *Contemporary Family Therapy* was devoted to 'Treating Indian Families: In India and Around the World'.

Nurturing Queer Youth: Family Therapy Transformed (Fish & Harvey, 2005) addresses the issue of working with *sexual minority youth*. The authors prefer this term or, more simply *queer youth*, to terms such as *gay*, *lesbian*, *bisexual* and *transgendered* because they consider the former terms to be more inclusive. They point out that young people are 'coming out', to themselves, to their families and to their wider environment at ever younger ages. Fish and Harvey discuss the challenge of working with such young people and their families.

The second edition of *Family Therapy in Changing Times*, by Gill Gorell Barnes (2004) takes a broad look at the diversity of family forms created by such things as:

- New cohabitation and marriage patterns
- The choice by some of lone parenthood
- Divorce and repartnering
- Gay and lesbian parenting
- Migration
- Cultural diversity

The book discusses methods of working with families affected by such circumstances.

The family forms that Barnes considers are but a few of the many that exist around the world. Religious practices and cultural traditions vary enormously. For example, in the Muslim faith the sexes worship separately, whereas Christian couples can worship together (Hünler & Gençö, 2005). In some countries polygamy is accepted and indeed, as this is written, King Mswati II of Swaziland has 11 wives and two fiancées. By the time you read this he will probably have more, though among the Swazi population at large, three is the usual maximum number of wives. (Perhaps we should hope that the king does not seek family therapy!)

The 1990s saw the emergence of the 'post-modern' approach to therapy. This was well described in Harlene Anderson's (1997) book *Conversation, Language, and Possibilities*. The 'post-modernists' reject the concept of the therapist as the expert with the skills and knowledge to promote change in the family so that it becomes more 'functional'. Instead, therapy becomes a collaborative endeavour involving family and therapists as equals. Anderson (1997, page 32) writes:

> 'In the modern perspective therapy constitutes a dominant cultural-truth-informed, *therapist-led endeavour* and yields *therapist-determined possibilities*. These truths determine and actualize a priori, across-the-board diagnoses, goals and treatment strategies.' (Anderson's italics)

Anderson (1997, Chapters 5 and 6) goes on to provide one of the clearer descriptions of the post-modern approach to therapy. No longer is the therapist 'an objective, neutral, and technical expert who is knowledgeable about pathology and normalcy and who can read the inner mind of a person like a text' (page 93). This is in contrast with the collaborative approach in which the focus 'is on a relational system and process in which client and therapist become conversational partners in the telling, inquiring, interpreting, and shaping of the narratives' (page 95). Anderson continues:

> 'A client brings expertise in the area of content: a client is the expert on his or her life experiences and what has brought that client into the therapy relationship. When clients are narrators of their stories, they are able to experience and recognize their own voices, power and authority. A therapist brings expertise in the area of process: a therapist is the expert in engaging and participating with a client in a dialogical process

of first-person storytelling. It is as if the roles of therapist and client were reversed: *The client becomes the teacher.* A therapist takes more of an "I am here to learn more about you from you" stance.' (page 95)

Out of such collaboration, solutions to the client's problems are expected, by the post-modern therapist, to emerge.

Lynn Hoffman is a talented writer who has been intimately involved in the family therapy scene since 1963, when she was engaged to edit Virginia Satir's *Conjoint Family Therapy*. *Family Therapy: An Intimate History* (Hoffman, 2002) which recounts, as Hoffman puts it on page xi, her 'journey from an instrumental, causal approach to family therapy to a collaborative, communal one'. It is, however, more than this, providing an insightful, if somewhat selective, account of the development of family since 1963.

Summary

Family therapy has developed since the Second World War as a new way of dealing with the human problems that were previously dealt with by one of the various forms of individual or group psychotherapy. It was based on a new conceptualization of how these problems come to exist. Formerly they were thought to be mainly the result of intrapsychic processes, or the 'psychopathology' of individuals, which was believed often to have its roots in early childhood experiences.

The family approach, by contrast, is based on the belief that these problems are related to the current interactions taking place between the individuals in the family and, sometimes, between these individuals and other social systems. It also takes into account multigenerational and extended family factors.

Initially, family therapists worked mainly with patients suffering from schizophrenia and their families, but they have come to apply their methods to the full gamut of psychiatric disorders. In its early days family therapy was divided quite sharply into schools of thought and practice. These divisions are now less clear, and a common body of knowledge has emerged and continues to expand. Family therapy methods are nowadays being applied to an ever increasing number of cultural and ethnic groups and family forms.

Recent years have seen the development of 'post-modern' approaches, in which therapy is seen more as a collaborative endeavour between clients and therapist. This is in contrast with the 'modern' approach, in which the therapist plays the role of 'expert' who has the training, skills and insights to intervene so as to resolve clients' problems.

Chapter 2
Healthy Families and their Development

As we have seen in the previous chapter, families vary. There is no one type of 'normal' family. But can we define a 'healthy' family? Perhaps, but well functioning families also come in many forms. The most important consideration is the extent to which the family provides for the needs – material, emotional and spiritual – of its members. It can be difficult, though, to know when the needs of the members of a family are being adequately met; indeed any cut-off point must inevitably be arbitrary.

The second edition of this book, published in 1986, had an outline on the front cover of a four-member family – a father and mother and two children, a boy and a girl – the archetypical nuclear family. But nowadays such families are in the minority in many cultures and societies. Twenty-three per cent of UK families with dependent children are lone female-headed households (Gorrell Barnes, 2004, page 47). In recent years I have rarely seen families in which the child or children are living with their two natural parents, neither of whom has been married previously. While this might be partly because such families have fewer problems and thus seek help less often, the statistical fact is that such families are becoming ever rarer and make up a smaller and smaller proportion of the population.

There have been substantial increases in the rates of divorce, of single, never-married women raising children on their own, of blended families and of other 'atypical', but not necessarily unusual, family constellations. In addition, increasing numbers of women work outside the home, so that many young children spend much of their time in day care.

'Normal' family functioning

There have been many suggestions as what the criteria for normal families should be. These were addressed from various theoretical viewpoints in the book *Normal Family Processes* (Walsh, 1982). A decade later, in the second edition of her book Walsh (1993, pages 3–4) writes:

'Over the past decade, attempts to define family normality have become more complicated and more important . . . clinicians and family scholars have been further humbled in addressing normality by our increasing awareness that all views of normality are socially constructed, influenced by our own world view and by the larger culture.'

The time may have come for us to abandon the search for the 'normal' family and seek instead the 'healthy' family. Perhaps that is what Froma Walsh, the editor of the above book, was really looking for when she discussed criteria for 'normality'. She distinguished families that function asymptomatically; those that function optimally; and those that function in a way that is statistically average. Normality may also be defined in terms of the processes occurring in the family of which Walsh wrote:

'Basic processes involve the integration, maintenance, and growth of the family unit, in relation to both individual and social systems. What is normal – either typical or optimal – is defined in temporal and social contexts, and it varies with the different internal and external demands that require adaptation over the course of the family life cycle.' (Walsh, 1982, page 6)

Fleck (1980) suggested that five parameters of family functioning should be considered. These are:

(1) Leadership: this is a resultant of the parents' personalities, the characteristics of the marital coalition, the complementarity of the parental roles, and the parents' use of power, i.e. their methods of discipline.
(2) Family boundaries: this covers ego-boundaries, generation boundaries and family–community boundaries.
(3) Affectivity: important in this parameter are interpersonal intimacy; the equivalence of family triads; family members' tolerance of each others' feelings; and unit emotionality.
(4) Communication: relevant here are the responsiveness of family members to each other; the extent to which verbal and non-verbal communications are consistent; the ways in which family members express themselves; the clarity of the form and syntax of their talk; and the nature of members' abstract and metaphorical thinking.
(5) Task/goal performance: this covers the nurturance given to members by the family; the ways in which the children master the process of separation from the family; behaviour control and guidance; the nature of family members' peer relationships and the guidance they are given in these; leisure activities; how the family copes with crises; and the adjustment of members after they leave the family of origin.

These criteria seem helpful, but they may be based upon an outdated view of the family. We can no longer assume that there is a 'marital coalition'. Often there is but one parent caring for the child(ren).

Ethnic variations

The importance of ethnicity has long been recognized. What is acceptable and functional in one ethnic group may not be so in another. As therapists, most of us probably, at least at an unconscious level, tend to lean towards norms and values similar to the culture in which we have grown up. This may lead to problems in engaging families from other cultures and ethnic groups and thus to therapeutic failure. A good knowledge of the ethnic variations to be found in the population with which one is working is therefore important.

McGoldrick, in the first edition of *Ethnicity and Family Therapy* (McGoldrick et al., 1982), reviewed the relationship between ethnicity and family therapy. She pointed out that ethnicity is 'deeply tied to the family' and is transmitted by means of the family. She emphasized that family therapists should pay careful attention to the cultural influences on families. This is surely even truer now than it was when McGoldrick wrote these words.

The third edition of *Ethnicity and Family Therapy* (McGoldrick et al., 2005) reviews some 47 ethnic groups and is by no means exhaustive. Its emphasis is on immigrants to America from other parts of the world. Thus the chapter dealing with 'Families of African Origin' does not consider in any depth African families that have remained on that continent. That may be because in much of Africa families are too poor and preoccupied with the tasks necessary for physical survival to seek help with family relationship problems. But in some parts of Africa, notably South Africa, family therapy is practised.

Yet another challenge is provided by the ethnically mixed marriage. It is common enough for the therapist to be confronted with families in which the partners come from families of origin with different standards and values. The challenge can be even greater when they also come from different ethnic groups. It is usually helpful to approach such families with an attitude of respectful curiosity, valuing and validating the uniqueness each partner brings to the union.

The functions of families

The functions a family should serve include:

- The provision of the basic necessities of life for its members
- The rearing and socialization of children
- Provision for the legitimate expression of the marital couple's sexuality
- The provision of mutual comfort and support for its members
- Reproduction and the continuation of the species

The above do not all apply to every family. Some couples elect not to have children; in others the children have grown up and left home.

Societies, especially in the 'developed' world, help with the rearing and socialization of children by providing schools, which socialize as well as educate, and sometimes other institutions – youth groups, boy and girl scouts, church groups, summer camps and so on – which supplement what the family does. They also wait in the wings for families to run into trouble, providing social service agencies to assist families, or to take over the care of children, when families fail to do this properly. In varying degrees they provide financial and material help to needy families.

In the past, and even today in many parts of the world, many of the functions now carried out by society's agencies were performed by the extended family. This consisted of a kinship network of grandparents, uncles, aunts, adult siblings, cousins and other relatives. Sometimes people unrelated by blood, but living in the same social network, also participated. But in industrial, especially large urban societies, a smaller role is generally played by the extended family and the neighbourhood community. Thus the parent or parents are faced with bigger tasks to perform than used to be the case. This is not to say that extended family networks no longer exist. They are fewer, however, especially in large urban communities and where there is a high level of migration.

Family therapists are concerned with all forms of family life, whether traditional or not. All these forms aim, explicitly or implicitly, to meet the needs of their members, but what these are seen to be may vary. Pre-marital sex may or may not be considered acceptable, for example, and the increasingly common practice of unmarried couples living together is no longer frowned upon in many societies. The family therapist must be sensitive to, and take into account, the standards and the moral and cultural values of the families coming for treatment.

AIDS has had devastating effects on family life. In sub-Saharan Africa, for example, there are millions of 'AIDS orphans'. Consequently many families are headed, not by lone mothers but by children, some as young as 11 or 12 years.

Family development

Families are not static entities; they are continually changing. There is a cycle of formation, growth, decline and dissolution which they all follow, with various diversions possible along the way. Our therapeutic approaches must take into account the current developmental stage of the family. Nichols (1996) emphasizes this, in *Treating People in Families: An Integrative Framework*, in successive chapters dealing with:

- Families in formation
- Expanding families

- Contracting families
- Postparental couples
- Families in transition due to divorce
- Families in transition due to remarriage

Previous descriptions of family development include those of Haley (1973), McGoldrick and Carter (1982) and Duvall and Miller (1985). However these seem increasingly outdated in that they assume, implicitly if not explicitly, that the normal process is that of a young couple meeting, courting, getting married, having and rearing children, then retiring and becoming grandparents. While this sequence of events still sometimes occurs, it is far from the current norm. It does not take account of the teenage girl who gets pregnant as a result of a casual sexual encounter; nor of 'arranged' marriages and other marriages that result from parental pressure; nor of gay couples who, in some jurisdictions, may be legally married and who adopt children. And as we have seen, in some countries polygamy is still legal and practised.

The current reality is that families rarely develop in smooth and entirely predictable ways. Apart from situations such as those mentioned in the previous paragraph, development may be affected by the death of family members; the separation or divorce of the spouses; the late birth of a child or children after the others have grown up; the arrival of new children in a reconstituted family; chronic illness; financial set-backs; migration from one culture to another; natural disasters; military service; war; and many other circumstances.

The clinical importance of family developmental stages

Two main areas need to be considered when a family presents for treatment. One is the family's developmental stage. The other is the family's structure and way of functioning.

Many of the clinical problems with which families present are related to difficulties in making the transition from one developmental stage to the next. When this is the case the therapist needs to consider how the developmental process can be freed or assisted. Are there any road blocks, either in the family's social context, or within the family itself, which can be removed with the help of the therapist?

Barnhill and Longo (1978) defined nine *transition points* which need to be negotiated as the family passes from stage to stage. Despite the changes in families and the wide variety of family forms we encounter nowadays, the concept of transition points remains useful. Those suggested by Barnhill and Longo were:

0–1   Commitment of the couple to each other.

1–2   Developing new parental roles, as husband and wife become father and mother.

2–3   Accepting the new personality, as the child grows up.

3–4   Introducing the child to institutions outside the family, such as school, church, scouts, guides, sports groups and so on.

4–5   Accepting adolescence, with the changed roles associated with this, and the parents' need to come to terms with the rapid social and sexual changes occurring in their son or daughter.

5–6   Allowing the child to experiment with independence in late adolescence and early adulthood.

6–7   Preparations to launch, the term used by Barnhill and Longo for the process whereby the parents come to accept their child's independent adult role, which includes starting his or her own family.

7–8   Letting go: facing each other again, when child-rearing is finished and the couple face each other as husband and wife alone again.

8–9   Accepting retirement and/or old age, with the changed lifestyle involved.

While accepting that many families are headed by single parents rather than couples and that family forms are more variable now than when Barnhill and Longo (1978) put forward the concept of transition points, the fact remains that any family is faced with the need to negotiate transitions. Just as an individual's development may be fixated at a particular stage – when it has failed to proceed beyond that stage at a time when it normally would have done so – so may a family fail to make one or more of the needed transitions. A family may also regress, that is go back to an earlier transition point, usually when faced with some stress. Barnhill and Longo also put forward the concept of 'partial fixation', when a family life cycle transition has not been successfully achieved, although a partial and even superficially satisfactory, though often precarious, adjustment has been made.

Optimal family functioning

Kirschner and Kirschner (1986, Chapter 2) introduced the concept of 'optimal functioning'. They considered the marital transactions; the rearing transactions; and the independent transactions. The latter refers to the functioning of the individual family members in their own activities, be they vocational, educational, social or recreational.

In two-parent families, the *marital transactions* are the foundation on which everything else rests. The marital couple first need to meet each other's needs. As 'reparental' figures for each other, each spouse can provide inputs that were lacking in the partner's family of origin. A spouse may programme the other for self-confidence and success through suggestions and directives regarding productive behaviours. Education, modelling, confrontation, validation, encouragement and inspiration may also be provided (Kirschner & Kirschner, 1986, page 30). If the marital relationship is a poor one, the foundations for a successful, well-functioning family unit are lacking, or at least shaky. It is hard for a couple who do not get along well together to function effectively as a parental team. An important part of the assessment of a family, therefore, is the assessment of the quality of the marital relationship. The essential question is whether the marital partners get satisfaction out of their relationship. Ideally, they nurture, affirm and support each other, and the relationship should be one of mutual trust and respect. Elements of romance and intimacy are involved in this, and the couple need also to have effective ways of recognizing and resolving conflict.

Nowadays many families are headed by single parents. Such parents need to perform the same tasks as couples, but must find the support they need elsewhere than in the marital relationship. An important part of the process of working with one-parent families is identifying the sources of support, and the social networks, available to such families; and involving those supports, directly or indirectly, in the treatment process. The estranged parent of the children may be important in this regard.

The *rearing system* comprises the way the parental couple work together to rear and care for their children. The parents should be agreed on the principles to be used in doing this, and the care provided according to these principles should meet the needs of their children and foster their healthy development. It is the transactions, or the network of relationships, between the parents and the children, and also those between the children, that largely determine how the children develop.

Finally, the therapist should consider the relationships that exist between the members of the family and the wider community of which the family is a part. In the terminology of the 'comprehensive family therapy' of Kirschner and Kirschner (1986), these are the *independent transactions*. In an optimally functioning family these enable family members to function autonomously outside the family. A successful outcome of childrearing is one which produces children who can do this.

In view of the enormous variety of family forms and ethnic variations with which therapists may be called upon to work, and the fragmentation of families that occurs in many of the troubled areas of our planet, the above considerations may be somewhat simplistic. Moreover, only some of the ethnic variations that exist are discussed in McGoldrick et al. (2005).

Summary

Families vary greatly in their composition. Healthy family functioning can take many forms and the variety of forms has been increasing. The cultural values of families, and their ethnic backgrounds, are also relevant factors. Families pass through a series of developmental stages as they are formed, bear and rear children, then launch the children into the world, leaving the marital couple alone again, although perhaps with the new role of grandparents. The family therapist must always consider the stage that has been reached by a family presenting for treatment, and whether the family is having, or has had, difficulty surmounting a particular developmental hurdle.

The concept of 'optimal family functioning' is helpful. It is concerned not just with the absence of problems, but also with whether the needs of the marital couple and the children are being met as well as they might be. A family should both meet the current emotional and psychological needs of all its members, and prepare the children for an autonomous existence in the wider world into which it will, at the appropriate time, launch them.

Chapter 3
Some Basic Theoretical Concepts

Every therapist needs a theory of change. This determines how that therapist behaves in the therapy room with clients. As family therapy developed it quickly became clear that it needed theoretical underpinnings, and thus clinical approaches, different from those suited to other types of psychotherapy. Those that had been used in the conduct of individual therapy were less useful in work with family groups. Theories were needed of how *families* function, what may go wrong with their functioning and how change in their functioning may be promoted. This is not to say that the psychological and biological make-up of individuals – their intelligence levels, personality types, emotional states and mental defence mechanisms – are irrelevant. Far from it! These are matters to be taken into account when we work with families, but considering them alone is not sufficient. The family is more than a collection of individuals.

In attempts to conceptualize the functioning of the family group, family therapists have pressed into use ideas derived from such theoretical schemes as general systems theory, cybernetics, learning theory, communications theory and theories about the relative functioning of the right and left cerebral hemispheres. Let us look first, however, at some of the attempts which have been made to use pre-existing psychological theories in family therapy.

Theories derived from individual and group psychotherapy

Psychodynamic theory

Many of the early family therapists relied heavily on psychodynamic theory in their work with families. Ackerman (1956) introduced the idea of 'interlocking pathology', arguing that the psychopathology of the different members of a family fitted together to produce the family system the therapist encountered. Bowen's concept of the 'undifferentiated ego mass', is another example of the application to families of ideas derived from the study of the psychopathology of individuals. Bowen originally used this term, which he later discarded, to describe the 'central family oneness' he observed in many families, especially those of patients suffering from schizophrenia. The family members, he believed, had not become emotionally autonomous to a healthy and appropriate degree (Bowen, 1961).

Virginia Satir (1967, Chapter 2) wrote of the relationship between individual psychopathology and family dynamics. She believed that people whose views of themselves are poor depend on what others think of them. They present a 'false self' to the world, rather as Winnicott (1960) defined the term. This false self is designed to present to others the impression the person wants them to have. It is based on the identification by the subject with others. Such people, Satir said, are liable to marry each other. Each partner is deceived by the psychological defences of the other; that is, by the false self the other presents to the world. At the same time each has fears of disappointment and difficulty in trusting others, including their respective mates. This may lead to marital difficulties.

While many other early family therapists came into the field with psychoanalytic training – for example Lidz, Wynne, Minuchin, Dicks, Boszormenyi-Nagy, Skynner and Epstein – according to Nichols (1984, page 223), they 'traded in their ideas about depth psychology for those of systems theory'. It is hard to know how far such therapists have used their understanding of individual psychodynamic processes to facilitate their work with families. Consideration of the psychopathology of individuals is, however, evident in the work of many of them, for example in that of Dicks (1967) and Skynner (1976). Psychodynamic theory does not, however, seek to explain the workings of family systems.

The 'Milan' team were a striking example of psychoanalysts turned family therapists. Starting with the ideas they set forth in *Paradox and Counterparadox* (Palazzoli et al., 1978a), they probably had more influence on family therapy in the 1980s than any other group.

Group therapy

The aim of much group therapy is to help the members of the group gain insight through the process of group interaction. The therapist's role is principally that of facilitator and, sometimes, interpreter of what is happening between the group members.

While family members can certainly learn things of value to each other in a 'group therapy' setting, the family situation is quite different from that which exists when a group of unrelated strangers starts to meet: the context in which most group therapy methods have been developed. The long shared history of family members, their established, and often shared, psychological defences, and their set attitudes towards each other may make it hard for them to engage in the process of interaction and confrontation which is the essence of most group therapy. It is likely that, instead, the family will simply re-enact the same scenarios that are characteristic of its usual way of functioning – unless the therapist does something active to change this, which is not typical of most forms of group therapy.

Other theories that have been used in therapy with families

Cybernetics

Cybernetics is a term that was introduced by Weiner (1948) to describe regulatory systems that operate by means of feedback loops. This process requires a receptor of some sort, a central mechanism and an effector. These are connected to form a feedback loop. An example is a thermostatically controlled central heating system. The thermostat is the receptor; it constantly measures the temperature in the space that has to be heated. It is connected to a central mechanism, the furnace. When the temperature drops to a certain level, the furnace is switched on and heat is distributed, via the effector channels, to the area to be heated. When the temperature rises to another predetermined level, the reverse process occurs and the furnace is shut off. This process provides an illustration of 'homeostasis': the tendency of systems, or at least some of them, to maintain themselves in a fixed, steady state.

Quite early in the development of family therapy some of the ideas of cybernetics were adopted by therapists trying to understand the fixed, but dysfunctional, processes occurring in many of the families they saw. The difficulties many families experienced when faced with the need to make changes were 'explained' by saying that the homeostatic mechanisms in the system tended to maintain the *status quo*, rather than permit needed changes to occur. But whether introducing a concept such as homeostasis really *explains* anything, rather than simply describing a process, is open to question.

A development of cybernetics was *control theory* (McFarland, 1971). This considers not only feedback mechanisms, but also 'feedforward' control. This latter type of regulatory activity is governed by factors which are independent of the results of the activity. Feedforward processes include the deliberate, conscious planning designed to reach a future goal. By way of example, Tomm (1980) cited the planning of certain families who send their children to private schools in order to have them attain particular educational or social goals. The accomplishment of these goals will not lead to any modification of the original plan.

Feedback may be either positive or negative. If it is positive it is 'deviation amplifying', and if negative 'deviation minimizing'. Positive feedback often operates within a certain range, while negative feedback comes into play at the limits of the range, as with a couple who get progressively more angry with each other until a certain maximum intensity is reached, but who stop short of physical violence, or at least of murder! Thus in families there are often periods of positive feedback regulation which are limited by negative feedback. A change in the relationship between those involved implies that there is also a change in the regulatory limits of the control system.

Cybernetics presents a superficially attractive model for understanding some of the phenomena we observe in families, but it is far from being an adequate theory of family functioning. The addition of McFarland's (1971) control theory ideas strengthens it somewhat, but many questions remain. For example, it is not clear what determines that people are going to make the deliberate, conscious plans which can lead to 'feedforward' processes.

Tomm (1980) described a model of therapy, which he dubbed the 'Calgary model' and which paid particular attention to cybernetic regulatory mechanisms. This was a systems-based model and it took into account such factors as interpersonal and subsystem boundaries, attachments and coalitions, control mechanisms, family rules, collective beliefs and goals. Stress was, however, placed on the control mechanisms within the family. These were illustrated by circular pattern diagrams (CPDs). These illustrate the repetitive, stable and self-regulating interaction patterns within families. An example is given in Figure 3.1. Tomm points out that the control mechanisms operate through multiple channels, largely non-verbal.

CPDs can be of value in therapy in that they facilitate circular, rather than linear, thinking in the therapist. They can also direct attention to parts of a circular pattern which may not be immediately obvious; and they help the therapist choose the point at which to intervene. Linear thinking (the distinction of which from circular thinking is discussed in the next section) may present problems because it tends to mobilize feedforward mechanisms and may fail to make use of the constructive potential of negative feedback.

The ideas of cybernetics and control theory, then, have contributed to the development of an epistemology for work with families, but they are

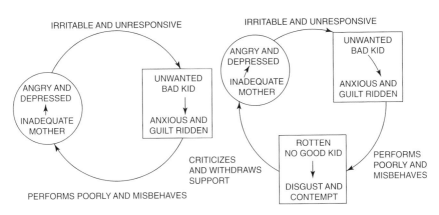

Figure 3.1 Dyadic and triadic parent–child patterns (reproduced with permission from 'Towards a cybernetic-systems approach to family therapy at the University of Calgary' in Freeman D.S., ed., 1980, *Perspectives on Family Therapy*, Toronto: Butterworth).

far from being adequate for this purpose. Tomm (1981, 1984a, 1984b) himself subsequently went on to develop a more systemic approach to family therapy, influenced largely by the work of the Milan group (Palazzoli et al., 1978a, 1978b, 1980).

Systems theory and its application to family therapy

General systems theory was proposed by von Bertalanffy as a general theory of the organization of parts into wholes. A system was defined by von Bertalanffy (1968, page 55) as 'a complex of interacting elements'. Hall and Fagan (1956) worded the same concept slightly differently. They defined a system as 'a set of objects together with the relationships between the objects and between their attributes'. These definitions place no limits on what the 'parts' or 'objects' may be. They may be living or non-living. The theory is designed to cover physical phenomena and machines as well as biological systems.

von Bertalanffy (1968) distinguished *open* from *closed* systems. Closed systems are those in which there is no interaction with the surrounding environment, as in a chemical or physical reaction in a closed container. Such systems obey rules different from those obeyed by open systems. Closed systems, for instance, show *entropy*, the tendency to reach the simplest, least ordered possible state from whatever may be the starting situation. Thus if two gases that do not react chemically with each other are introduced into a closed container, the result will be a diffuse, complete mixing of the two. Once this process is complete the system is said to be in a state of *equilibrium*.

Open systems, such as families, do not show entropy. Instead there is a steady inflow and outflow of relevant information across the boundary of the system. If the characteristics of the boundary remain the same and the outside environment is also unchanged, a *steady state* is reached. The environment of most open systems is, however, liable to change. There may also be alterations in the characteristics of the boundary. These properties of open systems make change and evolution possible. To make things even more complicated, the individual family members may change.

For family therapy purposes, the term *systems thinking* (Beckett, 1973) is probably more appropriate than systems *theory*. The importance of systems theory to family therapy lies in the ideas and concepts it has brought to the field. These include the following:

(1) Families (and other social groups) are systems having properties which are more than the sum of the properties of their parts.
(2) The operation of such systems is governed by certain general rules.
(3) Every system has a boundary, the properties of which are important in understanding how the system works.

(4)   The boundaries are semi-permeable; that is to say some things can pass through them while others cannot. Sometimes certain material can pass one way but not the other.

(5)   Family systems tend to reach relatively, but not totally, steady states. Growth and evolution are possible, indeed usual. Change can occur, or be stimulated, in various ways.

(6)   Communication and feedback mechanisms between the parts of a system are important in the functioning of the system.

(7)   Events such as the behaviour of individuals in a family are better understood as examples of *circular causality*, rather than as being based on *linear causality*.

(8)   Family systems, like other open systems, appear to be purposeful.

(9)   Systems are made up of *subsystems* and themselves are parts of larger *suprasystems*.

Some characteristics of systems

Systems thinking (the use of von Bertalanffy's (1968) ideas without employing the mathematical models he proposed) has more to offer family therapy than cybernetics, which is mainly concerned with feedback mechanisms. The idea of *circular causality*, as opposed to *linear causality*, as a basis for understanding the processes occurring in families, is however common to both. Linear causality describes the process whereby one event causes another. Thus when it starts to rain a man may put up his umbrella. But putting up an umbrella is not generally believed to have any part in determining whether it rains. This is a case of linear causality because event A (the onset of rain) is seen as the cause of event B (the umbrella being put up), while event B does not affect event A.

Circular causality is the term used for the situation that exists when event B does affect A. Thus if person A tells another person B to do something, and that person does it, this in turn will affect the behaviour of person A – who, for example, may then be more likely to ask B to perform the task again when the need arises.

A slightly more complex example of circular causation is that of a family containing a boy who is anxious about going to school. His mother, too, is worried and she turns to her husband who fails to give her reassurance or support. Instead he speaks angrily to his son. This seems to make the boy more anxious still. The boy's increased anxiety then leads to a further increase in the mother's anxiety. The son's school refusal worsens and the mother turns with greater force to her husband who gets even more angry with the boy, and so the circular process continues.

In this case, who is 'causing' the problem? Indeed what is the problem? Is it the mother's anxiety, which is communicated to both father and son? Is it the boy's school refusal? Is it the father's unsympathetic and angry behaviour towards the boy and his failure to support his wife? To the systemic therapist the problem is none of these things; to such a therapist the problem lies in the family system as a whole. A circular process is occurring and it is the system that must be addressed in therapy, not any one person, nor even any one dyadic interaction.

An important concept derived from systems theory is that of the relationship between systems, subsystems and suprasystems. All living systems are composed of subsystems (Figure 3.2). So if a family is the system under study, it will be found to consist of various individuals or groups of individuals which function as subsystems. Examples are parental, marital and child subsystems; there may also be boy and girl subsystems, or subsystems consisting of older and younger children. Such subsystems have their subsystems too; an individual human being is also made up of various systems, whether physical (renal, cardiovascular, nervous and so on) or psychological (ego, id, superego).

Suprasystems to which families may belong include the extended family, the village, the neighbourhood, the tribe, a church community and so on. These in turn are part of larger suprasystems, until we get to nations, groups of nations and planet earth itself. The earth, of course, is but part of a still larger celestial system.

The system upon which family therapists usually concentrate is of course the family. But family therapists are interested also in the subsystems and,

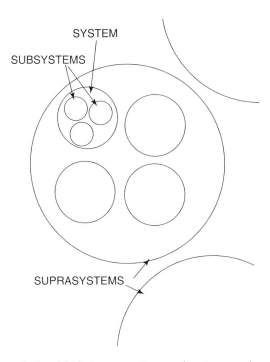

Figure 3.2   The relationship between systems, subsystems and suprasystems.

usually, the suprasystems of the families they are treating. There may be problems in a family's subsystem pattern. Figure 3.3 illustrates a pattern which may be associated with problems. The diagram represents over-close involvement (or 'enmeshment') of mother and son and underinvolvement of the parents with each other. The two subsystems are circled. A more satisfactory situation might be that shown in Figure 3.4. Many other, more complicated, subsystem patterns are possible, and indeed common.

Every system has a *boundary*, which marks it off from its surroundings. Living systems have readily identifiable physical boundaries, consisting of skin, mucous membranes, the bark of trees and so forth. The boundaries of emotional and psychological systems are not visible in the same way, but they are equally important. They control emotional interchanges, closeness and joint actions. The boundary between one subsystem and another is characterized by restricted emotional interchange, compared with that between those individuals within the one subsystem. Similar considerations apply to the boundaries between systems and their suprasystems.

Some families have relatively impervious boundaries, so that they are quite isolated from the social environment in which they exist. Others have highly permeable boundaries and so may be unduly susceptible to events and changes in their wider social environment. The boundaries of all open

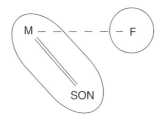

Figure 3.3   A problematic subsystem pattern.

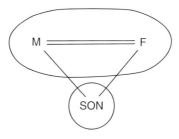

Figure 3.4   A satisfactory subsystem pattern.

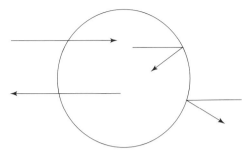

Figure 3.5 Semi-permeable boundaries in an open system.

systems are, in some degree, semi-permeable, that is they allow some things to pass through and prevent others from doing so (Figure 3.5). By this means the integrity of the system and its distinctness from the surrounding environment are maintained.

Subsystems have boundaries too, and work on subsystem boundaries is often an important part of family therapy, particularly when a structural approach is used. The structural therapist's approach to the situation in Figure 3.3 might be to establish a clearer boundary between mother and son and a closer relationship between mother and father, leading to a situation such as that depicted in Figure 3.4. Now there are clear boundaries around each of the two subsystems: that made up of the parents and that comprising the son.

Boundaries distinguish systems from other related systems and determine how they relate to each other. The nature and amount of communication, verbal and non-verbal, that occurs across them, is important in establishing boundaries. Much of this communication is concerned with emotional issues, rather than cognitive ones. Structural therapy, which above all else deals with boundary issues, and communication theory (discussed below) thus have much in common.

Feedback

Systems thinking takes in the ideas about feedback which form the basis of cybernetics, but it goes further; the systemic therapist considers not just the feedback processes that are occurring, but also the processes whereby change occurs in the family system. Referring to the 'recursive loops' which are characteristic of living systems, Hoffman (1981, page 339) pointed out that these loops 'are never totally closed, since there is always space for new information. Each cycle comes round to a new position, sometimes so minutely different from the previous one as to be imperceptible, but sometimes representing a major shift.' Family therapy is in part a matter of promoting this process.

Equifinality

The term 'equifinality' describes the process whereby an open system maintains the same steady state with differing inputs. The chemistry of the body is an example. The concentration of most electrolytes and other chemical compounds remains within narrow limits regardless of dietary intake. This is because of regulatory mechanisms involving the kidneys, lungs and other organs. Similarly families tend to have their set methods of functioning, regardless of what is happening around them, or what information or stimulation is coming in from outside. Although the principle of equifinality seems to have relevance to the way families function, the term is not nowadays much used in the family therapy literature.

Learning theory

Much human behaviour is learned, the remainder being biologically determined. Several processes by which learning may occur have been identified. These may be summarized as follows:

(1) *Respondent conditioning*, which changes behaviour by altering the circumstances leading up to it. Pavlov's classical experiments with dogs are examples of this. By pairing the ringing of a bell with the presentation of food, the dogs were conditioned to salivate simply when the bell was rung.

(2) *Operant conditioning* changes behaviour by altering the circumstances following it. Thus if a person touches something hot and gets burned, that person is less likely to touch the same thing again. Similarly, the way family members respond to each other helps determine how they behave. For example, if a girl is told to leave the table and forfeit the rest of her meal whenever she misbehaves, she may modify her future behaviour so that she can enjoy her meals in their entirety. Parents regularly give their children rewards and punishments designed to bring about changes in the children's behaviour.

(3) *Modelling* is the process by which people learn by imitating the behaviours of others. A young child may pick up a key, insert it into a lock and try to turn it, despite never having being taught to do this; the child is just modelling what he or she has seen others doing. In a similar way, children will pick up a telephone and 'talk' into it just as their parents do, even though they may not yet have acquired speech. The family therapist can similarly be a powerful model for family members. For example, the way the therapist relates and talks to the children in a family can be a model for parents.

(4) *Learning by cognition* is what is sometimes termed 'figuring things out'. By thinking a problem through, or just noticing something and considering what its implications are, we come up with new ideas and behaviours. Sir Alexander Fleming noticed that the growth of

bacteria on one of his culture plates was inhibited around a mould he found growing on the plate. That started him thinking and led to the discovery of penicillin.

A fuller description of the principles by which change is believed to occur is to be found in *Basic Behaviour Therapy* (Murdoch & Barker, 1991).

All therapists probably make use of 'learning theory', even though they may not conceptualize what they do in such terms. They are likely, for example, to try to demonstrate clear and direct communication (modelling), and to respond positively, whether verbally or non-verbally, when they observe healthy changes in families they are treating (operant conditioning).

When learning theory is applied to families in a more formal, planned way the behaviour patterns of the family are first carefully studied. A plan is then worked out to use one or more of the above methods to promote change.

'Deviant' behaviour is regarded by many behaviour therapists as resulting from feedback processes in the interactions of family members. It is thus an understandable, even inevitable, response to the contingencies presented by the system, these contingencies being the circumstances that govern the behaviour. This leads therapists to look for reinforcing and discriminating stimuli from other family members which may result in the 'disturbed' behaviour of a particular member. This does not necessarily mean that the other members are *causing* the behaviour of the identified patient; that person's behaviour is also part of, probably, a number of feedback loops and so may equally be seen as causing the behaviour of the others.

Wahler (1976) considered the possible operation of larger cybernetic systems. The 'contingency pattern' of one parent interacting with a child may, he suggested, depend partly on the cues and reinforcers provided to that parent by the other one, and *vice versa*. Moreover similar processes may occur throughout the family. He also described the 'positive reinforcer' and 'negative reinforcer' traps. In the former, one or more family members find the identified patient's behaviour reinforcing and in turn provide reinforcers for it. Thus a mother may find a 'clinging' child's behaviour reinforcing and so may, in her turn, reinforce that behaviour by cuddling or otherwise indulging the child; this will increase the clinging behaviour. Such a process may ultimately lead to refusal to leave the mother's side and even to the development of school refusal.

The negative reinforcer trap is said by Wahler (1976) to be the most common process involved in the development of deviant child behaviour. Giving in to tantrums is an example. A small boy in a supermarket wants one of the chocolate bars on a shelf and screams when he sees them. His mother does not want him to have any chocolate but, perhaps to quieten him down or avoid embarrassment, lets him have the chocolate bar. The screaming, which to the mother is an aversive stimulus, ceases temporarily; but the child has received reinforcement for his behaviour. So too has the mother for hers, since the screaming has stopped. Such a sequence of events can lead to escalation of such behaviours by both partners in the interaction, and the process can become generalized to other situations. Eventually the child may come to be regarded as having a severe behaviour disorder.

Couples and families with a range of problems have been successfully treated using behavioural interventions. Examples include the work of Jacobson & Margolin (1979), Gordon & Davidson (1981), Falloon et al. (1984), Patterson et al. (1992) and Dishion & Kavanagh (2003).

Patterson et al. (1976) reported that many marital relationship problems are characterized by the use by each partner of aversive stimuli to control the other's behaviour. Thus when a husband disapproves of his wife's behaviour he may speak harshly to her or shout angrily at her. This may be followed by a temporary cessation of the behaviour. The wife, however, may retaliate in a similar way when he does something she dislikes. Over time, as they become accustomed to shouting at each other, the intensity of the shouting may increase. Thus although they may be successful in controlling the undesired behaviour in the short term, aversive behaviours tend to be ineffective in the longer term. Instead a situation of chronic conflict may develop.

Behaviourism's emphasis on change, as Nichols (1996, page 40) pointed out,

'. . . is highly consistent with family therapy's focus on change. This is opposed . . . to the traditional accent in psychoanalysis, and in much of continuing psychodynamic psychotherapy, on insight as being essential to behavioural and personality alteration.'

Cognitive behavioural methods have increasingly been used for a variety of family problems (Epstein et al., 1988; Dattilio, 2005; Dattilio & Epstein, 2005; Tildin & Dattilio, 2005).

Communications theory

The identification of communication problems in families, and their remediation, have been central to family therapy since its early days.

In *Pragmatics of Human Communication*, Paul Watzlawick, Janet Beavin and Don Jackson (1967) defined the three aspects of human communication: syntax, semantics and pragmatics. *Syntax* refers to the conventions used when words are put together in sentences and paragraphs to express meaning; it comprises the grammatical rules of the language. *Semantics* is concerned with the meanings of words; it deals with the principles that govern the relationship between words or sentences and their meaning, the clarity of language and its use in particular situations. While the meanings of words may be defined in dictionaries, in practice people do not always stick to such definitions. In many families (and other settings) there are private languages and shared systems of communication which it is helpful for the therapist to understand.

Pragmatics is the study of the behavioural effects of communication. These are related as much, perhaps even more, to the non-verbal behaviour of those involved and to the context of the communication as they are to the semantic content of what is said. It is well known that non-verbal cues, as well as the context of a communication, can convey, for example, that something is being said as a joke, or a threat, or an apology, and so on, even though the words used are the same.

Watzlawick and his colleagues (1967) proposed some 'tentative axioms of communication'. They considered that these properties of communication had 'fundamental interpersonal implications', and they have certainly been used as the basis for much work done by family therapists. They include the following points.

It is impossible not to communicate

All behaviour occurring when one person is in the presence of another carries some sort of message. There is no opposite of behaviour, no 'non-behaviour', so there can be no 'non-communicating'. A man sitting silently ignoring everyone around him is communicating, at the very least, that he does not want to speak with those around him. Depending on the context, and how far it would normally be socially appropriate to speak under the circumstances, he may be communicating a great deal more also. Moreover communication is more than just what is said; it takes in posture, gesture and tone of voice, as well as context.

The relationship aspects of communication

Communication *has relationship aspects*, as well as content. Communications do not just give information; they also define the relationships between those communicating. Thus the statements, 'I wonder if you would mind shutting the door?' and 'How many more times do I have to tell you to shut that damned door?' are both requests to the person addressed to close the door, but the relationship defined is clearly different. Often the same sentence, spoken in a different way, can imply a different relationship. Compare 'I *think* you're wrong' with 'I think you're *wrong*'.

Punctuation

Punctuation is an important feature of communication. In a series of interactions it is not always clear what is stimulus and what response. Thus a wife may nag because her husband comes home late, while the husband comes home late because his wife nags. Each may thus consider the other the 'cause' of the conflict. How the series of events is perceived depends on how the sequence of behaviours is punctuated. Each partner may punctuate it differently, and thus come to consider the other to be the 'cause' of the problems. In such situations a major problem may be the inability of the marital pair to discuss the question of the punctuation of such processes – that is to 'metacommunicate' (or communicate about the communication) on the issue.

Digital and analogic communication

Communication may be divided into *digital* and *analogic* varieties. In digital communication, messages are coded into spoken or written words. The meaning of the messages is clear from the nature and ordering of the words, as in sentences such as, 'John is entering the theatre' or 'The show starts at 8.00 pm.' In such sentences facts are being communicated by the use of the verbal code.

Analogic communication is non-verbal. It is mediated by gesture, body and limb postures, facial expression, tone of voice and the sequence, rhythm and cadence of the words themselves. It also takes in poetry, music, painting and other forms of artistic expression. Other modes of analogic communication are caresses, blows, kisses, hugs and other forms of contact. Also the ways people dress, use make-up and generally present themselves carry their own analogic messages. Analogic communications are very relevant in family therapy, for the therapist must be fully alert to and understand, to the greatest possible extent, the messages the family members are sending each other. 'Fats' Waller, the jazz musician and singer, summed up the difference between digital and analogic communication in one of his recordings many years ago, with the phrase, 'Tain't what you say, it's the way that you say it'.

The distinction between these two types of communication is discussed further by Watzlawick (1978) in *The Language of Change*. Watzlawick reviewed the evidence that digital and analogic communications are associated with, respectively, the left and the right cerebral hemispheres. When a person's digital and analogic messages conflict, it is usually the analogic message that is the more accurate reflection of how the person is feeling. It also tends to be the one that is received by the person being addressed.

Symmetrical and complementary interaction

Any relationship between two people, or between two groups of people, may be, in varying degrees, symmetrical or complementary. When an interaction is described as symmetrical this implies that the participants are on an equal footing. Complementary interaction occurs on the basis of inequality. Examples are many doctor–patient, penitent–confessor and servant–master interactions. In these cases the complementary relationship conforms to the customs of the culture. Marital couples and other pairs of people may relate and communicate in complementary or symmetrical fashion, though of course there are differing degrees of each. Either style of relating is compatible with healthy functioning. Flexibility is however generally to be desired and if patterns of relating become rigid and inflexible, problems may develop.

When one person addresses a communication to another, the latter may respond in one of three ways. The first is *acceptance* of the communication: the person responds to the question or remark in an appropriate way. The second is *rejection*: the person addressed does not reply but may continue reading, listening to something else or looking out of the window. This is still communication, of course, but it is less direct and clear. The third, and generally the most pathological, is *disconfirmation*. This is the giving of offhand, uninterested, illogical, irrelevant or contradictory replies. Such replies may be delivered in a bored, laconic or sarcastic way. The person replying is, by means of the reply, labelling the original speaker as a person of no account.

Symptoms may themselves be communications. In other words, having the symptom conveys a message. Sleepiness, feeling tired or frail health may be an individual's way of saying he or she doesn't want to listen to another person, or participate in a particular activity.

Paradoxical communication

Finally, communication may be paradoxical. Watzlawick et al. (1967) defined a paradoxical communication as a 'contradiction that follows correct deduction from consistent premises'. Examples of paradoxical remarks are, 'I am lying' or 'I will visit you unexpectedly this evening'. The logical fallacy of such statements was pointed out by Whitehead and Russell (1910) in their 'theory of logical types'. This states that anything that involves all of a collection cannot be one of the collection. In the same way we cannot deal with language and metalanguage as if they were of one class. Thus the statement 'I am lying' is both a statement and a statement about the statement (that is a metastatement). It is therefore meaningless. The same applies to the remark 'I will visit you unexpectedly this evening'. To say that I will visit you is fine, but to say that the visit will be unexpected is a communication at a different level in the language hierarchy. It could only be logically stated by someone observing the events from outside the interaction.

Heirarchies

Haley saw relationships as involving struggles for power, and he asserted that, 'When one person communicates a message to another he is manoeuvring to define a relationship' (Haley, 1963, page 4). According to Haley (1976, page 103), 'When a child has temper tantrums and refuses to do what his mother says, this situation can be described as an unclear hierarchy.' Creatures of any sort who are organized together make up a status, or power, ladder. Confused hierarchical arrangements, as exemplified by the above mother–child communication sequence, tend to be associated with symptoms. A hierarchy may be confused or ambiguous, or there may be a coalition between members at different levels.

The *sequence* of communications is related to the hierarchy. Thus if A repeatedly tells B to do something, and B does it, B is probably lower in the hierarchy than A. If this hierarchy is inappropriate and associated with symptoms, a goal of therapy might be to change the sequence of events or, in other words, the hierarchy or power structure. This, incidentally, cannot usually be done simply by providing the family members with insight into their situation. More creative and, often, less direct methods may be needed.

Some other concepts and terms

Epistemology

'Epistemology' is a term much loved by family therapists. It refers to the theory on which a body of knowledge is based. It represents the underlying assumptions which people make when they seek to understand something. The search for new theoretical models for use in the treatment of families has thus involved the development of new epistemologies. (Whether the use of the term itself has been helpful is a different matter.)

As we have seen, family therapy has needed a new theoretical basis, different from that traditionally used to understand individuals. This led to the use of the term 'the new epistemology' by some therapists, but it is misleading because it suggests the existence of a specific, new, generally accepted way of thinking about and understanding families. But there is no one 'new epistemology'. The evolutionary process in our understanding of families is an ongoing process.

Lynn Hoffman (1981) ended *Foundations of Family Therapy* with a thoughtful chapter entitled 'Toward a New Epistemology'. She pointed out that there had been a shift from the study of homeostatic mechanisms, that is those processes that promote stability in systems, to a concern about how change occurs. She, too, seemed to foresee a continuing evolution of new ideas and thus of new epistemologies as the study and treatment of families develop. Her later book (Hoffman, 2002) did indeed review this continuing process.

Coherence

'Coherence' refers to one of the concepts that have emerged as part of the quest for new epistemologies by those who work with families. Dell (1982) used 'coherence' as a sort of shorthand term for 'organized coherent system'. He defined it as follows:

> 'Coherence simply implies a congruent interdependence in functioning whereby all aspects of the system fit together. It would seem to be adequate for describing the behaviour of a system-being-itself without inadvertently implying anything more than that.' (Dell, 1982, page 31)

Dell advocated the abandonment of the concept of homeostasis. He said that homeostasis is 'an imperfectly defined explanatory notion'. Indeed he went on to criticize many of the other concepts and terms which have become associated with various schools of family therapy. He wrote:

> 'In fact, the family therapy field is awash with such notions: family rules, resistance, therapeutic paradox, hierarchy, negative feedback, perverse triangle, and so on. All of those are imperfectly defined explanatory notions that hang in the air. There is a desperate need for some fundamentals that can begin to explain the data of family interaction, psychopathology, and therapeutic intervention.' (Dell, 1982, page 38)

Dell's objection to the use of the term 'homeostasis' was that it suggests a process, 'homeostasis', which prevents change occurring in the system. But he asserted that there is no such specific thing as homeostasis. It is just an 'imperfectly defined explanatory notion'. He recommended that we should simply accept systems as they are. He sided with the noted Chilean zoologist, Humberto Maturana (1978), who asserted that everything is 'structure determined'.

That means that individuals behave out of their coherence; they can behave in no other way. Control is impossible. Their coherence determines how they will behave, and no amount of determined attempts to control them will ever change that fact. Moreover, an individual's coherence specifies his reaction to the other's attempts to control him. The coherence will, in most cases, 'respond' in a different way than was intended by the attempt to control. You can lead a horse to water, but you cannot make it drink. Each successive attempt to make the horse drink results in the coherence (which is the horse) doing whatever it does under that particular perturbation. The coherence always determines. The best that can be achieved is for the owner of the horse to discover the perturbation to which the coherence (the horse) 'responds' with drinking behaviour (Dell, 1982, page 37).

Dell is but one of a number of therapists, and other students of family systems, who put forward ideas about how we can better understand families and help them overcome the problems with which they come to us. His views have by no means been generally accepted. Indeed they were published in an issue of *Family Process* that also contained two other articles suggesting new ways of viewing families and the processes going on in them (Allman, 1982; Keeney & Sprenkle, 1982). All three were subject to criticism in a later issue of the journal (Coyne, et al., 1982; Watzlawick, 1982; Whitaker, 1982; Wilder, 1982).

Dell's article defined therapy as a matter of discovering what particular inputs (or 'perturbations') produce the changes required in those coming for therapy. This seems a helpful idea, more helpful that the concept of homeostasis. The concept of the 'resistant' family may also be unhelpful. It may be better to regard the failure of a family or an individual to respond to a therapeutic intervention (that is, a 'perturbation') as due to the selection by the therapist of the wrong perturbation for those particular circumstances, rather than labelling family or individual 'resistant'.

The above ideas do not tell us anything much about how to determine which 'perturbation' is likely to result in the desired response. This is the very essence of therapy, of course, and will be the subject of most of the rest of this book.

Our two brains and first- and second-order change

A concept which some therapists have found useful concerns the different functions the two cerebral hemispheres are believed to have. Many who present with problems do not accept reasonable suggestions about how they might rid themselves of their problems. This seems to be because much of what we do is determined not by our conscious, rational minds, but by our emotions, deep-rooted attitudes and habitual ways of reacting and behaving.

Watzlawick (1978), in *The Language of Change*, addressed the question of how change occurs in psychotherapy. He distinguished 'first-order change' from 'second-order change'. First-order change is simply the result of a conscious decision to do something differently; for example, to try harder to accomplish a task, or to tackle it in another way. Second-order change involves a change in attitude, or the reframing of a situation, so that things are perceived differently. It goes beyond the application of logical, rational measures to something much less logical, like laughing at one's earlier attempts to try harder, or responding to a paradoxical approach (Barker, 1981b, 1996).

According to Watzlawick (1978) the two cerebral hemispheres have different functions. Each also has its own language, corresponding to the digital and analogic languages mentioned above:

'The one, in which for instance this sentence is itself expressed, is objective, definitional, cerebral, logical, analytic; it is the language of reason, of science, explanation, and interpretation, and therefore the language of most schools of psychotherapy. The other, in which the preceding example is expressed (the example being a passage, rather poetic in style, from Kafka's *An Imperial Message*), is much more difficult to define – precisely because it is not the language of definition. We might call it the language of imagery, of metaphor, of *pars pro toto*, perhaps of symbols, but certainly of synthesis and totality, and not of analytical discussion.' (Watzlawick, 1978, pages 14–15)

Watzlawick goes on to suggest that the second of the two 'languages' is more effective in producing the kinds of changes which psychotherapy aims to help people achieve. This language is believed to be the business primarily of the right cerebral hemisphere which 'tends to draw illogical conclusions based on clang associations and confusions of literal and metaphorical meanings, to use condensations, composite words and ambiguities, puns and other word games' (Watzlawick, 1978, page 24). The left hemisphere, on the other hand, deals with the direct, logical, rational communication of ideas.

Second-order change, Watzlawick suggests, involves making contact with, and presumably producing changes in, the processes occurring in the right hemisphere. The left hemisphere functions as a sort of logical watch-dog, guarding the right hemisphere against undue outside influence. It must therefore be bypassed. Watzlawick (1978, Chapter 7) describes methods of 'blocking the left hemisphere'. This may involve reframing the problem or the use of paradox, metaphor or hypnosis, any of which may be effective when direct methods are not. Metaphors can be powerful aids to communication when direct methods prove ineffectual (Barker, 1985, 1996).

Modern, post-modern and social construction theories

Dell, whose ideas have been mentioned above, was one of a number of therapists who introduced a whole new theoretical approach to facilitating change during therapy. No longer is the therapist the 'expert' who assesses the family, forms an opinion as to the nature of its 'problems' and intervenes to help the family change its way of functioning. The aim, which may be implicit or explicit, is to help the family function in a way that conforms more closely to society's norms.

Narrative therapies, interventive interviewing (Tomm, 1987a, 1987b, 1988), the use of the reflecting team (Andersen, 1987, 1991) and social construction therapy (Atwood, 1997) all, in varying degrees, place therapist and clients on an equal footing. They work together, first to clarify what changes the family wish to make, and then on the task of finding ways for the family to make the changes they seek. To a certain extent this approach parallels that which is becoming the norm in most branches of medicine. The patient is no longer the passive recipient of the physician's diagnosis and treatment decisions, but an equal, or more nearly equal, and informed partner in the diagnostic process and in treatment decisions.

Harlene Anderson, in *Conversation, Language, and Possibilities* (1997), provided an excellent account of the post-modern therapist's approach. This was outlined in Chapter 1.

Style versus method

The family therapy literature is replete with discussions of the relative importance of the 'aesthetics' of therapy, as opposed to the techniques used. L'Abate (1986, page 7) put this well:

'These two major variables can be reinterpreted in terms of the two faces of family therapy: *style*, that is the aesthetic quality of the therapist's personality and techniques which, as a whole, are nonrepeatable events, and *method*, the pragmatic quality of the therapist's professional preparation and competence, which include repeatable types of interventions.'

It seems that, to be effective as therapists, we need *relationship skills* – affect, warmth, sense of humour; and *structuring skills* – directness, self-confidence and technical expertise (Alexander & Barton, 1976). In assessing the literature, though, it can be difficult to know whether the relative effectiveness of different therapists is due to their differing styles or their methods. The therapist's personality and interpersonal skills are certainly important whatever the type of therapy. While interpersonal skills can be learned, there is a limit to how far a person's personality can be changed, so it may be that some people are less suited to being therapists than others. Style however can to some extent be learned (though not from books) and students tend to model their teachers' styles. These are, however, matters on which there are more opinions than hard data.

Summary

The history of family therapy has been characterized by the continuing search for new theoretical schemes, sometimes referred to as new epistemologies, to aid in the study of the processes occurring in families. Theories derived from the study of individuals are of limited value when applied to families. Cybernetics, systems theory, control theory, learning theory and communications theory are among the models which have been pressed into use by therapists of various schools. All have proved useful, but none has been found to be entirely satisfactory.

The concept of coherence – the idea that families constitute 'organized coherent systems' determined by their structure – may be helpful. It implies that therapy should be a process of discovering what will perturb the organized system, or 'coherence', in a helpful way. Ideas about the respective functions of the left and right cerebral hemispheres may also be helpful in devising effective ways of promoting change.

It seems likely that family therapists will continue to use ideas from a variety of theoretical schemes, much as carpenters, electricians and other technicians carry around a variety of tools and pieces of equipment.

Chapter 4

Choosing an Assessment and Treatment Model

We have seen, in Chapter 3, that various theoretical models have been proposed as the basis for therapy with families. This leads each of us to the question: which model should I use? The answer will depend, at least in part, on the theory of change to which we subscribe. In the present state of our knowledge, it is not possible to single out any one theoretical basis, or therapeutic approach, as being 'the best', even for specific problems, for several reasons:

- The research data on the relative effectiveness of different therapeutic approaches are limited.
- Families present for help with a wide range of problems. Thus an approach that may be helpful for a marital couple whose relationship is severely troubled may not be so useful for a family with a delinquent teenager.
- The willingness of families to take part in some of the many available types of therapy varies.
- The personalities and relationship skills of therapists vary. Some may be better suited to one approach than to another.
- The training and skills of therapists vary. A therapist's familiarity with, and experience of using, a particular approach is likely to affect that therapist's results.

There is increasing interest, in medicine generally and also in the mental health field, in ensuring that our practice is *evidence based* (Patterson et al., 2004). We owe it to our clients/patients to use the best available treatment approaches. We must therefore have access to, and examine, the available evidence regarding what is likely to be the most effective approach for each family we see. This represents a challenge, as the literature bearing on this question is both extensive and, often, contradictory. Approaches to confronting this challenge are discussed further in Chapters 16 and 17, and Williams et al. (2006) provide concise and valuable guidance on how the practising clinician can use research.

The therapy a family actually receives, and the results of therapy, are both hard to quantify. However there are some important factors that need to be considered when deciding upon the treatment approach to be used. These include:

- The aims of the therapy. It is important, even essential, that all concerned, the therapist and the family members, are agreed on the objectives of therapy. If there is no agreement there will be no way of knowing whether treatment has been successful.
- The therapeutic approach used should be consistent. For example, behavioural methods may not fit in well with a 'reflecting team' approach.
- Although a consistent approach is desirable, flexibility is also needed. It is not a good idea to persist doggedly in any particular approach if it is clearly failing to get the desired results. Although it is not realistic to expect every therapist to be skilled in every possible therapeutic method, we should surely each have more than one instrument in our therapeutic armamentarium.
- We should always be open to receiving feedback from family members and we should react sensitively to what they tell us. The last couple of decades have seen a steady move towards inviting the families to be equal, or at least more nearly equal, partners in the therapeutic endeavour. This is but part of a trend in medicine. Increasingly treatment of any kind, medical or surgical, is being seen as a joint endeavour in which physician and patient work together. The concept of 'doctor's orders' is becoming outdated. Nevertheless this may not suit all our clients, some of whom still prefer their therapist to take a more leading role. Another point to be borne in mind is that not all family members are comfortable with being observed through a one-way observation screen.

The role of the therapist

Many of the early family therapists were powerful, charismatic figures who assumed a strong leadership role during therapy sessions. It sometimes seemed that the sheer power of the therapist's personality played a major role in promoting change in the families being treated. Even therapists with less powerful personalities took a leading role in the therapy process. Not unreasonably perhaps, they saw it as their job to promote change in any way they could. Often there was not a lot of discussion of therapeutic goals. There tended to be an implicit assumption, on the therapist's part, that the objective of treatment was to restore, or guide, the family towards some sort of perceived 'normal' way of functioning. This assumption was often not spelled out.

For various reasons, mentioned in earlier chapters, the above approach has come to have less appeal. For one thing, our concept of the 'normal' family has taken a beating. The many family forms now extant preclude our considering any one family form as 'normal'. As we saw in Chapter 2, it may be more appropriate to consider whether a family is 'healthy' or, to use jargon that is popular with therapists, 'functional'.

Particularly in the 'post-modern' approach to therapy, the therapist is no longer the master of the therapy room, but an equal, or even a humble, member of the group of people gathered there. But why humble? Basically because we cannot know everything that is relevant about any family. This is especially true when we are working with members of ethnic, cultural or religious groups other than those to which we belong. Most therapists have no first-hand experience of life as a member of many of the ethnic groups whose members may seek help with family problems. Most of us have not lived as a member of a gay or lesbian family. Still less can we know what it is like to be a member of a family in which the marital partners belong to different ethnic or other backgrounds. In such situations we need to seek guidance from the families with which we are working. As Anderson (1997, page 131) points out, they are the experts. (As an aside, it is worth mentioning that the 'one-down' position can be a powerful one – see Chapter 9.)

Changing therapeutic attitudes

Therapists generally, and perhaps family therapists in particular, are increasingly seeking the strengths and potential for healthier functioning, in their clients. This approach is not new. The late Milton Erickson (see Haley, 1973; Erickson, 1982; O'Hanlon & Hexum, 1990) was not primarily a family therapist but he was inclined to view his patients' problems in their family context. Although, early in his career, he received psychoanalytical training, he came to prefer to look for the strengths in his patients and their families, rather than dealing with supposed repressed conflicts and resolving these in the context of the transference relationship. Today's therapists are increasingly following Erickson's lead, though many may not be aware they are doing so.

Although therapy has been changing in the ways outlined above – that is to say becoming more a collaborative endeavour in which therapist and client(s) work together on the issues that have brought the client(s) to the therapist – many options remain. In the fourth edition of this book, this chapter contained sections on the various approaches that have been used by therapists of differing theoretical orientations:

- Psychodynamic approaches
- Behavioural family therapy
- Family systems therapy
- Structural approaches
- Extended family systems approaches
- Approaches using communications theory
- Strategic therapy
- Experiential approaches

To these there might now be added:

- Narrative approaches
- Approaches using social construction theory
- Postmodern approaches

The above approaches are discussed in later sections of this book. They are not all mutually exclusive. Even approaches that might, on a superficial view, seem totally different may have something in common. Behavioural family therapy and the 'post-modern' approach, outlined in Chapters 1 and 11 are in many respects quite different. But when we read Harlene Anderson's (1997) account of her post-modern therapy it seems that she is modelling a particular style of communication that might, with benefit, be adopted by some of her clients. Modelling is, of course, a behavioural technique.

Anderson (1997) advocates strongly that we should not enter into our therapy sessions with too much in the way of preconceived notions. She mentions (page 138) a consultation sought by a 'competent and creative, yet frustrated psychiatrist' with Harry Goolishian, a colleague of Anderson and one of the foremost developers of the post-modern approach. Lars, the client, was a Norwegian merchant seaman who was convinced he had a disease he had contracted as a young man when he had sex with a prostitute in the Far East. Goolishian asked him, 'How long have you had this disease?' Colleagues who were watching the interview were critical of this question. They would have preferred Goolishian to have asked, 'How long have you *thought* you've had this disease?' They feared that Goolishian's question reinforced Lars's 'hypochondriacal delusion'. Anderson (page 138) goes on to explain:

> 'The not-knowing position (one advocated by Anderson and other postmodernists) . . . precluded the stance that Lars's story was delusional. Lars said he was sick. Thus, Harry wanted to learn more about his sickness. To do this required not-knowing questions . . .
>
> 'Trying to understand Lars and what could appear as his "nonsense" or "psychosis" was an essential step in a continuous process of establishing and continuing a dialogue. It meant moving *with* the narrative truth of Lars's storied experience rather than challenging it and assigning meaning to it such as *delusional*.' (pages 238–239)

It seems that this intervention by Goolishian marked a turning point in Lars's therapy. At last someone believed him. The therapy could now proceed without getting hung up on the issue of whether or not Lars had a disease.

I should point out that although this approach is termed 'post-modern', it is not new. Milton Erickson was a master at meeting his patients where they were. The oft-told case of the man who was a long-term patient in a mental hospital and believed he was Jesus Christ illustrates just how 'post-modern' Erickson was. Erickson did not question whether the man was Jesus Christ. Instead he pointed out that Jesus was a carpenter and got him working on building a bookcase in the doctors' lounge (See Haley, 1973, page 28).

Another case that also dates back to the period when Erickson was working at Worcester State Hospital (1930–34) is that of two patients, both of whom were convinced they were Jesus Christ. Again, Erickson did not argue with them about this. Instead, he got them to sit together and had each explain to the other that he was the *real* Jesus Christ (Erickson, 1982, pages 201–202). As a result at least one of the patients was discharged free of psychotic symptoms 6 months later.

What approach should the novice family therapist take?

There is certainly no lack of choice. It is reasonable to start with the therapy approach in which you have been trained. It is to be hoped that this has been wide-ranging and flexible. Also the novice should not be practising family therapy without the help of a supervisor. If it can be avoided, you should not, while a novice, work on your own without support and contact with experienced colleagues. Many therapists work in clinics where they are part of a team. This may provide opportunities to work as a co-therapist or to be part of a 'reflecting team'.

The best family therapy training programmes seek to make their students 'scientist-practitioners'. This involves integrating research into the curriculum and the supervision process (Hodgson et al., 2005). Research is discussed further in Chapter 17.

In Chapter 13, I describe a method of therapy that I find useful, though I do not stick rigidly to it. It is not presented as 'the' way to approach therapy, but simply as an illustration of how theoretical ideas and practical techniques may be brought together and can form a rational method of dealing with troubled families.

My first family therapy teacher and supervisor was Duane Bishop of McMaster University. He was one of the developers, with Nathan Epstein, of the McMaster Model of Family Therapy. I believe that was a good starting point for me. I went on to study the work of Salvador Minuchin, Ivan Boszormenyi-Nagy, Jay Haley, Milton Erickson, the Milan Group and many others. More recently I have collaborated with colleagues using the 'reflecting team' and other post-modern approaches. Over the years I have attended conferences, conventions, lectures and demonstrations. I have also done much reading and have viewed videotapes by a wide range of therapists. These experiences are what have made me the therapist I am today. Similarly each of us has had a unique series of learning opportunities, starting with our initial training, followed by experiences such as those mentioned above. But I have to say that family therapy has often seemed to be developing at such a frenetic pace that it is sometimes hard to come to terms with one approach before the next one arrives and demands attention. Whatever experiences and opportunities to learn we have had, when a family presents asking for help, we must select from all of this the approach we will take with that family. In so doing, it is essential that we consider also the relevant research evidence that will help us in deciding upon our approach.

Lyn Hoffman in *Family Therapy: An Intimate History* (2002) describes her own journey from being editor for Virginia Satir's *Conjoint Family Therapy* in 1963, to becoming one of the most insightful writers on family therapy some 40 years later. Her book is a virtual history of the evolution of family therapy as it is today. Her account provides a fine example of open-mindedness to new ideas and the constant quest for answers and for better ways of helping families.

Summary

Over the course of the past 50 years many approaches to helping families have been proposed and practised. The array of options is both impressive and at times confusing. It is not always clear which approach or method of therapy is most suitable for each of the wide varieties of families, with their disparate problems and their many family types. It is important that we learn about, and have experience of, a variety of therapeutic approaches and techniques. We need also to ensure that our clinical practice is evidence based, making use of the latest research findings to guide us in our work.

Chapter 5
Models for the Assessment of Families

While a number of formal family assessment schemes have been developed, the clinical interview with the family remains the primary means by which most therapists assess families. During a clinical interview the therapist can both observe the behaviour of the family members, and learn about their views and beliefs, and the concerns that have brought them to the therapist.

As family therapy developed, various formal assessment models were devised. These can be useful as screening devices, in research and in drawing attention to the various aspects of family functioning that need to be considered in work with families.

The *McMaster Model of Family Functioning* (Epstein et al., 1978) addresses the *current functioning* of the family, rather than its past development or present developmental stage, and considers the following aspects of family functioning:

(1) Problem solving
(2) Communication
(3) Roles
(4) Affective responsiveness
(5) Affective involvement
(6) Behavioural control

The Process Model of Family Functioning (Steinhauer et al., 1984) is closely related to the McMaster model. Its categories are quite similar:

(1) Task accomplishment, which is similar to the McMaster model's 'problem solving'
(2) Role performance
(3) Communication (including affective expression)
(4) Affective involvement
(5) Control
(6) Values and norms

To illustrate how more formal assessment models approach their task, we will review these schemes in a little more detail.

Task accomplishment and problem solving

These functions are viewed in similar ways in each of the above two schemes. In both, the following processes are considered to be involved:

- Identifying the tasks to be accomplished
- Exploring alternative approaches and selecting one
- Taking action
- Evaluating (or monitoring) results and making any necessary adjustments

The McMaster model has an additional stage in the process of 'problem solving', namely that of communicating the existence of the problem to whoever needs to know about it.

Both models divide family tasks into *basic*, *developmental* and *crisis* varieties. *Basic tasks* include the provision of food, shelter, clothing and health care – the essentials for survival in society. *Developmental tasks* are those that must be performed to ensure the healthy development of members as the family life cycle unfolds. The well-functioning family is sensitive to what its members' needs are and makes the necessary adjustments as it passes through the family life cycle. Symptoms in family members are often found to be associated with problems in making the transition from one family developmental stage to the next.

Crisis tasks tax the family's skills and resources to the limit and sometimes beyond. They include dealing with unexpected or unusual events, such as the death of a family member, serious illness in the family, job loss, natural disaster, loss of the family home through fire or foreclosure, or migration from one culture to another. In some families, however, events which other families might deal with calmly may precipitate a crisis, for example receiving a bad school report about a child, or discovering that a teenager has been shoplifting or is smoking marihuana. As the authors of the Process Model put it, 'A family's capacity to accommodate to stress and avert potential crises is an excellent indicator of family resilience or health' (Steinhauer et al., 1984, page 79).

Roles

Roles have been defined as 'prescribed and repetitive behaviours involving a set of reciprocal activities with other family members' (Steinhauer et al., 1984). Task accomplishment requires that there is a suitable allocation of roles and that the family members do what their roles require. Roles should be assigned, mutually agreed and enacted; and they must be integrated with one another. For satisfactory task accomplishment they must also cover all the things that need to be done. In most families many of the roles to be performed are not allocated in a formal way; rather they become habitual patterns of behaviour carried out by particular family members. Sometimes, however, it is necessary for family members to get together and agree upon who is going to do the shopping, clean the house, mow the lawn, feed the cat, or whatever needs to be done and is not being done.

The McMaster Model distinguishes 'necessary' family functions – roles that must be performed for healthy family functioning – and 'other' family functions. Necessary functions include the provision of material resources; nurturance and support of family members and the sexual gratification of the marital partners; and life-skill development and the maintenance and management of the family system. 'Life skills' refers to such matters as supporting children through school, helping members obtain and keep jobs, and assisting them in their personal development. 'Systems management and maintenance' refers to the provision of leadership in the family and to the process of decision making, maintaining the family's boundaries and establishing and maintaining its standards.

'Other' family functions are those unique to a particular family, such as 'scapegoating' or idealizing a family member. In the description of the Process Model, roles are described as 'traditional' and 'idiosyncratic', the former covering similar ground to the 'necessary' family functions mentioned above, while idiosyncratic roles are often the expression of individual and family pathology. The authors of this model also cite the role of scapegoat as an idiosyncratic one. Role problems are discussed further in Chapter 10.

Communication

The authors of the McMaster Model consider mainly verbal communication, not because they discount the importance of non-verbal communication, but because of the practical difficulties of measuring and collecting data on non-verbal content. The Process Model does however consider non-verbal, or what they refer to as 'latent' content, which includes 'meta-communications' expressed by voice tone, facial expression, eye contact or its lack, body language and choice of words.

Critical aspects of communication, whether verbal or non-verbal, are the clarity, directness and sufficiency of communications sent by family members to each other, and the availability and openness of those to whom the communications are addressed. Communications may be affective (the expression of feeling), instrumental (related to the ongoing or needed activities of everyday life), or neither affective nor instrumental (for example, the expression of opinions on works of art).

Clear, as opposed to masked, communications are generally desirable, since 'masked', that is vague, disguised or ambiguous, ones increase the likelihood of confusion and distortion by the receiver. It is also generally better if communications are sent directly from sender to receiver, rather than through a third person. When messages are sent indirectly they may be distorted, and the third party involved may be placed in a difficult position, trapped between sender and receiver. Finally, it is helpful for the therapist to discover whether sufficient information is being communicated between family members, or whether the family has a problem disseminating needed information among its members.

Affective involvement

Affective involvement is a matter of 'the degree and quality of family members' interest and concern for one another' (Steinhauer et al., 1984). Ideally a family will meet the emotional needs of all its members, until they reach a stage of development at which some of these needs are met by people outside the family group, as increasingly happens during normal adolescent development.

Both the McMaster and the Process Models distinguish various *types* of affective involvement, as well as being concerned with the degree to which family members are involved with each other. The following types of involvement are listed in both schemes:

(1)   Uninvolved (or lack of involvement, in the McMaster Model). This implies that the family members live rather 'like strangers in a boarding house'. They are frequently alienated and unfulfilled.

(2)   Interest (or involvement) devoid of feelings. In such families involvement of family members with one another seems to arise from a sense of duty, a need in one member to control another, or curiosity.

(3)   Narcissistic involvement. Here one family member is involved with another in order to bolster his or her own feelings of self-worth, rather than because of real concern or caring for the other person.

(4)   Empathic involvement. This is based on a real understanding of the needs of those with whom the subject is involved, resulting in responses which meet those needs.

(5)   Enmeshment. This term is used in the Process Model, although the McMaster model has two categories which describe a similar concept: 'overinvolvement' and 'symbiotic involvement', the latter being seen only in seriously disturbed relationships.

According to Steinhauer and his colleagues (1984) the types of involvement, as set out above, are related to both the degree of involvement and its quality, which can be either nurturing or destructive; although, as with all these terms, we are not dealing with 'either/or' situations, but with an infinite number of possible variations along the various continua.

The McMaster scheme has a separate dimension called 'affective expression', but the Process Model incorporates this into the 'affective involvement' dimension, since the former is an expression of the latter.

Control

'Control', as described in the Process Model, is similar to 'behaviour control' in the McMaster Model. These terms refer to the influence family members have on one another. The Process Model distinguishes 'maintenance functioning' and 'adaptations of functioning'. In order that these can be accomplished, a means of controlling family members' behaviour is necessary.

These models each recognize four basic styles of behaviour control, namely rigid, flexible, laissez-faire and chaotic. Rigid control is high on predictability but low on contructiveness and adaptability. It may work quite well for maintenance functioning – the performance of day-to-day tasks and roles – but is less successful when change is required or developmental tasks need to be confronted. Steinhauer and his colleagues (1984) pointed out that its punitive aspects tend to encourage subversion, passive–aggressive behaviour, power struggles and the displacement of anger outside the family.

Flexible styles of control are predictable but constructive and can adapt appropriately to changed circumstances. In the words of Steinhauer and his co-authors (1984, page 83), flexible control 'assists task accomplishment because its supportive and educational tone encourages family members to participate and to identify with the ideals and rules of the family'.

Laissez-faire styles are fairly predictable but low on constructiveness. In 'laissez-faire' families 'anything goes'. Inertia and indecision are the watchwords, rather than organization and action. Task accomplishment tends to be poor and there are often problems of communication and role allocation. Children raised in these disorganized families are often insecure and attention-seeking in their behaviour and display little impulse control or self-discipline. Entry to school, where conformity to certain standards of behaviour is expected, can be hard for them.

Chaotic styles of control are low in both predictability and constructiveness. These styles are unpredictable, switching from rigid to flexible to laissez-faire, so that no one knows what to expect. Changes occur more according to the whim or mood of family members than on the basis of changes in the family's situation and needs. The instability and inconsistency which characterize these families usually result in poor functioning on the other parameters.

Values and norms

This is a dimension of family functioning which is not included in the McMaster Model. The Process Model considers the family's moral and religious values, which are derived from a variety of social and psychological sources, and its norms, which are 'the sum total of what is/is not acceptable within that family'.

When these diagnostic schemes were developed there was less emphasis on this aspect of family assessment. Many of the earlier assessment schemes seemed to consider how the functioning of the family compared to that of a 'traditional' nuclear family, even though they did not necessarily make that explicit. Nowadays, as we have seen, family therapists are working with a wide range of ethnic, cultural and other groups (see, for example, McGoldrick et al., 2005). It is now widely recognized that family therapists, to work successfully, must understand the value systems of the families they see if they are to be effective.

The structural approach to assessing families

The structural model (Minuchin, 1974) considers six aspects of family functioning. These are:

(1) The family's structure
(2) The family's flexibility
(3) The family's resonance
(4) The family's life context
(5) The family's developmental stage
(6) The relationship of the identified patient's symptoms to the family's transactional patterns

The structural therapist joins the family system, though without becoming involved to the extent of losing objectivity, and experiences its structure through participating in its transactions. Boundaries are delineated both by observation of the family's transactions, and by planned interventions, such as attempts to create boundaries between subsystems, or to break them down, and noting the results. Structural assessment techniques are discussed later in the chapter.

The triaxial scheme of Tseng and McDermott (1979)

This identified three classes of family problems:

(1) Family development dysfunctions
(2) Family system dysfunction
(3) Family group dysfunction

This scheme is quite complex and the original article should be studied by anyone who is considering using it. It does not appear to have been widely used, perhaps because of its complexity.

The Circumplex Model

Olson et al. (1979, 1983) described the use of a 'circumplex' model for the assessment of families. They identified two aspects of family behaviour, *cohesion* and *adaptability*, which they believed to be of fundamental importance. *Cohesion* measures the 'emotional bonding that family members have toward one another'. It is similar to the 'enmeshment–disengagement' described by Minuchin (1974). *Family adaptability* is a measure of how far the family permits change (referred to by these authors as morphogenesis), and how far it is characterized by stability ('morphostasis').

After assessment, families are rated on the two axes, for each of which there is a four-point scale, as follows:

	COHESION	FAMILY ADAPTABILITY
High	Enmeshed	Chaotic
	Connected	Flexible
	Separated	Standard
Low	Disengaged	Rigid

The creators of this model developed a series of assessment tools to assess family cohesion and adaptability. The first, a 111-item, self-report scale, named the Family Adaptability and Cohesion Evaluation Scales (usually referred to by the acronym FACES), was introduced with the model. It was succeeded by FACES II, a 30-item measure (Olson et al., 1983); and later by FACES III, a 20-item measure (Olson et al., 1985). The Circumplex Model also recognizes a dimension of *family communication* (Olson et al., 1983). This is called a 'facilitating dimension', and is 'considered critical for facilitating couples and families to move on the two dimensions' – cohesion and adaptability.

The Circumplex Model and the three versions of FACES have been studied, and used clinically, quite extensively. It is not clear how far the FACES I, II and III actually measure what the Circumplex Model postulates. As Green and colleagues (1991) pointed out, 'Correspondence between family models and measurement devices designed to measure these models is more frequently assumed than it is empirically established.'

The Beavers Model

The Beavers Model (Beavers & Voeller, 1983) has been claimed to have certain advantages over the Circumplex Model. It has two axes. One is concerned with the 'stylistic quality of family interaction', which is classified as either 'centripetal', 'mixed' or 'centrifugal'. A fuller description of this model, and discussion of its clinical application, are to be found in *Successful Families: Assessment & Intervention* (Beavers & Hampson, 1990).

The Darlington Family Assessment Systems (DFAS)

This model was described by Wilkinson and Stratton (1991). It aims to consider not only the family system as a whole, but also the functioning of the

Table 5.1   Dimensional structure of Darlington Family Rating Scale: perspectives and problem dimensions (reproduced from Wilkinson & Stratton (1991) by kind permission of the editors of the *Journal of Family Therapy*).

Perspectives	Problem dimensions	
Children (sibling subsystems)	1.	Physical health
	2.	Child development
	3.	Emotional behaviour
	4.	Relationships
	5.	Conduct
Parenting system (executive subsystem)	1.	Physical health
	2.	Psychological health
	3.	Marital partnership
	4.	Parenting history
	5.	Parents – social
Parent–child interaction (interface major subsystems)	1.	Care
	2.	Control
Whole family (total system)	1.	Closeness and distance
	2.	Power hierarchies
	3.	Emotional atmosphere and rules
	4.	Family development

children and the parents. The assessment is done using a structured procedure, the Darlington Family Interview Schedule (DFIS), which is then rated on the Darlington Family Rating Scale (DFRS). Table 5.1 outlines the structure of the DFRS.

The DFIS and DFRS appear to have reasonable reliability and validity (Wilkinson & Stratton, 1991). The model does not seem to have been widely adopted by family therapists.

Summary

This chapter has outlined a few examples of the many existing schemes for the assessment of families. These schemes help us clarify our thoughts and diagnostic ideas about the families we see.

Hard data on the relative merits of the different diagnostic systems are lacking, but whatever theoretical scheme is used, it is important to come to an understanding of how the family system functions. We also need to be clear about the developmental stage the family has reached, and whether its current problems are associated with difficulties surmounting a developmental challenge.

Chapter 6
The Family Diagnostic Interview

While the procedures therapists follow in assessing families depend in part upon their theoretical orientation, the following is suggested as one possible approach to this task. When talking with a family when I first meet them, I prefer to call the process of assessment that of coming to an 'understanding' of the family. The terms 'assessment', and even more so 'evaluation', have judgmental overtones that may be better avoided.

The diagnostic interview is best considered in stages which, however, may overlap:

(1) The initial contact.
(2) Joining the family and establishing rapport.
(3) Defining the desired outcome.
(4) Reviewing the family's history, determining its present developmental stage and constructing a genogram.
(5) Assessing the current functioning of the family.
(6) Developing a diagnostic formulation.
(7) Offering the family feedback and recommendations.
(8) Arranging whatever further interviews, diagnostic procedures or referrals are recommended.
(9) Informing a professional colleague who has referred a family of the results of the assessment, and of any recommendations arising from it, including any proposed treatment plans.

The initial contact

The initial contact may come from a family member seeking help or from a professional colleague. When colleagues refer I like to receive a written request with all available relevant information. If the referring professional is to have an ongoing professional relationship with the family, there should be open communication between that person and the therapist, subject to the agreement of the family members.

The importance of the initial contact with the family can scarcely be overstated. The family should be told how the therapist works, who should come to the first interview, how long the interview will take and what will happen when they arrive at the clinic or office. If fees are payable, they should be explained and it should be established whether they are to be paid by a third-party insurer or by the family. Some therapists like to make the initial contact themselves, while others leave it to a receptionist or secretary. The latter can work well if that person knows how the therapist works, can discuss the above issues knowledgeably and has good skills in communicating over the telephone.

Many of those referred to programmes where family therapy is practised do not realise why the therapist will want to see the whole family. In many cases, only one family member is perceived as having problems. Several points may be made to explain why all family members should attend:

- The problems of an individual family member can often be best understood in the context of that person's family.
- The behaviour of any one family member inevitably affects other members.
- Other family members can often be part of the solution to the problem. It is usually unwise to suggest that they are a part of the problem, even though that may be the case.

When a child is the identified patient, it may be easy to persuade parents that *they* are important, but they may be reluctant to bring children whom they consider to be well adjusted and problem-free. In that case the point can be made that the well-functioning children may have much to offer the problem child, in that they have the skills to function well in the family – skills the identified patient may need to learn. They may also be able to help the therapist develop a more complete understanding of how family members interact and influence each other.

Reluctance to attend on the part of certain family members may arise from a fear that they will be blamed for the family's problems. They may also harbour feelings of shame or fear that they will be embarrassed. In dealing with reluctance to attend, these possibilities should be borne in mind.

Joining the family and establishing rapport

Establishing rapport starts with the initial contact. It should be a main objective of the first interview, perhaps the first several interviews, and rapport must be maintained throughout treatment. Psychotherapy probably fails more often because of the failure to establish or maintain rapport than for any other reason.

Establishing rapport has been given other names. Minuchin (1974) writes of 'joining' the family. Karpel and Strauss (1983) refer to 'building working alliances'. Nichols (1996) uses the term 'therapeutic alliance', this implying that 'the family system comes into the therapist's world and the two systems interdependently construct the basis of trust and co-operation necessary for working together to achieve desired change' (page 98).

As rapport develops, the participants become increasingly involved with each other. Hypnotherapists have long recognized the importance of rapport, and know that failure to induce an hypnotic trance is usually due mainly, if not entirely, to the lack of sufficient rapport. Erickson et al. (1961, page 66) described rapport as:

'... that peculiar relationship, existing between subject and operator, wherein, since it [hypnosis] is a co-operative endeavour, the subject's attention is directed to the operator and the operator's attention is directed to the subject. Hence, the subject tends to pay no attention to externals or the environmental situation.'

When rapport is well developed, therapists can say almost anything, even quite outrageous things, to clients without their becoming upset. Even remarks that could be construed as insulting will be taken to have been meant caringly or in jest, or not seriously.

Rapport may be achieved by both verbal and non-verbal means. The non-verbal are probably the more important. The *non-verbal communications* the therapist offers a family start at the first contact, even if it is a telephone conversation, since one's tone of voice and manner of speaking convey powerful messages. A warm, friendly tone of voice and a respectful, interested and accepting approach are important. When a family arrives I like to greet them personally in the waiting room and make the acquaintance briefly of each family member. I address them by name, if I know their names, and shake hands with each (except for very small children). If I do not know their names I ask for them as I greet them, at the same time telling the family who I am and expressing pleasure at their arrival. It is important, of course, to *appear* pleased to see the family, not just to say so.

Comfortable physical surroundings can assist in promoting rapport. The therapist's mode of dress carries its own message. People seeking therapy generally like their therapist to be respectably dressed and well groomed, though dress that is too formal can be off-putting to some, as can the white 'lab' coats doctors tend to wear in hospitals.

The therapist's manner and behaviour are by far the most important factors, and excellent rapport can be established in prison cells, classrooms, public parks or on the beach. Rapport is promoted by matching or 'pacing' the behaviour of those with whom you wish to establish rapport. You can do this by matching your clients' body posture and movements, respiratory rhythm, speed of talking, and voice tone and volume. You can also either 'mirror' or 'cross-match' their movements. Mirroring is the moving of, say, your left arm or leg in response to similar movements of the client's right arm or leg. 'Cross-matching' occurs, for example, when the therapist's hand or finger is moved in rhythm with movements of the client's foot. Movements which may be matched include such things as crossing and uncrossing the legs, the tilting of the head to one side or the other, and leaning forward or settling back.

You do not need to match all the behaviours of those with whom you seek to establish rapport. Matching should be done sensitively and unobtrusively. If it is, clients do not become consciously aware of it. While it is not possible to match simultaneously the behaviours of all members of a family, you may observe common things about their behaviour which you can use. Otherwise you may match the behaviour of the different family members in turn, perhaps as you speak to each one; and many of the other behaviours I have mentioned are shared with the whole family: your courteous, respectful manner, mode of dress and so forth.

The developers of 'neuro-linguistic programming' (NLP) paid much attention to rapport-building processes. NLP was developed from the study of such highly effective communicators as Milton Erickson and Virginia Satir. The above matching and mirroring devices are part of what the authors of the literature on NLP call 'pacing'. They write:

'When you pace someone – by communicating from the context of their model of the world – you become synchronised with their own internal processes. It is, in one sense, an explicit means to 'second guess' people or to 'read their minds', because you know how they will respond to your communications. This kind of synchrony can serve to reduce resistance between you and the people with whom you are communicating. The strongest form of synchrony is the continuous presentation of your communication in sequences which perfectly parallel the unconscious processes of the person you are communicating with – such communication approaches the much desired goal of irresistibility.' (Dilts et al., 1980, pages 116–117)

Your *verbal communications* can also assist or impede the development of rapport. It is important to listen carefully to the family's language. How they understand their world and their problems will be reflected in their language. By using this you can powerfully promote rapport.

Rapport is also helped by matching the predicates used by those with whom you wish to establish rapport (Bandler et al., 1976; Bandler & Grinder, 1979). A predicate is a word that says something descriptive about the subject of a sentence. Predicates include verbs, adjectives and adverbs. Some people tend to use visual rather than auditory or feeling predicates; as, for example, in the phrases, 'I see what you mean', 'things are looking brighter', or 'that is a pretty hazy idea'. Examples of the use of auditory predicates are, 'I hear what you're saying', 'that sounds terrible', or 'it was like music to my ears'. Sentences such as 'I'm facing a lot of heavy problems', 'that feels like a good idea', or 'that's a big weight off my shoulders', illustrate the use of 'kinesthetic' or feeling-type predicates.

Rapport can be enhanced by matching your predicates with those of the person with whom you are in conversation. Of course most people use predicates of all three types, as well as some olfactory ('this business smells fishy to me') and gustatory ('it leaves a bad taste in my mouth') ones. But most have a preferred way of processing information and it can be helpful to note this and use it to enhance rapport.

As well as matching predicates, it can be helpful to listen carefully to the vocabularies of the family members you are interviewing, noting the kinds of words and expressions they use. This enables you to match their vocabularies. Few things impede the establishment of rapport as much as repeatedly using words and expressions with which those with whom you are speaking are unfamiliar. This is especially important when you are dealing with children, whose vocabulary is partly a function of age, but it applies also to adults. Thus the vocabulary of a university professor is likely to be different from that of an unskilled labourer who left school at the age of 15.

Other useful rapport-building devices include accepting family members' views of things without challenging them in the early stages of your contacts with them; adopting a 'one-down' position; and talking of experiences and interests you have in common with members of the family.

The 'one-down' position is especially helpful when family members see the therapist as a powerful figure who, they may feel, threatens them in some way. Many such people may have a long history of problems with authority figures. With them, a one-down approach may help. It might consist simply of saying that you know little about the job a family member has and asking that person to explain something about it to you, or asking children to spell their names for you. Or it could be a matter of expressing doubts about how fully you understand the family or its situation. In such situations it may be appropriate to offer interventions in a tentative, doubtful way. Nowadays therapists often find themselves working with clients from ethnic minorities and various 'non-conventional' families. Asking them, from a 'one-down' position, about their family values and traditions is both a way of obtaining information that is essential for understanding and working with them, and also a means to establishing a co-operative, equal role, rather than an authoritarian one.

Therapists of the 'post-modern' school, for example Anderson (1997), prefer to take a 'conversational' approach. This involves speaking *with* their clients rather than interviewing them in any sort of formal way.

It may be unclear what the true nature of a family's problems is. The therapist may have a view that is different from that of the family members, but it is the family members' views that are more important. It can be tempting to impose our opinions on the nature of the family's problems on to the family but that is usually a mistake. It is unhelpful to get into arguments or disputes with our clients. Initially, at least, we should accept the family's view of their situation.

Identifying common experiences can be useful with any family. These might consist of having lived in the city, county, province or state the family come from. I was once seeing a family at a time when I had a stiff and painful back. I mentioned this as I eased myself slowly into my chair, and it transpired that the mother in the family also had back problems. This at once gave us something in common on which to exchange a few words. Common hobbies, sports and pastimes may be used in similar ways.

Defining the desired outcome

Psychotherapy generally goes better if it has well-defined goals. Indeed there is no way to define success if no desired outcome has been agreed. Nevertheless therapy goals may be modified as treatment proceeds, and the family's potential for change becomes increasingly apparent. The defining of therapy goals is discussed in the next chapter.

It is important, at this stage, to give family members the opportunity to express their concerns. Turning too rapidly to the family history and or raising issues can put some families off. This is an aspect of the 'pacing' mentioned above.

Reviewing the family's history, determining its developmental stage and constructing a genogram

In many cases, these tasks can conveniently be tackled together. The emphasis placed on them varies from one therapist to another. I find it helpful to have an understanding of how the family has come to be where it is. Much of this information can be gathered in the course of the construction of the genogram.

I like to start by establishing the make-up of the family. Who are its current members? A good beginning is to ask first who lives in the family's current home. Are all the members of the household present? If not, who is absent from the interview? How are the family members related? The following questions need to be modified, for example if you are dealing with a one-parent family, or a blended family.

A good way to approach the family's history is to start with the parents' births and childhoods. It may be helpful to preface these questions with an explanation. You may say that you are interested in how the present family came to be, and want to understand something of its background. You may then ask the parents where they were born and brought up, what their family lives were like when they were children, how they got along at school and what they did when they left school. As they answer these questions they will probably speak of their parents and siblings. If not, you may prompt them to do so. They can next be asked how they met and courted, and then asked to outline the course of the marriage or common-law relationship so far.

It may be convenient to ask next about the births of the children, and the children's development to date. It will probably be clear by now what stage in its life cycle the family has reached. Evidence may also have emerged of any difficulty the family is having in surmounting any of the family transition points mentioned in Chapter 2.

The genogram

A *genogram* (sometimes called a geneogram), or family map, is a useful adjunct in both assessment and treatment. Guerin and Pendagast (1976) drew attention to its value, and it has become widely used since then. It gives a concise, graphic summary of a family's current composition. It should also show the extended family network, the ages of the family members, the dates of the parents' marriage and of any divorces or separations. It indicates how all the family members are related and it can also show who the identified patient is, although I usually omit this information when I am engaging family members in constructing a genogram. The geographical locations of the family members can be indicated, together with brief summaries of the salient points concerning each family member, for example occupation, school grade, health and important points from individuals' past histories (illnesses, accidents, losses, incarcerations and so forth).

While some therapists prepare the genogram later using the information they have obtained from the family during sessions with them, I prefer to prepare it with the assistance of the family members during the first session or two, often the first one. Specimen genograms are shown in Figures 6.1 and 6.2. Figure 6.1 shows a relatively uncomplicated family situation. The oldest child is adopted, the maternal grandfather is dead, the paternal grandparents were divorced when the father was aged 8, the paternal grandfather remarried 4 years later and his second wife died in 1973.

Figure 6.2 shows a more complex family constellation. In this family the parents of the identified patient, Brad (distinguished by a double boundary), cohabited in a 'common law' relationship from 1965 to 1969, after which they got married. They separated in 1973 and were legally divorced in 1980. Carmen, Brad's mother, has since had a common law relationship (with Eric) and is now married to Ken, with whom she lives with her two children by Eric and a 3-year-old by Ken. Brad and his father, Dave, live with Katrina and her 10-year-old daughter by her former husband, Len. She also had a previous pregnancy which ended in a miscarriage in 1974. Carmen is an only child and both her parents are dead. Dave is the fourth in a family of one girl and four boys.

A genogram can contain information about the health, behaviour, strengths or problems of the people shown in it. These points can be written beside the symbols representing the family members. While such information is not an integral part of a genogram, I find it helpful to include it.

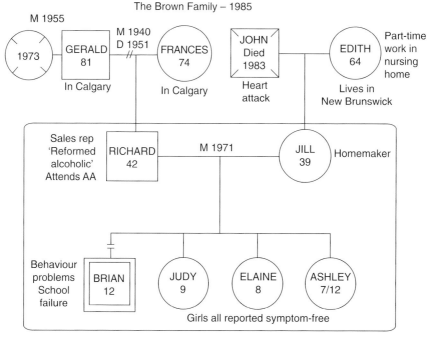

For interpretation of symbols see Figure 6.2

Figure 6.1 An uncomplicated genogram.

I like to involve all family members, except those too young to understand, in the preparation of the genogram. The establishment of rapport can
often be advanced during this process, and much information about how the
family functions is often obtained. Even reticent family members are generally willing to share abundant information and are often surprised to recognize that while they know much about some areas of the family history,
they know little about others. As information is discussed, it may become
clear that spouses are unfamiliar with information about each other's
families that it was assumed they knew (Holman, 1983, page 69).

Genograms in Family Assessment (McGoldrick and Gerson, 1985) is the
definitive source for information on the construction, interpretation and
clinical uses of genograms, with many illustrations.

Friedman and colleagues (1988) described the 'time-line genogram'. This
has a vertical axis that is a time scale which may go back 100 years or so.
Life events and relationship data are recorded along the time line. There
is a 'progeny line' which extends diagonally below the horizontal 'marriage
line' and records the dates of birth of the children. The data is thus spread
out according to the temporal relationships of the events charted on the
genogram.

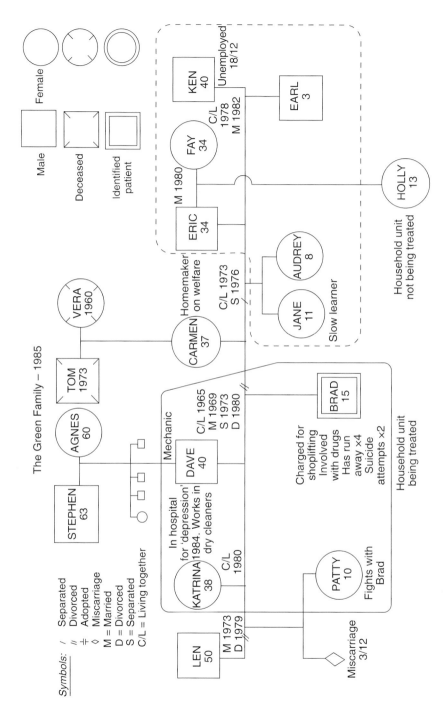

Figure 6.2 A complex genogram.

The time-line genogram is an interesting idea but does not seem to have been widely adopted. It is more complex than a regular genogram and takes longer to construct. It also takes longer to interpret. It may thus be less suitable for routine clinical practice.

Assessing the current functioning of the family

The assessment process aims to achieve an understanding of the current functioning of the family. There are only two reliable ways of obtaining information about family relationships. One is to observe the interactions between family members; the other is to ask questions which bear on the relationships between the members, and study carefully the family's responses, both verbal and non-verbal. It is advisable to do both, but the therapist usually learns more about how a family functions from the experience of interacting with it than from asking questions of the family members.

A family's description of its functioning is only one aspect of a complete assessment. The formal organizational structure may be described, but this says little about how the different parts habitually interact and about the functioning of the system as a whole. The questions asked of family members are not, therefore, usually about *how* the family functions as a group or organization; instead they are designed to reveal this indirectly.

There are many ways of interviewing families, some direct, others, in varying degrees, indirect. Palazzoli et al. (1980) suggested 'three guidelines for the conductor of the session'. They recommended that the interviewer first develop some *hypotheses* about the family system. One always knows something of a family, even before the first interview; for example, its composition and the fact that it contains, for example, a rebellious child, an anorexic adolescent or a depressed adult. Whatever information is available is the basis of the hypotheses with which the therapist starts.

Palazzoli and her colleagues (1980, page 5) define an hypothesis as 'an unproved supposition tentatively accepted to provide a basis for further investigation, from which a verification or refutation can be obtained'. Having developed such suppositions the therapist then proceeds to test them. This is an active process, the therapist asking a series of questions designed to explore the patterns of the family's relationships, beliefs and attitudes. The Milan authors believed that if the therapist were to behave in a passive fashion, that is as an observer rather than a mover, the family, 'conforming to its own linear hypothesis, would impose its own script, dedicated exclusively to the designation of who is "crazy" and who is "guilty", resulting in zero information for the therapist' (Palazzoli et al., 1980, page 5).

Hypotheses, the Milan group believe, must be systemic, that is they must concern the family system as a whole. It is not enough to say that somebody may be depressed, or anxious about something. This may be the case, of course, but to treat a family system successfully it is necessary to consider the *relationships* between the family members, and how these fit together to make up the family system as a whole. This does not mean that the mental states and psychopathology of individual family members are irrelevant. Far from it! They may be of great significance, though information about them is obtained in different ways. It is also information of a different order.

This brings us to the concept of *circularity*. The Milan associates derived many of their ideas from the work of Gregory Bateson (see Ruesch and Bateson, 1968). A 'Milan-style' interview is a circular process. The therapist responds to information the family gives about relationships by formulating more questions, to which the family then responds again, and so on. The questions are framed in a circular way too. Their method is to ask one member of the family to describe the interactions or relationships between two others.

Many of the questions concern differences between such things. The therapist seeks information about differences in how family members react to particular events, view certain behaviours, worry about things, handle children, understand the family's problems and so on. This style of interviewing has considerable therapeutic potential. For example it:

- Opens up the system to new information.
- Allows members to learn about themselves from others: it gives them a 'third person' perspective.
- Allows members to take a reflective rather than a reactive stance to other members. This can lead to increased understanding and empathy between family members.

Triadic theory, which is the idea that two people (or groups or even agencies) in conflict tend to involve a third person or group in the conflict, has been described as 'one of the cornerstones of many models of family therapy' (Coppersmith, 1985). Bowen's views on 'triangles', outlined in Chapter 1, and the concepts labelled alliances, coalitions and detouring, described in Chapter 3 as part of structural therapy's theoretical basis, are also examples of triadic thinking. The process of bringing in a third person is sometimes referred to as 'triangulation'.

Coppersmith (1985) points out that the ability to think in terms of triads (or triangles, which are essentially the same thing) is an important skill for the family therapist. It is the basis of the style of interviewing practised and advocated by Palazzoli and her colleagues (1980). The therapist is always thinking of the various triads in the family and how they function. The questions asked of a family member, or group of members, are often about differences between the behaviours or responses of two other members or groups of members; and the emphasis is on relationships between people rather than on the behaviour of individuals.

There are some other important practical points about interviewing families using the ideas of Palazzoli and her colleagues (1980):

(1)   It is better to ask questions about specific behaviours which occur between family members, rather than about how people feel about the situation, or about how they interpret or understand it. For example the therapist might ask one of the children in a family questions such as the following:

> What does your father do when Billy loses his temper and swears at his mother? (Then, when the father's reaction has been described.) And what does your mother do then? And if your big sister is around, what would she be doing?

(2)   As well as asking about them directly, differences may be highlighted by asking people to rank the family members in terms of specific behaviours. For example the members of a family in which one child is physically aggressive to a younger one, might be asked the following questions:

> When Chad hits Dorothy, who is most likely to step in and try and stop him? And who is the next most likely to do this? And then? . . . (And so on, until it is determined who is least likely to intervene.)

(3)   It can be helpful to ask questions about changes in the patterns of relationships. These may concern differences before and after certain specific events. Thus members of a family that has recently moved from one place of abode to another might be asked about differences in the behaviours of members relative to one another before and after the move. Similarly the situation before and after a marital separation, a remarriage, an illness or accident affecting a family member, or a child's entry into school or departure to university, might be explored.

(4)   Questions can be asked about how the behaviour of family members varies in different circumstances, whether these are real or hypothetical. For example:

> Who would be most upset if Eric was seriously ill?
> Do Frances and Gillian fight more when Dad is at home than when he is not?
> What does Mummy do when Harry misbehaves? Does she react in any way differently when Dad is at home?

Neutrality is the last of the three attributes that the Milan group recommend. When asking questions in the way described above, the therapist may seem to be allied with the person being questioned, while that questioning is occurring, but the alliance shifts when the questioning moves to another family member. During the session the therapist will be allied in turn with all the family members, and 'the end result of the successive alliances is that the therapist is allied with everyone and no one at the same time'. The Milan authors also advise that the therapist declare no judgments, whether implicit or explicit, while interviewing the family. To do so would have the effect of allying the therapist with one or more of the individuals or groups within the family.

There are other approaches to interviewing families, and not everyone uses the methods advocated by the Milan associates. Karpel and Strauss (1983), for example, in their book, *Family Evaluation*, described a more direct style of questioning. They recommend questions and remarks like:

> 'Can you tell us a little bit about how you were feeling after your father died?'

Or,

> 'So when he died you felt responsible?' (Both from page 124)

These authors sometimes address intrapsychic processes quite directly. They are clearly concerned with intrapsychic processes (which the above questions address), as well as interpersonal ones. The Milan group therapists might have preferred to ask other members how they thought the person concerned felt when the father died. They might also have asked each member to rate the family in terms of who was most upset, down to who was least upset. Similarly each member could have been asked who they thought felt most responsible for the father's death, who came next, and so on.

Karpel and Strauss (1983) also describe a series of 'probe questions', designed 'to probe the broad area of family structure in a routine, organized fashion that is both direct and non-threatening' (page 136). The probe questions cover such subjects as the layout of the home; a typical day in the life of the family; rules, regulations and limit setting within the family; and the alliance and coalitions within the family. Thus Karpel and Strauss might say:

> 'I'd like to get a better idea of who spends a good deal of time with whom in the family, whom each of you is most likely to talk to when something is on your mind?' (page 142)

It seems these authors use many more direct questions than the Milan group. For example they describe asking a daughter how she reacted when her mother behaved in a particular way, whereas the Milan associates would probably have asked this question of another family member.

Other areas that Karpel and Strauss suggest as subjects for probe questions are family disagreements, previous family crises and the changes the family members desire to make (which we will consider in Chapter 7).

Assessing how a family functions is by no means simply a matter of asking questions and getting replies. Families tend to reveal more by what they do than by what they say. The therapist will observe who sits where in the room; who plays, or talks to whom; who tells who to do what; whether the children do what their parents tell them; who laughs; who cries; what the other family members do when one of them is upset; whether the parents agree or disagree, for example about a misbehaving child; how outgoing or inhibited are the various family members; and so on. The extent to which the family is well ordered or 'chaotic' is often evident before any questions are asked.

We may summarize by saying that there are many ways of obtaining information about families, and there are few scientific data to tell us which is best. Some interview styles seem to suit certain families better than others. Therapists develop their own personal styles, and use techniques with which they are comfortable and which fit their theoretical models of how families can be helped to change. However we achieve it, we need to come to an understanding of the family system as well as of the individuals in it. The relationship patterns and habitual ways of interacting are a major focus.

The last decade or two have seen the adoption by therapists who term their approach 'post-modern' of a 'conversational' approach, a gentler collaborative way of finding out about the family (Anderson & Goolishian, 1988; Goolishian, 1990; Anderson, 1997).

Developing a diagnostic formulation

At this stage it is necessary for the therapist, or team, to review the information that has been obtained. Many find it helpful then to develop a *diagnostic formulation*. This involves considering how the family functions, whether the presenting problems are related to its way of functioning and, if so, how they are related.

While the human systems to which a person belongs are always relevant, therapists should always bear in mind that sometimes other factors are more important. Physical conditions, such as hyperthyroidism, hypothyroidism, porphyria, cerebral tumours and many other diseases of the nervous system, have particular psychiatric manifestations. Whatever the state of the family system, such conditions require their own specific medical treatment. Referral for assessment and any needed treatment of co-existing medical disorders may be appropriate.

Some psychiatric disorders also appear to have causes which are physical, rather than being related primarily to family factors. In many cases of bipolar affective disorder, the swings between moods of depression, normality and mania occur in a regular cyclical pattern with little or no apparent relationship to external circumstances. In such cases, family therapy may not be the principal treatment needed. However, family therapy may be required even when the presenting problem in one or more members has a predominantly biological cause, since the presence of such a condition does not provide immunity from family dysfunction. Indeed, the reverse is true. Such disorders make family dysfunction more likely, since they are stressful. Emotional factors, which are often closely tied in with the family situation, can also be important in the genesis, and the exacerbation, of physical conditions (see Minuchin et al., 1978).

An important issue that the formulation should address is the extent to which the presenting problems are a feature of family dysfunction and how far they are due to other, perhaps physical, perhaps intrapsychic, causes. In many instances it is not an 'either/or' question that must be answered. Even if there are no relevant physical *disorders* affecting any of the family members – and often none is evident – the temperaments, cognitive styles and physical characteristics of the family members are relevant and important factors.

The formulation should summarize the therapist's understanding of the family. It is not just a listing of factors but a description of their interplay and relative importance. It should include a description of the family system, using whatever theoretical model the therapist favours. The family's developmental stage, and whether it is having difficulty dealing with one of the 'transition points' discussed in Chapter 2, should be considered.

There is much to be said for making a written formulation. It should be concise and clear, and should provide a logical explanation of the case but with mention of areas of uncertainty. It should lead to a treatment plan or, perhaps, a plan for further assessment or investigation. In most cases it will contain the following information:

- A brief description of the problems which have led the family to seek help, and of the changes they hope will result from therapy.
- Mention of the family's constitution, with the members' ages, relationships and occupations, and the family's developmental stage. Much of this information may be provided by attaching the genogram to the formulation.
- The therapist's understanding of the family, the nature of its current problems and how these are being maintained, using whatever theoretical model the therapist finds helpful. The relative importance and interrelation of the various factors maintaining the current situation should be described.
- The family's strengths, assets and motivation for change.
- Information about the family's ecological context or suprasystem, and how this is affecting the family.

When treatment appears to be needed the formulation should lead logically to a treatment plan and, usually, a prognosis: a statement of the expected outcome, with and without treatment.

Offering the family feedback and recommendations

I like to give the family a short break while I develop the formulation. When one or more observers have been watching the session, or colleagues have been participating, the formulation will be developed by the group. Co-therapists will of course want to discuss their findings and develop a joint formulation.

The form the feedback takes will depend on the theoretical orientation of the therapist(s), as well as on the nature of the family's case. It is not simply, or even mainly, a matter of explaining the formulation to the family. Generally, insight in itself is not particularly helpful. Knowing how the therapist understands their problems does not necessarily lead to change. Indeed when a strategic approach to treatment is planned it may impede it.

The feedback should always include any recommendations the therapist has regarding further investigation or assessment of the family, and it should state whether treatment is recommended and, if so, what type. The feedback is often the start of therapy. Depending upon the therapist's theoretical orientation, it may take the form of agreeing a contract for the family to do certain things, as is the practice of those who use the McMaster Model of Family Therapy; or it may be less direct and intended to reframe the situation in a therapeutically helpful way. A narrative approach may be suggested, or one based on social construction theory.

I often find it useful at this stage to 'positively connote' what the family members are doing. What is positively connoted is the *intent* behind the actions of family members, not necessarily the actions themselves. For example, parents may be using inappropriate methods in their attempts to discipline a child, and may even be physically abusing the child, but their intent, namely to rear their child to behave in a socially acceptable way, is nevertheless commendable.

The concept, derived from the work of Milton Erickson and described by Lankton and Lankton (1983), of 'best choice' may be helpful at this stage of the assessment. Erickson believed that people always make the best choice of behaviour available to them in their particular circumstances. It may prove unfortunate, even destructive, but is the best available to those concerned, taking into account their state of mind and situation. Therapy, therefore, is a matter of giving the family members more choice, and alternative, more effective options. Sometimes the therapy plan can helpfully be presented in this way.

Discussing and arranging the next step

It is important that the family leave the first interview knowing what is to happen next. This will often be a matter of setting the date and time of the next appointment. Sometimes other recommendations may be made, such as referral to a colleague for further investigation or specialized treatment. When the family contains a child or children who are having social or academic problems at school, contact with the school, and perhaps a visit to the school, may be suggested. Indeed, Aponte (1976) recommended that when the main problems are at school, the first interview should be a family–school interview. The therapist may sometimes wish to obtain information from professionals who have previously treated the family, or members of it. In that case the necessary forms of consent, authorizing release of this information, should be signed by the appropriate family members.

The question of who should attend future sessions sometimes arises at this stage. If one or more important people were absent from the first interview, the therapist should either ask the family to bring the missing person(s) to the next session – which is quite appropriate if the person concerned is a child – or discuss with the family how to approach the missing individual(s). If these are adults, it may be better for the therapist to make the approach, with the permission of the family. I have outlined a metaphorical approach to this issue elsewhere (Barker, 1985, pages 25–27).

At times it may be helpful to have extended family members who do not live in the household present at certain sessions. On the other hand the therapist may wish to see fewer people, perhaps just the marital couple, next time or even for a series of sessions. In that case, also, the plan should be explained and agreement sought.

Feedback to referring professionals

When a family is referred by another professional person it is both courteous and good clinical practice to send that person a written report of the results of the assessment. This should make it clear how the therapist thinks the referrer can assist in the ongoing treatment of the family. This may involve no more than the referrer not getting involved in the issues the therapy is addressing, but referring questions the family may ask about those issues back to the therapist. It may be helpful to supplement the written report with a telephone call. I believe it is good practice to let the family have a copy of my report to the referring professional. This provides a model of open communication, as well as making the statement that all concerned – family, therapist and referring professional – are part of a team.

Sometimes more active participation, such as joint planning and action, with family physicians, paediatricians, child welfare social workers, school staff and others may be important. In that case the appropriate contacts should be made with the outside people and agencies concerned at this stage, with the family's permission.

Summary

The assessment of families needs to be both systematic and flexible. The initial contact should lead to the establishment of rapport and the gaining of the family's trust. Whatever model of family functioning is employed, the main focus is on the family system: the pattern of the relationships between the members. The construction of a genogram is usually a valuable part of the assessment process. At the same time, the therapist should not overlook the characteristics of the individual family members.

A 'triadic' approach to interviewing families, which involves thinking about groups of three individuals, or collections of individuals, and how they interact, is helpful. The family's developmental stage, and whether it is having difficulty making the transition from one stage to the next one, should be considered.

The assessment leads to a diagnostic formulation. Feedback is then provided to the family. Any treatment recommended is explained. Referring sources should be kept informed, especially if they are still involved. Other outside professionals may need to be contacted and, in some cases, their involvement in the treatment endeavour may be helpful.

Chapter 7
Establishing Treatment Goals

Family therapy is a meeting of therapist(s) and family members for the purpose of working together to achieve changes in the family. These changes may be in the behaviours of family members, in their emotional states or relationships, or in the family's overall functioning. Such an endeavour requires clearly defined and agreed goals.

The 'strategic' and 'solution-focused' approaches to therapy are based on strategies or plans that aim to lead to the changes the family seek. They therefore require well-defined objectives. But the same applies to all other approaches including the 'collaborative' approaches that are being increasingly used. Without defined objectives family and therapist have no way of judging whether and when therapy has been successful.

Negotiating the objectives of treatment and reaching agreement is not always easy, especially when there is pre-existing disagreement between family members. It may take a whole session, sometimes several, but the time is well spent. Indeed, the process itself can be therapeutic.

> Steve and Terri had been married eight years. They had two daughters, one aged 7 years and the other 6 months. Steve was a busy professional man and Terri a homemaker who worked occasionally as a receptionist. They presented with concerns about the behaviour of their 7-year-old daughter, Vivienne.
>
> Vivienne was an attractive, highly intelligent but rather sulky and sullen girl. She was having relationship difficulties with other children at school, where she also exhibited mild behaviour problems and was thought not to be performing up to her academic potential. A much bigger problem, it soon emerged, existed in the marital relationship.
>
> Steve and Terri had met hitch-hiking at a time when Steve was still a student and Terri had just left a home where she had not been happy. They married soon afterwards, both still in their teens. At first things went well for the couple. Until Vivienne's birth Terri worked as a waitress, then as a receptionist, helping support Steve as he continued his studies at university. Terri realized that Steve had to study hard and for long hours, and at first accepted without protest that she got little of his attention. Vivienne arrived sooner than the couple had planned to start a family, and with her birth Terri started to feel increasingly unhappy and lonely. Her parents disapproved of her marriage and also looked down on her, she felt, because she was the only child in their family who had not gone on to higher education.

> Eventually Steve completed his university studies and graduated. He obtained a job working for a large company which demanded much of its trainee executives. He also started attending evening classes, playing squash with colleagues after work and staying out drinking with his friends after these activities. Terri was left, literally, holding the baby at home. She felt trapped in the relationship, estranged from her family of origin and powerless.

My first session with this family was spent exploring the situation and what the couple wanted from therapy. As the seriousness of the marital situation became clear, I asked each spouse to paint a word-picture of his or her desired outcome. They both found this an interesting experience and each was surprised by the picture of the 'ideal marriage' which the other presented. This exercise took up the remainder of the first session, so that no time was left for any other therapeutic work. I therefore made an appointment to see them again the following week.

When they came, Steve and Terri reported a big change for the better in their relationship. While not all their problems were resolved, and Vivienne continued to cause them some concern, they had clearly been helped by learning what each other wanted of the marital relationship.

Even if agreement is never reached, and treatment is not started, time spent discussing treatment objectives may not be wasted. Therapy embarked upon on the basis of misunderstood goals seldom produces results that are satisfactory to any of those concerned. The one possible exception to this is the long-running therapy into which some clients get to achieve 'emotional growth' or 'make gains' – the 'gains' never being defined in any precise way. Such therapy resembles a hiking trip embarked upon with no idea of where the hikers want to go, nor of what they will do when they finally arrive somewhere. Such therapy, like this sort of hiking, can be enjoyable, of course, but it may not be the best way to achieve particular results quickly.

The setting of objectives and the description of an outcome frame do not always have as positive an effect as they did in the above case. Indeed that family was a little unusual in that the marital partners were able to make significant changes simply in response to the discussion of the desired objectives. But it does show how some relationships suffer because the partners are unaware of what each other wants.

Defining the desired state

It is helpful to obtain a clear picture of the 'desired state' which families coming for therapy wish to reach. How this differs from the present situation should also be defined as precisely as possible.

Many family members, and individuals too, come to therapy with negative goals. Parents want their children to stop having tantrums, or fighting with each other; or a spouse wants his or her partner to stop arguing; or a couple want their teenage daughter to stop refusing to eat the food they offer her. These are all valid reasons for seeking professional help, assuming that common-sense measures have proved ineffective, but they are not adequate as outcome descriptions. To put it another way, a description of your 'desired state' requires more than a statement of what you *don't* want to be happening. A comprehensive picture of how you *would* like things to be is as useful to both client and therapist as an architect's mental image is, to the architect, of the building for which plans must be developed.

So it is often useful to ask family members to reframe their objectives in positive terms. If the children are not to have tantrums, how should they react in situations in which they have been having tantrums? If they are not to fight, how should they deal with their disagreements? What should replace the arguments the couple have been engaging in? Presumably the arguments have served some purpose. So too, we may assume, has the teenage girl's refusal to eat. While the objective of having the girl eat more is perfectly reasonable, it might be helpful to consider also the purpose her refusing food has served, and how that purpose might be served in other ways.

Such questions seem scarcely to have been considered by many families seeking therapy. Even when families' goals are stated in positive terms, these are often vague and ill defined. Perhaps they want 'to be a happy family', or 'to get along well together'. These are reasonable enough things to want, and they may be useful starting points for the discussion of treatment goals, but they are not in themselves adequate outcome descriptions. What do the family members believe a 'happy family' to be like? How, exactly, would they be relating to each other if they were getting along 'well'?

Families sometimes describe their objectives in comparative terms. They want to be 'happier' or 'to do more things together'. I ask them to elaborate on such statements. If they are to be happier, the next question may be 'happier than what?' And in what circumstances? What would the family look like, and what would it be doing, if it were happier? What things would they choose to be doing together, where would they be done and how often? And how does all this differ from the way things are now? There may prove to be disagreement on such points, so that what looks like an agreed objective is not really one at all. Indeed fundamental differences may be concealed in such statements. If so, resolving these differences might become a goal of therapy.

I have found it helpful to get families to describe, in as much detail as possible, how things will be when (and not if!) therapy is successfully concluded. This is the process described above in the case of Steve and Terri.

The descriptions you ask for should be sensory based. Ask your clients how they will *sound* when therapy is complete and even have them act it out. The more the family members act out their aimed-for state, the easier it is likely to be for them to achieve it, for they have already, if only briefly, done so.

By talking about how things will be *when* therapy is complete, you embed in your statements the message that it will end successfully. On the other hand, if you discuss how things will be *if* therapy reaches a successful conclusion, you are implying doubts about this, which is not the way to inspire confidence in those who come to you for help.

Once the desired state has been described there are still some questions to be considered:

- Will there be any drawbacks to the desired state? Will anything that at present offers gratification to someone in the family, or serves some useful purpose, be lost, without being replaced by a satisfactory alternative? For example, if the daughter who at present won't eat starts to eat the food her mother prepares, will this result in less closeness between mother and daughter, since there will be no further need for battles or discussions about the daughter's diet? Or will it mean less closeness between the parents because they will no longer need to spend long hours discussing their daughter's eating problem?
- What other consequences will follow once the changes the family seek have occurred? Careful consideration of how things will be for all members of the family when the specified changes have been made may lead to second thoughts. This in turn might lead to further modification of the objectives.
- What has so far stopped the family making the changes they say they would like to make? This question is closely related to the foregoing ones but asking it in this way may place the issue of what is causing the symptoms to continue in a different perspective.
- Under what circumstances are the changes desired? Context is important in the setting of objectives. Thus while it is generally a good thing to be happy, there are circumstances in which this may not be appropriate, for example following a bereavement or other loss. Disagreements and even arguments, especially if they are constructive, can be useful in the right context. So can most other behaviours. Aggression may be needed to defend your loved ones, or even yourself, and there probably are occasions for the telling of 'white lies', for example when the secret police want to take your loved ones away for execution. Most 'symptoms' may therefore have value in some circumstances. There are times when it is appropriate to refuse food, or to get angry, or to feel tired, or to be undecided about something – even to lie.

■ How quickly does the family want to change? This is not only a useful thing to know, but it is also a good question to ask because of the statement embedded in it, namely that change *will* occur if therapy is undertaken. By asking such a question you dismiss, by implication, the issue of whether change is possible, and replace it with that of how quickly the changes should, and will, occur.

Intermediate and final goals

Sometimes it is helpful to distinguish short-term from long-term goals. Psychotherapy may be likened to travelling through a jungle, where it may not be possible to see your final objective and where you cannot survey, from your starting point, the route that will get you there most quickly and easily. So it is often best to plan your journey in stages. A good way to proceed is to climb a tree, survey your route to the next landmark – it may be another large tree – and then repeat the exercise as often as necessary until you reach your objective.

Family therapy, too, is often best approached in stages. Intermediate goals, equivalent to the trees the jungle traveller climbs to survey the next stage of the journey, may be set and reached along the way. Each is an opportunity to review progress and even to set a new course. The intermediate goals may not always need to be made explicit to the family, but the point that every journey starts with the first step can sometimes usefully be made. Setting goals should also be done in such a way as to suggest that they are attainable.

The metaphor of an avalanche, which starts with the movement down the mountain of a small quantity of snow or a few rocks, leading to a massive shift of material down the slope, may be useful. Similarly what look like small therapeutic interventions may have disproportionately large results.

Motivating families to consider and set objectives

Many families readily understand the desirability of defining their objectives, but some question it and seem satisfied with vague ideas and ill-thought-out notions about what they want from treatment. In such cases the importance of well-defined objectives can be explained metaphorically. The following story, reproduced from *Using Metaphors in Psychotherapy* (Barker, 1985), illustrates the value of careful preparation.

Norman, a man who was well skilled with his hands, wanted to build a garden shed. So he went to a store that sold materials and supplies for the 'do-it-yourself' market and asked for advice. The salesman he spoke to asked him a lot of questions, many of which he was not immediately able to answer. He wanted to know what kinds of things Norman planned to keep in the shed, how big it should be, on what sort of ground it was to be built and with what materials, what kind of floor Norman wanted it to have, what tools and equipment Norman already had at home and how much he could afford to spend on the shed.

Norman realized that he needed to give a lot more thought to his project than he had done so far. So he first gathered together all the items he intended to keep in the shed, including his lawn-mower, electric hedge-clipper and wheelbarrow, his garden tools, the fertilizer spreader and a couple of bags of fertilizer, his children's bicycles, some flower pots and seed boxes and sundry smaller items. He was now able to estimate the size of shed he would need.

Next Norman assembled all his wood-working and other tools. These had been scattered in various parts of the house, and some had not been used for years. Indeed he was surprised by some of his finds, tools he had long forgotten acquiring. The total was impressive and it seemed as if Norman might have just about all the equipment he needed.

Norman now examined carefully the site where he planned to erect the shed. It was damp and it seemed safer to plan to have a wooden floor raised up, perhaps on concrete blocks, above ground level.

Finally Norman reviewed his financial situation. The salesman had given him a rough idea of what sheds made of different materials would cost and it seemed that he would be able to afford a cedar wood shed, which was what he had originally hoped to build.

Norman now had a pretty clear idea of what the shed he was going to build would look like, the work that would be involved in constructing it and what it would cost in time and money. He decided to go ahead with it, and was ready to return, properly prepared, to the store to buy the materials he needed, to receive instructions and a plan of how to build the shed; also to purchase those few additional tools he required.

Maintaining and developing a family's motivation is important at all stages of therapy. The period when goals are being set is one during which this process can often be actively promoted. Sometimes certain family members do not believe that the changes they desire can be achieved. Sometimes the whole family thinks this. Some families even come to therapists with the expectation that there will be no change! Their aim seems to be simply to prove that nothing can be done. (I believe they are the sort of people Watzlawick (1983) wrote about in *The Situation is Hopeless but not Serious*.) The process of goal-setting and the discussion of the outcome frame can, if approached optimistically and in a business-like fashion, greatly reassure families that they, along with the rest of the human race, have the potential for change.

Summary

Family therapy, like most human activities, is more likely to be successful if it has clear goals. Time and effort spent in defining goals are usually well repaid. Well-defined goals assist the therapist in developing a treatment plan, and they offer encouragement to the family, especially if the result is an agreed set of objectives which appear realistic.

The 'desired state' is that which, when achieved, will constitute a completely satisfactory therapy result. It should be stated in positive, rather than negative, terms. That is to say it should describe how things *will* be at the successful conclusion of treatment, rather than how they will *not* be.

Other important points about goal setting are:

(1)   Aim for specific, definable objectives.
(2)   Determine the context in which the new behaviours are desired. The old ones may still have their uses under certain circumstances.
(3)   Have the family consider whether there will be any drawbacks to the desired state. If there will be, are the changes worth making?
(4)   What other consequences will follow once the changes desired have been made?
(5)   What has stopped the family making the desired changes so far?
(6)   How quickly do the family want to change?

It is sometimes helpful to have intermediate goals, to be achieved during the course of therapy.

Chapter 8
When Should We Use Family Therapy?

Family therapy aims to change the functioning of families. That might seem a simple enough concept, but families do not usually come complaining of the way they function. Usually someone comes, or is brought, with particular symptoms or behavioural problems. The therapist must then decide which therapeutic option, of the wide range which nowadays exists, will best meet the needs of the case.

Family therapists tend to understand human problems in relationship terms. This may explain why discussion of the indications for family therapy is more often found in textbooks of psychiatry, and in journals not devoted primarily to family therapy, than in texts on family therapy. In the early days of family therapy this approach was seen by some of the pioneers as almost a panacea for all human problems. Indeed as recently as 1980, Haley, in his book *Leaving Home*, claimed that his methods were equally appropriate whether the identified patient is schizophrenic, anorectic, delinquent, addicted to heroin, antisocial, violent or mentally retarded. While the families of such patients may have problems requiring attention, claiming family therapy as the primary treatment modality for them all seems to be going beyond what the evidence supports. By contrast, Steinberg (1983), in his text on adolescent psychiatry, paid much attention to the question of when family therapy should be used. He considered family therapy a distinct form of treatment, with its own particular place within the wider range of therapies. This is probably the current thinking among mental health professionals generally.

In a sense, all therapy with any one or more persons who belong to a family group is family therapy, since change in any one family member inevitably has its impact on the whole family group. But how can we know whether we should be working with the whole family, with a part of it, or just with one member? In practice the various forms of family therapy *are* different from therapies which take the individual as their focus, even though the latter, when effective, have effects in the family as a whole. Moreover, therapists skilled in working with families are often less skilled in work with individuals than those who concentrate on individual psychotherapy, and *vice versa*.

A second issue is that of physical illness. As we have seen in Chapter 6 psychiatric symptoms can be due to endocrine disorders (for example hypothyroidism and hyperthyroidism), metabolic disorders (such as porphyria), infections (for example syphilis) and many other diseases of the brain. Medical and surgical therapies are available for such conditions, and family therapy should not be the primary treatment for them; the families of those with such conditions may, however, need therapy.

A third point is that other psychiatric treatments, pharmacological as well as psychotherapeutic, are available. It is therefore necessary to consider when one of these may be the treatment of first choice. Schizophrenia is nowadays usually treated pharmacologically, and most psychiatrists caring for such patients do not see family factors as being the principal ones to be addressed in treatment. Yet the family environment has its effects and its characteristics may help determine whether the schizophrenic patient relapses. (This is discussed further in Chapter 11.) Similarly, antidepressant drugs are sometimes the best treatment for depressed individuals, and the use of anxiolytic drugs for anxious patients may have to be considered, if only as a short-term crisis measure.

Finally, it seems that systems theory, as Searight and Merkel (1991) put it, 'may have significant limitations in accounting for family dysfunction and for guiding intervention'. Nichols (1987) pointed out that in the last analysis it is individuals that change, not systems. Change in the system is a result of the changed behaviour of the individuals in it. Intervention in the system, which is the basis of so much family therapy, may not always be the only or even the best way of promoting change.

It is remarkable how many textbooks on family therapy gloss over the issue of the indications for family therapy. For example, *Integrating Family Therapy* (Mikesell et al., 1995); *Treating People In Families* (Nichols, 1996); and *Family Therapy Techniques* (Carlson et al., 2005) are all silent on the issue of when family therapy, rather than some other treatment method, is indicated. One might expect that this would have been the subject of research, but no such research is included in *Research Methods in Family Therapy* (Sprenkle & Piercy, 2005).

Basic criteria for employing family therapy

Two conditions should exist before family therapy is recommended. These are:

(1)   Evidence of a malfunctioning family group.
(2)   Evidence that the family dysfunction is related to the problems for which help is being sought.

For these criteria to mean anything, the terms 'malfunctioning' and 'dysfunction' have to be defined. Unfortunately, as we saw in Chapter 2, there are no agreed norms for the functioning of families. Some families which seem to be functioning in quite unusual ways appear to be free of clinical problems, while others appear relatively 'normal', at least at first acquaintance, and yet contain members with severe clinical problems. In addressing issues of this sort the models of family functioning reviewed in Chapter 5 are useful. They direct our attention to specific aspects of family interaction which can be the focus of therapy. This is more important than deciding whether a family is 'normal' or not, although the attempt by Beavers (1982) to define 'healthy, midrange, and severely dysfunctional' families was a bold attempt to do this. Another helpful concept is that of 'optimal family process', described by Kirschner and Kirschner (1986). These authors also addressed in a helpful way the issue of when whole family groups should be treated, and when therapy should focus on individual members.

Whether or not you choose to compare the families you see with some theoretical norm, it is important to make the best judgment possible of whether the presenting problems can be understood on the basis of the way the family functions. In doing this, it can be helpful to use as a guide one of the models suggested in Chapter 5, or one of the several other models that are available. Occasionally families present themselves as family units and define their problems in family terms, and with increasing public awareness of family therapy this may be happening more often. In such cases family therapy is usually the best approach. Often, however, involvement of the whole family, when it occurs, happens at the therapist's initiative.

Differing views on the place of family therapy

Some therapists pay more attention than others to the assessment of whether or not family therapy is indicated. Beal (1976) investigated the differences between therapists, using a modified version of a scale developed by the Group for the Advancement of Psychiatry (1970) when it rated the theoretical orientation of therapists. He found that therapists at the A end of the scale, that is those who are primarily concerned with the appropriate expression of emotion in the family, are more concerned about the indications and contra-indications for therapy than are therapists at the Z end, those concerned chiefly with family structure and communication pathways. To this latter group problems are interactional (they do not reside in individuals but in the processes of interaction going on in a family or other social system); and behavioural (consisting of behaviour 'which is stimulated and shaped by the behaviour of others') (Weakland, 1977, page 23). Weakland (1979, page 57) also wrote of how the family approach to treatment has come to be applied to 'the whole spectrum of recognized psychiatric problems, except the manifestly organic'.

Unfortunately the question of what is 'manifestly organic' is often hard to answer. The system of an identified patient with an obviously organic problem, for example cerebral palsy, may or may not be badly functioning. Moreover, many medical problems are nowadays seen as having multiple and complex causes. Bronchial asthma is a good example. In severe cases there are often structural changes in the lungs and in all cases the physiological control of respiratory function is abnormal. In addition allergy and infection are important factors in precipitating attacks. A comprehensive treatment plan cannot overlook these factors. In a sense, asthma is 'manifestly organic', certainly once there are structural changes in the lungs, but there is reason to believe that attacks of asthma can be precipitated by processes occurring in the family system (Minuchin et al., 1975).

Haley (1976, pages 170–178) explains the difference between orientation A and orientation Z in his usual lucid way. The A therapist, he says, is attempting to achieve understanding of the problems and emotional growth in individuals, whereas the Z therapist is working to produce specific changes in particular behaviours without being concerned about understanding or insight. The indications which each type of therapist considers appropriate are therefore bound to be different. In addition the A therapist is typically willing to use traditional group therapy techniques, whereas the Z therapist sticks to the family or other naturally occurring groups.

Then there is the question of schizophrenia. Is *it* organic? Many, probably most, psychiatrists would say 'yes'. There are certainly genetic factors involved. There is also evidence pointing to various biochemical abnormalities in the brain. Yet there is also reason to believe that the likelihood of relapse in schizophrenic patients discharged from hospital is influenced by family factors (Leff & Vaughn, 1985). The *Clinical Practice Guidelines – Treatment of Schizophrenia* (Canadian Psychiatric Association Working Group, 2005) has a chapter on 'psychosocial interventions' that includes a section on family interventions. So in developing a comprehensive treatment plan for the subject with schizophrenia, and indeed for those suffering from a variety of other disorders, family therapy is often one element.

Some views on indications

The indications for family therapy, like the objectives of treatment, should be positive ones. Walrond-Skinner (1978), defining family therapy as 'the psychotherapeutic treatment of the family system, using as its most basic medium conjoint interpersonal interviews', identified four approaches to the subject. The first is the *exclusive approach* position. This is very much the Z therapist's position. Disturbance in an individual is to be dealt with by treating the system of which the individual is a part. Family therapy, perhaps better called systems therapy since systems other than family groups may be the focus of treatment, thus becomes a new orientation to both understanding and treating psychiatric disorders, and one suitable for almost universal application.

At the other extreme Walrond-Skinner defined the *treatment of last resort* position, family therapy only being employed when all else has failed. If this view of the place of family therapy is taken, it may be applied only to particularly severe and serious disorders, so that its chances of success are likely to be limited.

The *diagnostic aid* position is taken, according to Walrond-Skinner, by those who see family therapy as an adjunct which may be used to assist in treatment selection and to promote the more effective use of individual, group or inpatient treatment. It may also be used intermittently, perhaps during 'a crisis phase of therapy', and can be useful in overcoming intra-psychic or interpersonal resistance to therapy.

Finally there is the *differential treatment* position taken by clinicians who consider family therapy along with other treatments which might be used. Whether it is selected depends in part on whether the therapist's theoretical model suggests that it will be effective. Such clinicians also take into account their clinical experience and their understanding of the literature on the subject in deciding what treatment to recommend.

Neither of the first two of the above positions seems tenable. While the 'systems approach' to families and their treatment is indeed a new way of tackling mental health problems, it does not mean that all other approaches must be abandoned or are of no value. Indeed, many family therapists use other approaches when these are needed by the individuals or families they are treating. It is clear also that family therapy can be more than a treatment of last resort. Indeed there are probably few therapists who nowadays take that point of view. The 'diagnostic aid' position may be tenable if family therapy is not conceived as limited to it. It does seem, however, that family therapy can be a powerful treatment when properly used in the right cases. But it should only be embarked upon after a careful consideration of the relative merits of the full range of available treatments.

Walrond-Skinner (1978) went on to suggest the following indications:

(1) Symptoms considered by the therapist to be embedded in a dysfunctional system of family relationships. If the symptoms appear to be expressing the 'pain or dysfunction' of the family system, family therapy will probably be the best treatment. There remains the difficulty of assessing whether this criterion is met. How to set about this has been discussed in Chapter 6.

Tracie was a shy, timid and anxious 8-year-old, the third child and youngest daughter in a family of four children. She was referred because of her inhibited behaviour and social isolation at school. Her mother also felt that she was slow learning to read, though the teachers at her school disagreed with this opinion. This was a consequence of the mother's belief that Tracie was 'super-intelligent', a view not substantiated by intelligence testing, which showed her cognitive functioning to be within the average range.

There was much emotional distance between the parents. The father disagreed with the mother's attitudes towards the children, which he thought were overcontrolling, but he let her do as she wished. Tracie had always been a difficult, frail and rather special child, in mother's view, and a close, anxiously enmeshed relationship between her and her mother had developed, apparently at the expense of the relationship between mother and father.

In this case it was easy to understand the presenting problems in the light of the family's way of functioning. In structural terms, mother and Tracie had an enmeshed relationship. Using the McMaster or Process Models, Tracie had a special role, that of frail, special child, regarded by mother as 'super-intelligent'. Father was relatively disengaged from the rest of the family, and there was a poorly functioning parental system.

Tracie's inhibited behaviour and over-dependence on her mother were integral parts of the pattern of family functioning. It was unlikely that her behaviour would change much, if at all, until the family system changed. The situation could also be formulated in family developmental terms: Tracie had remained dependent on her mother to a degree more appropriate to the infant or toddler years. The normal emotional separation of mother and child which occurs as toddler becomes schoolchild had not taken place. Just how the presenting clinical picture had arisen was unclear. Such situations often turn out to have multiple causes. Temperamental and/or physical factors in child and parents may interact with relationship difficulties in the nuclear family, extended family systems problems, and perhaps extra-familial factors. The causes are however less important than the cure, and if there is a family systems problem related to the presenting symptoms, family therapy may be helpful.

(2) Problems presented by those seeking help to produce some change in a relationship rather than to deal with problems in an individual family member. Examples are marital difficulties, including those involving sexual problems, child–parent relationship problems and problems between siblings.

(3) Separation difficulties. These are considered by many therapists to be best treated by family therapy. Indeed they are really no more than examples of the kind of relationship difficulties mentioned above. Thus a

family containing an adolescent girl trying to separate from her family, or an overprotected younger child who is having difficulty growing up, may be helped by family therapy. Family therapy may be equally useful when members need to become closer to each other; that is when the process of separating has gone too fast, or when marital partners have never become sufficiently close. During the latter parts of the family life cycle, however, many of the tasks with which families have difficulty concern the separating out process as children leave the home and go their various ways.

(4) Family therapists with a psychoanalytical viewpoint believe family therapy to be of value with families 'functioning at a basically paranoid-schizoid level, with part object relationships, lack of ego boundaries and extensive use of denial, splitting and projection' (Skynner, 1969b). Such families bear similarities to those in which Bowen (1966) described an 'undifferentiated ego mass'. The idea is that basic psychological functions are scattered among the family members, who are not properly functioning individuals in their own right. It may be that such a description is only another way of referring to many of the families covered under items (1), (2) and (3) above.

(5) Family therapy has been used for severely disorganized families, functioning badly and in poor socioeconomic circumstances. A project to help such families was described by Minuchin and his colleagues (1967) in the important book *Families of the Slums.*

The 'decision tree'

Clarkin et al. (1979) reviewed the limited research literature on the indications for family therapy and employed this to construct a 'decision tree' for use in determining whether family therapy or some other form of treatment should be used. These authors proposed four steps, as follows.

Step 1. Is family or marital evaluation indicated?

The authors defined family evaluation as one or more family interviews designed to assess the structure and process of family interaction, in order to discover how this is related to the behaviour and symptoms of individual members. They concluded that situations in which family or marital evaluation are almost always essential include the following:

(1) When a child or adolescent is the presenting patient.
(2) When the presenting problem is sexual difficulty or dissatisfaction.
(3) When the presenting problem is a serious family or marital problem, especially when the future of the marital relationship, the adequate care of the children in the family, or family members' vocational stability or health are at stake.

(4)   When there has been a recent stress or emotional disruption in the family, caused by such family crises as serious illness, injury, loss of job, death or the departure from the home of one of the family members.

(5)   When the family or the marital pair, or an individual within the group, defines the problem as a family issue and family evaluation is sought.

Clarkin and his colleagues (1979) also suggested that family evaluation is usually indicated when admission of a family member to hospital for psychiatric treatment is being considered. In such circumstances family evaluation is of value for history-gathering, to clarify the relationship between family interaction patterns and the course of the identified patient's illness, and in order to negotiate a treatment plan with the whole family. Other 'less powerful' indications for family evaluation include:

(6)   Situations in which more than one family member is simultaneously in psychiatric treatment.

(7)   When improvement in a patient coincides with the development of symptoms in another or a deterioration in their relationship.

(8)   When individual or group therapy is failing or has failed, and the patient is very involved with family problems, has difficulty dealing with family issues or shows evidence of too intense transference to the therapist; or when family cooperation appears necessary in order that the individual can change.

(9)   When, during individual evaluation, it appears that the advantages to the family of the patient's symptoms can be understood in the light of the psychological functioning of the family.

Step 2. Deciding whether either family or marital treatment is required

This next step involves deciding whether treatment using a family or marital therapy approach, as opposed to individual treatment, sex therapy or in-patient treatment in hospital, is required. Clarkin and his co-authors suggested that family or marital therapy may be indicated:

(1)   When marital problems are a presenting problem.

(2)   When a family presents with current problems in the relationships between family members.

(3)   When there are chronic and severe problems in perception and communication. These include projective identification, in which members blame each other for the problems and disclaim their own parts in them; paranoid-schizoid functioning, as mentioned above; and various severely disturbed forms of communication such as are seen in schizophrenia.

(4)   In the presence of adolescent antisocial behaviour, such as promiscuity, drug abuse, delinquency or violent behaviour.

(5)   When there are adolescent separation problems.

(6)   When there is found to be control or manipulation of the parent by the child.
(7)   Following the failure of other treatment, for example when individual therapy sessions have been used mainly to discuss family problems.
(8)   When the family group is motivated to accept treatment but an individual is not.
(9)   When improvement in one family member leads to symptoms or deterioration in another.
(10) When more than one person needs treatment and resources are available for only one treatment.

The next choice is between family and marital therapy. In making this choice the therapist must consider whether the main problems are in the spouse subsystem or in the family as a whole, and also the motivation of the different family members to become involved in one or other type of therapy.

If marital therapy is selected, the decision then has to be made whether or not to include sex therapy as a part or even the major part of this. The decision will depend upon whether sexual problems are present, how severe they are and whether the marital problem is clearly centred about the sexual difficulties. In addition the couple must be motivated to have sex therapy and be willing and able to carry out the appropriate tasks.

Finally the therapist must decide whether 'family crisis therapy' should be considered as an alternative to admission to hospital. Family crisis therapy is an approach described by Langsley et al. (1968, 1969). It consists of an intense but brief family intervention performed at the time of crisis. It is discussed further in Chapter 17.

Timing is another issue, though it is not directly addressed by Clarkin and colleagues (1979). The selection of a particular approach to therapy does not preclude the use of another one at a different time. Decisions regarding the timing of therapeutic interventions can significantly affect outcome.

Step 3. Deciding on the duration and intensity of therapy

The choice here is between family crisis therapy, brief family therapy and long-term family therapy. The former is most likely to be indicated when the problems with which the family presents are associated with a developmental or other crisis, and particularly when the problems are acute and urgent.

Brief family therapy, which the authors defined as lasting less than 6 months and consisting of sessions no more often than once a week, is indicated for less urgent problems. These include the following situations:

(1)   When there is a focal symptom or conflict involving a child, adolescent or marital pair and the family is highly motivated to change.

(2)   When family involvement is necessary to support another method of treatment, such as regular attendance at a day hospital.
(3)   When a couple presents seeking help in deciding whether to separate.
(4)   In family situations too complex to be understood in a brief evaluation. In this situation brief family therapy may enable the therapist to learn more about the situation and test the response to treatment.

Long-term therapy may be indicated for more complex and chronic problems, especially where a family's motivation to change is strong and in instances where the family has failed to respond to family crisis therapy or brief treatment.

Step 4

This step is not explored by Clarkin and his colleagues (1979), but consists of determining which family therapy approach is likely to be most useful in a particular case. Currently there are few sound data on this.

The practical value of the 'decision tree' is unclear. While it was derived from an extensive review of the literature, this in turn had many limitations. It consisted largely of personal views arising out of therapists' own clinical experiences, rather than being based on scientifically sound studies. I have summarized it here because the principle of using a decision tree along the lines suggested seems a sensible approach. One first considers the circumstances in which family or marital evaluation is indicated; then considers a number of steps, leading up to the selection of a particular form of treatment, if any is required.

In addition to the above indications certain authors have advocated the use of specific approaches to family therapy in particular disorders, for example psychosomatic conditions (Minuchin et al., 1978) and 'families in schizophrenic transaction' (Palazzoli et al., 1978a).

Contra-indications for family therapy

There are even fewer hard data on the contra-indications for family therapy than there are on the indications. Walrond-Skinner (1976) commented that lists of contra-indications may say more about therapists' own areas of defensiveness than about the likely effectiveness of the therapy. She also commented that what to one therapist is a contra-indication may to another be a challenge. Nevertheless she did suggest the following contra-indications:

(1)   There may be practical limitations to family therapy. If key family members are unavailable for geographical or other reasons, or are completely unmotivated to become involved in treatment, family

therapy may have to be ruled out. Another factor is the availability of a suitably trained and experienced therapist. Family therapy is a complex and often difficult undertaking, and it is important that the skills of the therapist be matched to the needs of the family. If this is not so it may be better not to start until a suitably skilled therapist is available, either to carry out the treatment or to provide 'live' supervision behind a one-way screen.

(2) Family therapy may be contra-indicated because the family presents too late in the course of the disorder. The outlook may be too poor to justify the necessary expenditure of time and money, though this is very much a value judgment and the question of whether a family wishes to spend its money on family therapy is perhaps its decision, rather than the therapist's. Ackermann (1966) mentioned as a contra-indication 'the presence of a malignant, irreversible trend towards break-up of the family which may mean that it is too late to reverse the process of fragmentation'. Yet the fact that a family is likely to break up, or is in the process of breaking up, does not necessarily mean that family therapy is inappropriate. Sometimes people seek help in separating or divorcing amicably and with as little damage as possible to all concerned, and the therapist may be able help them achieve this.

(3) It may be dangerous to attempt family therapy when 'the emotional equilibrium is so precariously maintained that attempts to change the relationship system may precipitate a severe decompensation on the part of one or more family members'. It is certainly the case that many families maintain themselves in a precarious and stressful adjustment. In some cases an alteration in the family situation could increase the stress faced by one or more individuals. This in turn could lead to a worsening of their condition with perhaps depression or even suicide. These are issues requiring mature clinical judgment, including careful assessment of suicidal and other risks. Such risks should always be borne in mind when deciding whether or not to embark on family therapy or any other treatment. Walrond-Skinner (1976) also mentions that it may be felt unwise to embark on family therapy when one or more members are organically ill, lest this raises hopes of a 'magical' cure of the organic illness. This risk can usually be avoided by the clear setting of objectives, as discussed in Chapter 7.

(4) Some therapists consider that family therapy may be contra-indicated in the presence of depression or severe emotional deprivation in one or more members. Walrond-Skinner suggested that the combination of individual treatment for the members with these symptoms may in such cases be combined with sessions for the whole family. Kirschner and Kirschner (1986) described an approach taking into account, and providing treatment for, both family systems problems

and individual psychopathology in family members. Comprehensive family therapy (abbreviated to CFT by the authors) seems to offer the prospect of helping families in which there is severe psychopathology in one or more members. These are challenging families, hard to engage and to help and CFT may offer a rational approach to them. The need to consider the individuals in the family, as well as the functioning of the family system, is also the main theme of Nichols' (1987) book.

(5) Finally, Walrond-Skinner (1976) advocated caution when the family is referred by an agency such as a court or school. In such cases there may be a hidden agenda, for example the family's desire to avoid a more severe sentence, or to prevent a child from being expelled from a school, rather than a real wish to change. If the family is deeply involved with other agencies, the therapist's relationship with these agencies, and their role in the treatment and the disclosure of any information arising from it, should be clearly defined before therapy is begun. Sometimes it is found that it is the family/agency system that should be the focus of treatment.

Clarkin et al. (1979), in describing their 'decision tree' for the selection of patients for family therapy, also listed contra-indications which had been mentioned in the research literature. Many are similar to those mentioned by Walrond-Skinner (1976). They include various signs of lack of motivation for, or strong prejudice against, family therapy. The inclusion of members who are in the process of 'individuation', for example a young adult who has just left the family, may not be desirable, lest it compromise the individuation process (Glick & Kessler, 1974).

Summary

In the early days of family therapy, some therapists regarded family therapy as an effective treatment for virtually all non-organic psychological disorders. Nowadays it is generally looked upon as one of a variety of therapy approaches, each of which has its place in the treatment of emotional and behavioural disorders. While there is a school of thought which considers anything that produces change in a family system as family therapy, even the treatment of an individual family member, in practice it is necessary to decide whether or not to make the family system the main focus of therapy.

Family therapy should be considered when (a) there is a malfunctioning family group; and (b) the problems which therapy is to address are related to the functioning of the family. It is likely to be of value when the presenting problems concern children or adolescents; when families present complaining that members have problems in relating to each other; and when a family appears to be having difficulty making the changes required to pass from one developmental stage to the next, for example when adolescents start to become more autonomous.

Family therapy is neither a 'cure-all' nor a treatment of last resort, but an effective way of dealing with problems which are embedded in a dysfunctional family system. It may sometimes usefully be combined with the treatment of individual family members.

The 'decision tree' approach involves first deciding whether family or marital *assessment* is indicated, then whether family or marital *treatment* is required, and if so whether the family or the marital couple should be the focus of the therapy. Then the duration, intensity and type of family treatment needed are considered.

Chapter 9
Practical Points in the Treatment of Families

Involving reluctant family members

In Chapter 6 we considered some points which can be made to family members who do not understand why the whole family should come to the initial assessment interview. Making these points does not always result in everyone attending. Sometimes reluctance disappears once the key family members realize how interdependent family members are. The family members may also need to come to understand, perhaps by being given examples, that emotionally healthy and well-functioning family members usually contribute helpfully to the therapeutic process.

Karpel and Strauss (1983) discussed how a therapist may negotiate full attendance at a family assessment interview. They also made suggestions about when to compromise, and when not to do so, on the matter of full attendance. They recommended that, at least in the initial phone contact, the reluctant family members should be told simply that the goal of the interview is to gather as much information as possible about the presenting problem. They warn that:

> 'Going beyond a variant of the "information-gathering" rationale for the family evaluation . . . may lead the caller (usually a parent) to feel that he or she is being blamed for the family's troubles. Or it may cause the caller to become angry and defensive over someone implying that there is something wrong with his or her family.' (Karpel & Strauss, 1983, page 100)

Reluctance or refusal to attend may be met with at any point in the assessment or treatment process. The therapist then has various choices. One is to decline to start, or continue, with therapy. While this may occasionally be the best course of action, we must bear in mind that the refusal of the reluctant family member(s) to attend is probably but one manifestation of the family's problems. There is a certain lack of logic in declining to offer help to a family because of the very problems for which they require help. So what alternatives do we have?

There are four categories of family member who may decline to attend: parents or marital partners; dependent children; 'adult' children; and extended family members (grandparents, uncles, aunts, cousins and so forth).

A missing parent or marital partner

If the presenting problem concerns a child, or the marital relationship, and one parent (or marital partner) declines to attend while the other wishes to do so, this suggests that there may be marital problems, or major difficulties in the functioning of the pair as a parental couple. When one parent is reluctant to be involved from the start, direct communication with this person by the therapist may be effective. In making contact, taking a 'one-down' position may be helpful. That is, you say, in effect, that you need the help of the reluctant person. The message is, 'I need your help in order to be effective in helping your son (or your daughter, your family, your wife, or whoever is being presented as the problem).' Contrast this with saying that the person must come because the therapist, as an 'expert', insists, or because the person concerned is a part of the problem.

If marital difficulties are the main presenting problem it is important to involve both partners. If one asks for help and the other is unwilling to come, even after a direct request from the therapist, I am usually willing to see the partner who is asking for help, at least once. The purposes of such a meeting are, first, to explore in a face-to-face interview possible means whereby the other partner may be induced to attend; second, to assess the mental state of the partner who is seeking help, since that person may have a disorder which can be treated other than by marital therapy; and third, to explore whether there may be any possibility of starting treatment of the marital difficulties by seeing the one partner.

If the identified patient is a child, and it is a two-parent family, it is important to involve both parents from the start. If only one agrees to come, or actually shows up for the first interview, I usually see the children with the one parent, but during the first interview I focus on the issue of the missing parent and how that person might become involved in the treatment. Sometimes the reluctant parent becomes willing to attend when the family returns home and talks about the session, mentioning perhaps that the things the absent parent feared (perhaps that they would be told the family was a 'bad' one, or that the problem was the parents' fault) did not happen.

If after two or three sessions one parent is still failing to attend, a further direct approach by the therapist, perhaps by telephone, may be successful. Again it is often helpful to use the 'one-down' approach. In other words the therapist is saying, 'After two (or three) sessions with your family, I find I need your help more than ever. I'm sure the information you can give me will make things a lot clearer.' Another approach is to plead confusion. You may say you feel defeated by the problem the family presents, and can only make progress with the help of the person concerned. If this approach fails, and the presence of the missing parent seems vital if progress is to be made, this may be the time to suggest that there should be no further sessions until the missing parent is available. This is risky and may present ethical problems, but it may precipitate a crisis leading to the involvement of the missing parent. Or it may result in the family situation deteriorating further, or the child's symptoms worsening. Such developments seem sometimes to be necessary before change for the better can start. When the problems are marital and one partner fails to attend, a similar approach is indicated.

When parents are divorced or separated, and the identified patient is a child, therapy normally starts with the family in which the identified patient lives. But parenthood does not end with divorce, and involvement of the other parent is often desirable at some stage, even if the children do not have regular contact with that parent. When there *is* regular contact, problems in the relationship between the two parents, or families, often continue despite the separation. When this is so such problems usually need to be the focus of therapeutic attention. Having both parents present at some sessions may be helpful. This emphasizes that they each still have a parental role despite the separation or divorce. Unresolved issues between separated parents may persist for many years, and the children may be used as pawns in a game in which the parents continue to play out their feelings towards each other.

Achieving a joint meeting of two separated parents can be difficult, but is often worth working hard to achieve. I usually meet first with each parent, and any new marital partner either one may have. These meetings can be used to discuss how important both parents are to their children, and to explain the benefits that accrue when separated parents work together on parenting issues. The purpose of the sessions should be defined as that of dealing with children's issues, rather than aiming to repair the marital relationship. Once this has been made clear, parents often become more willing to come.

Missing dependent children

Children, including adolescents, who are living at home in the care of their parents sometimes object to coming to family therapy sessions; or their parents may be willing to bring only the identified patient, on the grounds that that child has the problem and therefore no one else need be involved.

We then have two possible problems. That of children or adolescents, and it is often adolescents, who object to coming is the simpler. If the parents have decided that the family should have therapy, and that the children should attend, the children should be expected to come, just as they are expected to go to school, or to bed at night, or to do any of the other things which parents reasonably expect of their children. If a child refuses to come, this is a therapeutic issue. It may be necessary to see the parents, and any children who will come, and work out a means of enabling the parents, or parent, to gain control of their child(ren).

The situation is different when it is the parents who are reluctant to have a child or children attend. They may not want the other children involved because they see the problems as residing in the identified patient. Involving anyone else in the treatment might threaten that assumption. Another question, which arises in many situations in which there are problems concerning who should attend, is that of who is to control the therapy process: is it to be the therapist or the family? It is a paradox that a family will seek the help of a therapist, but will then dictate how the treatment should proceed. Yet this often happens, probably because change, though desired, is also threatening. If the family remains in charge, the progress of therapy may be adversely affected. However, such situations are less likely to arise when therapy is presented as a collaborative endeavour, rather than one in which the therapist takes on the role of an expert who prescribes how the treatment process should go. 'Let's work together on this' is usually a helpful approach.

Many reasons are offered for parents' refusal to bring certain children. They do not want them to miss school, because they are already behind in their studies and may fail if they miss any more. Or the other children are unaware of the identified patient's problems (something which in reality is rarely the case) and should not be bothered about it, or might even be harmed in some way by knowing about it. Or the other children would miss out on some sporting or other activity which is important to them.

The simplest way of dealing with parents' objections to bringing the other children is to explain why it is helpful to see everyone, at least at the first session. Who should attend future sessions can be discussed at that meeting, and this can be an ongoing process as treatment proceeds. The therapist's interest in meeting everyone in the family and obtaining as much information about the family as possible can be emphasized, together with the point that no one will be compelled to reveal information or discuss topics they do not wish to mention.

Sometimes it is possible to achieve a meeting of the whole family by initially agreeing to family members' requests or conditions as a means of engaging them. It may then later be possible to get everyone to attend without the conditions. The following case illustrates this.

Jason, aged 11, his father, Ken, and his stepmother, Lynn, presented themselves for the first interview. One full sister, two stepsiblings and a baby recently born to Ken and Lynn were left at home, although Ken and Lynn had been asked to bring the whole family. The parents complained that Jason was presenting a host of behaviour problems and that these were getting steadily worse. As a result, he had recently been placed in a foster home. Ken and Lynn seemed unshakable in their belief that the problem was solely Jason's, though I thought there was evidence of a number of family systems' problems. Ken, supported by Lynn, insisted that Jason required hypnosis, which would solve all his behavioural problems.

I decided to go along with this idea and saw Jason three times, each time doing some hypnotherapy. Jason proved to be an excellent hypnotic subject and the sessions were used to help him gain access to some good feelings about himself, related to various successful past experiences, and improve his self-image. At the conclusion of these three sessions I suggested a meeting of the whole family to discover what changes the family members had observed in Jason, who had been spending his weekends at home.

Presented in this way, the parents found the idea of a family meeting quite acceptable. They even asked if they could bring the baby, before I had had a chance to tell them that I did want everyone, including the baby, to come. When at last the family meeting occurred, it proved possible to do a great deal more than ascertain the changes the other family members had observed in Jason, although the session started as an enquiry into Jason's recent behaviour. Moreover the family seemed to find the sort of family interview that was carried out neither alarming nor threatening to them. Nor did they feel they were being criticized, as they had apparently thought they would be.

Missing adult children

'Adult' children may be divided into those who have physically left home, and those who are still living in the parents' home. It may not be reasonable to expect the former group to come to sessions against their will, though many are glad to help resolve a problem in their family of origin. All the therapist should do in these cases is invite the independent children to come for sessions whenever it appears that this would be helpful. If the reasons for inviting them have been explained to them, and they refuse, this should be accepted.

The situation is different when adult children are still living at home, even if they are wage-earning and contributing their share of the household budget. Sometimes such children decline to come to therapy sessions. Whether the parents should expect them to do so, even unwillingly, depends in part on the 'contract', written or more probably unwritten, on the basis of which these children are still living at home. This contract may be unclear, and an aim of therapy might be to make it clear and achieve acceptance of it by all concerned. Such families may not have resolved the issue of whether these children should obey certain family rules, rather than doing exactly as they like in their parents' home. In practice there have always to be some rules family members must obey. Whether mandatory attendance at family therapy sessions should be one of them may be a matter for negotiation.

While the above issues may need to be dealt with in therapy, the decision as to whether children, young or adult, should attend rests ultimately with the parent(s). We must tell family members what we believe will lead to the best and quickest therapeutic outcome, and why. When our clients decline to accept our advice we have always to consider whether we can still hope to treat them effectively. If we believe we cannot, we must tell them so. What look like blocks to therapy, because our clients decline our advice, may however sometimes be overcome by careful development of rapport, and the use of treatment strategies such as those discussed in Chapter 10.

Extended family members

Extended family members are usually best contacted through the family member to whom they are most closely related. Most often this is one of the marital pair. Extended family members often attend willingly, but if they are reluctant to do so direct contact by the therapist, to explain why seeing them would be helpful, may yield results.

Maintaining a therapeutic alliance

In the second edition of this book this section was headed 'maintaining control of the therapy', but in the 20 years since that edition was written I have learned that a collaborative, rather then a controlling approach to families tends to yield the best results. It is true that some families have firm views on the form treatment should take, based on their understanding of the family's problems, and that their understanding of the problems has not led to resolution of the problems. The family's views are not irrelevant and we should always treat them with respect. Unfortunately the idea that the therapist can work some sort of 'magic' on the family has been encouraged by some therapists and authors. It is encompassed in the titles of such books as *The Structure of Magic, Volume 1* (Bandler & Grinder, 1975) and *Volume 2* (Grinder & Bandler, 1976), and *Magic in Action* (Bandler, 1984). Nichols (1987, page 53) observed that, 'Client families induce therapists to play magician because they long for a magically protective relationship.' He goes on to suggest that:

'Many therapists attempt to capitalize on their clients' idealization, realizing that it lends power to their directives, but ignoring that the complement of the powerful therapist is a humble and insignificant family. Authoritarianism bothers us least when we are the ones deferred to.'

Nichols (1987, page 55) also suggests that, whereas the pioneers of family therapy sought to rescue their patients from 'the Freudian vision of the person ruled by unconscious forces in the form of inexorable repetitions of the past', they have tended to replace this with a vision of rule by 'the system'.

The truth, of course, is that no one limited set of variables can explain anything as complex as human behaviour. The attempts by our families to control the treatment process must be recognized for what they are: manifestations of the family's way of functioning or, if you prefer, its 'psychopathology'. In most instances our response may need to be something between passively accepting the family's stance and directly confronting it on the basis of our supposed expertise.

In the early stages of therapy it is often best to go along with a family's viewpoint, at least in some measure, but without losing sight of what is happening. As rapport and trust develop, the family members may become more willing to follow suggestions. Taking a 'one-down' position, as described above, may be helpful. Strategic approaches, such as the use of paradox or of metaphorical ways of communicating a point of view, may also help. Telling stories such as the following can sometimes enable the family to view its situation differently, and get involved constructively in therapy.

I remember a very caring family I worked with before I came to this city. The parents were deeply concerned about their 13-year-old daughter, Patricia, who had started running away and getting into trouble with the law. Her mother brought her to see me and told me they suspected also that she was on drugs, though she denied it and the parents had no proof. There were two other children in the family, both girls and both older than the daughter who was in trouble. Neither of them had been in trouble and the parents had no particular concerns about them.

As none of the other members of the family appeared to have any problems the reasons for the daughter's behaviour were a real puzzle to the family. Their family doctor suggested that they bring Patricia to see me, and she came to my office with her mother. I had long talks with both of them and at the end of it all I was as puzzled as the family. The mother and daughter were pleasant people and they appeared quite open in the interview situation. From what the mother told me it seemed that the parents had handled their daughter's problem behaviour sensibly; they hadn't over-reacted, they'd spent long hours discussing the problems with her, trying to figure out what had gone wrong and what they could do about it, and they had imposed reasonable sanctions in response to Patricia's misdeeds, though these had not been effective.

In those days I didn't always ask the whole family to come when I first saw a child, as I do nowadays. But I now felt I needed more information. Naturally I first thought of the father. So I called him up and said I needed his help. I asked him to bring the whole family, including the other two daughters, to see me. I said I thought probably he, and perhaps the other girls too, could help me understand the youngest daughter's problems.

The father wasn't too keen on the idea nor, he told me, would the other girls be. He was very busy at his work and therefore reluctant to take time off. He feared losing his job, a fear which I felt probably wasn't fully justified as he had a long and excellent work record with his firm. The other girls were good students at school, they had exams coming up and didn't like missing school. I commented that this was interesting since Patricia had a negative attitude towards school and was not doing well there. Eventually, after a good deal of discussion, the father agreed to come and to bring the whole family.

I was quite new to family therapy in those days and was surprised by how much I learned from that first interview with the whole family. The father was a perceptive person. He told me a lot about the relationship between Pat and her mother that I hadn't even guessed when I just saw the two of them. The other daughters, too, gave me much new information. Seeing them together made me realize how close they were emotionally. The mother had said they were close, but it wasn't till I met them, and saw how they interacted, that I realized the true nature of their relationship.

It was also only when I saw the whole family that I appreciated how different the two older girls were in looks compared to Patricia. They were both strikingly attractive blondes with slim figures, whereas Pat was a little overweight, had mousy-coloured hair and an altogether less striking appearance. Seeing the whole family helped me a lot. The problem for me was to understand how, in what seemed a basically healthy, normal family, there could be one member with problems such as Patricia's.

This story, reproduced from *Using Metaphors in Psychotherapy* (Barker, 1985), makes a number of points which might help motivate reluctant family members to attend for an assessment interview. It also offers those to whom it is told a different way of looking at family situations, especially those in which there may appear to be only one person who has a problem. The various points it makes are discussed further in the book from which it is quoted.

Involving children in family sessions

It is important that all family members are involved in the treatment process, even very young ones. Dare and Lindsay (1979), Guttman (1975) and Ackerman (1970b) are among the authors who have addressed the issue of how to involve children in family therapy. Nichols (1996, page 99) is another author who has written of the importance of involving all family members, including the children. Even children who are preverbal should be acknowledged in some fashion.

Dare and Lindsay (1979) expressed two concerns. One was that family therapists may not learn the skills needed to communicate effectively with children and to provide them with settings in which they can express what is going on in their inner worlds, an issue also raised by McDermott and

Char (1974). The other is that the changes in personality structure which individual therapy seeks to bring about in children will not occur in the course of family therapy. But they believe that neither of these concerns is justified if suitable steps are taken to involve the children.

But why is it so important to involve children in the family therapy process? Dare and Lindsay (1979), like Satir (1967), Skynner (1976), Kirschner and Kirschner (1986), Nichols, M.P. (1987) and Nichols, W.C. (1996) are concerned both with the family system and with the psychological development of its members. A system cannot exist without transactional content and they believe that systems theory and psychodynamic views are complementary rather than antagonistic. Along with Boszormenyi-Nagi and Spark (1973) and Bowen (1976) they are interested in the relationship between the current interactional pattern in the family and the interpersonal patterns of the past. The way family members have interacted in the past often seems to be reflected in the present intrapsychic structures of the family members. In other words developing children take into themselves, and incorporate into their internal models of the world, patterns of behaviour, attitudes and beliefs, and also family myths, learned from their parents, and to a lesser extent from other family members. These in turn have been learned from *their* parents, and so on.

Byng-Hall (1973) discussed the role that family myths may play in the functioning of some families. He regarded their use as a form of defence against examination of the real issues facing the family. Children are often repositories of such myths, and through them a family's defences can sometimes be penetrated.

Children are, and should be seen as, active participants in the current interactional system and also as repositories of the history of the family. The content of their play and other communications is important, and many therapists believe that steps must always be taken to help child members of the family express themselves.

Dare and Lindsay (1979) recommended the provision of a few good-quality materials, chosen specially for each family. They keep the toys or play materials for each family in a separate locker. A small dolls' house has been found to be a useful adjunct for young children. A 'family' of people for the house provides a group upon which young children can project their family knowledge and fantasies. For older children, and those who are well defended against direct expression using family figures, domestic or zoo animals may be useful. A toy telephone, bricks, a dolls' tea set, plasticine, modelling clay, pencils, crayons and paper are useful items. Dare and Lindsay (1979) make it clear that the children's drawings will be kept as records of their work, not taken home by the family.

From the start of the first session any children present should be actively involved. They should be asked their names and greeted individually. Little ones can sometimes be held for a time by the therapist. Interest should be shown by the therapist in both the verbal and the non-verbal contributions of the children. By all these means the therapist shows that he or she is approachable at a childhood level, and that childlike feelings are acceptable.

Making free and accepting contact with the children need not undermine parental authority, though the latter must always be acknowledged and respected. Dare and Lindsay (1979) take care to refer to the parents either as 'mother' and 'father', or as 'Mr' and 'Mrs'. Interruption of their speech by the children is not permitted.

Throughout therapy Dare and Lindsay (1979) make every effort to attend to and understand the children's communications. Their play materials and drawings are given careful attention, and it is made clear that the therapists want everything to be understood by the children, who should ask about things which they do not understand. Giving children and childhood things high status sometimes produces scepticism or disbelief in the parents, but this is usually soon shaken by the accuracy, perceptiveness and unexpectedness of the children's knowledge. Dare and Lindsay (1979) state that the material produced by children can be 'extraordinarily forceful'. It can help overcome parental resistance, and historical and other data the parents thought were secret may be revealed.

Involving children in this way not only facilitates the production of content, but it also helps reveal the transactional patterns of the family and current interpersonal processes. Children, like adults, reveal a great deal non-verbally. Thus those who sit stiffly on their chairs during a therapy session raise questions about the family's control structure. Fear, dependency, depression, the seeking of attention and the response of parents to their children's play or the overtures they make to them – all these are indications of aspects of the functioning of the family.

The construction of the genogram during the first or second session provides an opportunity for the children to participate. They usually enjoy it and sometimes come up with valuable comments about the family and its members.

> Jackie, aged 10, was adopted at the age of 4, after living until then with various members of her natural family. During my first meeting with the family we constructed a detailed genogram of the family she was living in. When it seemed to be complete, I asked if there was anyone else who should be added. Jackie responded immediately with, 'Now, what about *my* family?'

All these devices are designed to prevent 'family' therapy becoming marital therapy in the presence of the children. There are of course times when marital therapy is needed, but Dare and Lindsay (1979) believed that many therapists move towards it because they are more comfortable communicating verbally with adults than they are making contact with children. Regardless of how frequently it is desirable to move from whole family to marital therapy, however, family therapists should certainly have the skills, and be familiar with the techniques, needed to contact and involve children in therapy as members of the family group. This applies whatever the orientation of the therapist, and whether or not intrapsychic processes are given prominent consideration by the therapist.

The therapist's use of self

Most traditional family therapy differs from many other forms of psychotherapy in the active role played by many of its therapists. This may however be less true of the narrative, constructionist and 'postmodern' methods currently in vogue.

In producing change in families the therapist's personality is important. Many of the pioneers of family therapy were powerful, charismatic figures. How far this is helpful or necessary is not clear, but every therapist must learn to use her or his personality to best advantage. Particular approaches may suit therapists with particular personalities and temperamental styles. Some therapists have difficulty using certain approaches effectively, but quickly become skilled with others. Properly supervised practice can enable the novice to gain confidence, and use effectively any of the ways of approaching families and therapy techniques mentioned in this book. (I still remember the trepidation with which I offered a family my first paradoxical injunction, though nowadays I feel quite comfortable using paradoxical methods when they appear to be indicated.)

Versatility and flexibility of style and the ability to use humour, playfulness, drama and passion are useful assets in the family therapist. It is important also for the therapist to be comfortable with the expression of emotion.

Transference issues

The term 'transference' is used here to mean the feelings projected on to a therapist by family members. These feelings are associated with previous relationships, often with parental or authority figures of whom the therapist may be an unconscious reminder. This process is not stressed in the family therapy literature but merits consideration.

Skynner (1976, pages 206–208) discussed the development of transference phenomena during family therapy. He did not recommend encouraging transference. He also points out that it is less likely to develop the less the therapist is a 'blank screen'. Family therapists are generally more active and spontaneous, and reveal more of themselves than individual therapists, so the projection of patients' own feelings on to them is less likely. Transference can nevertheless develop. Family sessions can, for example, cause hostility previously kept under control by mental defence mechanisms to be projected into the transference. This may need to be interpreted and discussed.

I was seeing a family consisting of James, a 13-year-old boy, who lived with his father, Tom, aged 35, and the 19-year-old young woman, Kate, with whom Tom had been living since he and James' mother separated 3 years previously. Many tensions existed between Tom and Kate, and these seemed to be exacerbated by James' violent resentment of Kate whose arrival in the family he had never accepted. He was not allowed by his father to express his anger directly, though he did so indirectly through various behaviours. The tensions between Tom and Kate were also kept under wraps and were not openly acknowledged. As the various unacknowledged feelings came to light during family therapy sessions, the whole family, led by Tom, attacked me with a variety of accusations. This process had to be worked through, and judiciously discussed, over the course of several sessions.

The transference process is two-way. Families can arouse feelings in their therapists in much the same way as therapists arouse feelings in their clients. This is called counter-transference. Such processes can be associated with the therapist's emotional needs. Skynner (1976) suggested that members of helping professions tend to have defensive systems that deal with inner conflict by taking 'parent' roles towards clients or patients. The latter then take the 'baby' role in response.

We should always bear in mind the possibility that transference or counter-transference issues may be interfering with our treatment. Such issues are more likely to surface the more the therapist takes a passive role, and the less intense and frequent the sessions the greater the chances of avoiding such problems. It is better if previously repressed feelings are expressed between family members rather than towards the therapist. They can then be dealt with in the course of therapy.

Contracts

Many family therapists establish specific contracts with the families they treat. These often concern the number of sessions proposed and their frequency, who should attend, the goals of therapy, the fee and other issues. Some, like Epstein and Bishop (1981), have family and therapist sign a written contract at the end of the assessment process and before treatment begins.

Establishing a contract, which specifies the number of sessions and their frequency, has several advantages. First, it can define the length of time the therapist considers will be needed to produce the changes sought. It thus sets a programme for change. Second, it can define the part to be played in the process by the family members and the therapist. Third, it can provide for 'homework' to be done between sessions, with the implication that the families will work on their problems between sessions, as well as during them.

A time-limited contract also provides an exit point for the family, which may therefore be less likely to feel trapped into extended therapy. Knowing that there is a projected end-point may make it easier for them to enter treatment.

Perhaps the most important part of a contract is the specification of the changes for which the family and therapist are meeting together in order to achieve.

The spacing of sessions

Therapists' views on the spacing of family sessions vary. In the early days of family therapy many therapists saw families weekly, even more often, perhaps because in individual therapy this had been the usual practice. Nowadays there is a tendency for therapists to see families less often, as infrequently as once a month, or sometimes even less often than that.

Palazzoli (1980) set out a rationale for seeing families less frequently, and demonstrated that, in her experience, families seen less often did as well, or better than, those seen more frequently. It seems that when strategic and systemic methods are used, more widely spaced sessions may be best, whereas when more direct, and especially behavioural, methods are employed it may be preferable to see families more frequently.

Spacing sessions at greater intervals has several advantages. One is that a therapist can handle a bigger caseload. Another is that, as we have seen, there is less likelihood of the family becoming over-involved with the therapist, so that transference problems are diminished or avoided. Modern family therapy may involve family members in carrying out tasks or performing rituals between sessions. These can often, with benefit, extend over the course of several weeks. Finally, systems change takes time, and a week, or even two, may not be long enough for a well-designed intervention to have its full impact on the family system.

Confidentiality

An important feature of family therapy is the openness it promotes. When all members of the family are meeting together and talking about the issues with which treatment is dealing, the question of keeping certain information confidential, as between family members, does not arise. We can model free and frank communication, and can encourage it. For example, a therapist might comment, when one person says something uncomplimentary to another, 'I'm impressed that you decided to clear the air and get those feelings out in the open.' This connotes positively the intent behind the statement, rather than the statement itself.

In family therapy information emerging in therapy naturally becomes available to all members of the family. So if a member is absent from a session, the others will feel free subsequently to share with that person what happened and what was said during the session. I find it helpful to make this clear at the start of treatment, especially when treating families that have had difficulty sharing information and communicating effectively with one another, that is disengaged families.

Family members sometimes try to obtain individual attention or communicate information to the therapist outside the therapy sessions. This may involve phone calls to the therapist, or taking the therapist aside at the end of a session and requesting a private talk. Another, healthier approach is to ask openly for a private talk, while the other family members are present. The meaning of such behaviours should be carefully considered. Whether private interviews should be granted, and how to respond to telephone calls, must be decided in the light of what is known about the family system. Such issues may be best brought to the family sessions for discussion.

Sometimes therapists see subgroups of families for certain sessions or parts of sessions, and ask those present not to share what is said with the other family members. This can be a way of strengthening boundaries that are too permeable or diffuse. If this is to be done it should of course be made clear to the other family members that this is a private talk the therapist and the family members concerned are having, and that its content may not be shared with the rest of the family. Their agreement should be obtained to this. Some strategic therapy plans involve such confidential talks with certain family members.

Jane, a 13-year-old with a severe sleeping problem and school refusal, had an enmeshed relationship with her mother, while her father was largely uninvolved with the family. He declined to come to therapy, but the mother and Jane were seen on one occasion, and during the latter part of the session I interviewed them separately. I told Jane, while I was seeing her on her own, to see how long she could stay awake each night and telephone me, without her mother's knowledge, at certain set times to tell me. She was not to discuss her sleeping habits with her mother at all. I told her mother, when I saw her alone, that she could talk to Jane about any subject except sleeping, which must not be discussed. She could however discuss it, when the children were not present, with her husband.

My plan was to separate mother and daughter, having Jane become involved with me by reporting to me how long she was staying awake, while at the same time promoting sleep by a paradoxical injunction. Because Jane's sleep problems were her mother's main preoccupation and something she could scarcely help talking anxiously about, she was given permission to discuss it with her uninvolved husband as a means of bringing him more into the family.

The strategy was successful and the sleep problem had resolved within two weeks. School attendance also became normal shortly afterwards, and the mother found that when she told her husband of her concerns regarding Jane he showed more interest than she had expected. In this case some secrets between family members were essential to the treatment strategy employed.

The content of family therapy sessions is of course strictly confidential so far as people outside the family group are concerned. Information should not be released by the therapist without the family's permission.

Observers

Family therapists make extensive use of one-way observation screens and closed-circuit television. By such means the treatment is observed by one or more other therapists. These can assist the therapist in understanding the family and devising intervention strategies. Dealing with families is a complex process. Many things, both verbal and non-verbal, are going on at once and it can be helpful to have several people watching and listening. de Shazer (1982) regards the total team as being 'the therapist' and refers to the member who goes into the therapy room with the family as 'the conductor'.

Observation through one-way screens is commonly used by supervisors in teaching family therapy. It enables them to watch their students in action and, using a telephone, to intervene in the treatment if necessary. Communication by telephone between therapist and/or family, and those observing, can also have other therapeutic uses (Coppersmith, 1980).

Closed-circuit television can serve a similar purpose to observation through a one-way screen, especially when a large audience, or one situated at a distance from the treatment room, wishes to watch a therapy session. Videotape recordings are often used, both for supervision and review of sessions, and to enable therapists to watch themselves in action. They enable therapists to learn more about their own functioning, as well as that of the families they are treating. Videotape recordings are not, however, a substitute for live observation, since intervention during sessions by supervisors or the other observers is not possible when a videotape is reviewed. Ideally sessions should be observed and also taped for subsequent review. Videotape replay has itself been used as a therapeutic device (see Chapter 12).

Whatever form of observation or recording is proposed should be explained to the family in advance and consent obtained. It is usual to get a signed consent to record sessions. Written consent is not usually considered necessary in order to have observers watch, but the family should always be told who is watching, and if they wish they should be allowed to meet the observers. Only rarely do families object to being observed, once it is explained that they have not just one therapist, but a team devoted to helping them. Families raising objections to being videotaped may be told that records are always kept of therapy sessions, usually in written form, and that the tape recording is only a better, more comprehensive form of clinical record. They should also be assured that the tape will not be released to anyone outside the clinical team without their permission.

What should the therapist do if family members do object to being observed and/or tape recorded? This depends in part on the philosophy of the institution in which the therapy is being conducted. If team therapy, as described for example by de Shazer (1982), is the basic approach of a centre, it might be better, unless the centre can offer other treatment approaches, to suggest that the family seek help elsewhere. On other occasions it may be quite appropriate for an experienced therapist to proceed without the help of observers or recordings, perhaps after warning the family that treatment might take longer, or be more difficult, without the additional help.

The situation is different when the family is to be treated by a student. In this case proper supervision, which might need to be 'live' depending on the nature of the case and the experience of the therapist, is essential. To proceed without it, when it is needed, would be unethical. In such cases it is necessary to consider whether any other way of treating the family is available.

Serious objections to being observed or tape recorded come mostly from individuals with paranoid personalities or paranoid psychoses. When this is the case the management of the paranoid person, or family system, becomes a clinical issue, often a difficult one, with which the therapist or team must deal.

Co-therapy

From the early days of the family therapy movement there have been those who have believed that a co-therapy team, that is two therapists working in the room with the family, is preferable to having a single therapist work with the family, at least in many instances. As with many other issues that arise in family therapy this is one on which there is a lack of good data. The advantages claimed for co-therapy include:

(1) Better observation of what is going in the family group. It is certainly true that a single therapist cannot observe all the events, verbal and non-verbal, that take place in a family interview. If two therapists are present, less may be missed.

(2) The therapists can supply each other with mutual support. Each can also watch for signs that the other is getting overinvolved with the family or is losing objectivity in dealing with the family system.

(3) The therapists can model healthier ways of relating and communicating than the family use. When the co-therapists are a man and a woman, they may help to model a better relationship for marital and parental couples.

(4) In that type of strategic therapy in which two incompatible alternative courses of action may be presented to the family, the therapists can say they disagree about which would be the better. One of them can present one alternative while the other presents the second.

(5) It can be a valuable learning experience for the therapists. Each may learn from the other, and a less experienced therapist may learn much from a more experienced one.

(6) Two, or even more, therapists may be required for very large families and, especially for multi-family therapy (see Chapter 12), simply to monitor events, keep the therapy process under control and maintain contact with all members of the family.

Most of these advantages have been questioned:

(1) It has been said that experienced therapists are able to observe enough of the family process to make appropriate interventions. There is no hard evidence that observing everything, or more than one therapist can observe, improves results.

(2) Experienced therapists in their day-to-day work do not require the support of co-therapists. When they require assistance with families they can seek consultation with colleagues. Students and other inexperienced therapists should receive support from their supervisors, either by means of live supervision or through review of videotapes of their work.

(3) Modelling can usually be done by therapists working on their own, using members of the family group as partners in the process. When family members do not have the appropriate skills these can be taught by the therapist. This can itself be a useful therapeutic strategy.

(4) It is not necessary to have two therapists in the room to present two different viewpoints to a family. One view can be put forward as the

therapist's while the other can be that of the observing team, or the two views can be presented as those of two groups within the team. Even if you are working without a team, it is still possible to say that you can see two possible courses of action but are unsure which would be better.

(5)   Other learning experiences are available without the use of co-therapy. One-way observation and review of videotapes enable students to watch skilled and experienced therapists at work without the necessity of being in the therapy room.

(6)   While it seems to be generally agreed that more than one therapist is needed for multiple family therapy, it is less clear that this applies with big families. My own experience in trying to see on my own a family of two parents, 14 children and the marital partners of two of these suggests, however, that it would have been helpful to have someone else present. It was hard even to remember everyone's names, let alone form a clear view of how the family system operated!

Two other problems with co-therapy are the additional cost of paying two therapists, and the greater complexity of the process. Careful planning is necessary, as well as subsequent review of each session by the co-therapists, who should also have similar theoretical orientations, comparable skills and a satisfactory working relationship.

It seems that co-therapy is used in some centres more than in others, perhaps more as a matter of policy than because of firm evidence that it yields better results than treatment by a single therapist. Most therapists work on their own. Of the 11 case studies in the book *Family Therapy: Full Length Case Studies* (Papp, 1977), only two were treated by co-therapy teams. In one of these Carl Whitaker started out as the sole therapist, but was joined by David Keith in the fourth interview. The decision to bring in a co-therapist was made because of the 'close lock-in' or 'profound intimacy' which Whitaker felt had developed between himself and the mother, herself a professional therapist. The other co-therapy case was a marital one treated by James Framo and his wife who had worked together as co-therapists for 5 years. There are other instances of marital couples working together as co-therapists, for example Robin Skynner and his wife (1976) and Stephen and Carol Lankton (1983).

While there are no clearly established benefits of co-therapy, it seems that it has its place in certain circumstances. For example co-therapy of a creative and fascinating kind was reported in the book *The Family Crucible* (Napier & Whitaker, 1978), which described the co-therapy treatment of a family (actually a composite of a number of families) in a singularly clear and well written way.

Summary

This chapter has considered some practical points that may require attention during family therapy. Attendance of the whole family for assessment, which is usually desirable except when the problem is purely a marital one, may be resisted. It can usually be achieved by persistence, careful explanation and avoidance of confrontation in the therapist's early contacts with the family.

Family therapists need to learn to use their personality assets to best advantage. We all have characteristics which we can turn to good use in family therapy, and we need to identify and capitalize on these.

Involving children in family sessions is important. Children are often repositories of their families' myths and histories, and much can be learned from their contribution to family sessions.

Family members may project their feelings and attitudes on to their therapist, though this happens to a lesser extent than in individual therapy. At times such transference issues require to be dealt with. Also discussed have been the spacing of sessions; issues of confidentiality; and the use of observers and of team members who are not in the room with the therapist. Co-therapy teams are sometimes used but their place in family therapy is unclear. It seems that they can be used creatively in some circumstances.

Chapter 10
Common Family Problems and their Treatment

This chapter considers some of the more common family problems and direct approaches to their treatment. Many family problems yield to relatively straightforward interventions. The more complex ones may require more sophisticated approaches. These are discussed in subsequent chapters.

Many of the concepts used in this chapter are derived from the McMaster Model of Family Functioning (Epstein et al., 1978), the closely related Process Model of Family Functioning (Steinhauer et al., 1984), the structural school of family therapy (Minuchin, 1974; Minuchin & Fishman, 1981) and from communications theory (see Chapter 3).

Task accomplishment problems

Task accomplishment problems (as defined in the Process Model), or problem-solving difficulties (the McMaster Model term) were discussed in Chapter 5. Failure to provide for the basic needs of family members can be severe and serious. An extreme example was reported by Oliver and Buchanan (1979). These authors presented a horrifying story of an extended family network, starting with a mentally retarded young woman and the six men with whom she successively lived and her children, and continuing with their descendants. Altogether 40 members of the family, and their spouses or partners, were studied. Throughout all the family groups there was a gross failure of basic task accomplishment, with physical neglect, assaults on the children, incest, prostitution – sometimes taught to the children by the parents – and a total failure to provide the basic elements of care.

Oliver and Buchanan's paper is replete with reports of assaults on children with hammers or knives, burns causing persisting poker marks, bites, beatings and hair pulling. Unfortunately cases as severe as this are by no means uncommon. The media continue to report such cases with, sadly, some of them resulting in the death of the child or children concerned. Such extreme cases require the attention of the child welfare services at least initially, but for every extreme example of the failure of a family to provide the most basic care for their children, there are many other serious, though milder, cases.

Families in which there is serious failure of basic task accomplishment tend not to present themselves voluntarily for family therapy. They may, however, be referred by the social workers employed by child welfare agencies. In some cases treatment is ordered by a court, though family therapy entered into involuntarily tends to be both challenging for the therapist and often unsuccessful.

Developmental tasks are those associated with the growth of individuals or changes in a family's composition or situation. Examples are the changes necessitated by the birth of children, their entry into school, the onset of adolescence or the departure of offspring from home as grown-up children. There may be problems in surmounting any of the 'transition points' described in Chapter 2. Certain families cope well at some stages in their development but have difficulty at others. For example, development may proceed smoothly until the children reach adolescence, a time when major adjustments in family functioning may be needed.

Crisis tasks, those that do not regularly or predictably present themselves in the course of family development, often present special challenges. Some families function well until faced with crises such as serious illness or death of a family member, job loss, migration from one culture to another, or the loss of the family home by fire or foreclosure. Others seem able to deal well with a whole series of disasters.

Basic, developmental and crisis tasks comprise a sort of hierarchy, in that if basic tasks are not performed well it is unlikely that developmental or crisis ones will be. Similarly, crisis tasks will probably not be handled well if developmental ones are not. The reverse does not necessarily apply. That is to say it does not follow that if crisis tasks cause a family difficulty, developmental ones will also do so, nor that the failure to cope with developmental tasks is likely always to be associated with failure in basic task performance.

In the *treatment* of task accomplishment problems, direct methods may be effective, although when there are severe problems affecting all three categories of task, therapy often presents great difficulties. Indeed 'multi-problem' families present some of the greatest challenges family therapists meet. It is important, however, not to be overwhelmed by the immensity of the problems some of these families face.

We must first, as always, establish rapport and develop a trusting relationship with the family members. Families with basic task accomplishment problems are often composed of people with poor self-images who readily feel criticized, and are easily threatened by authority figures. They may not have achieved the 'basic trust' in the world Erik Erikson (1965) wrote about. So trust is often a major issue. The collaborative approach described by Anderson (1997) is often helpful for such families.

'Positive connotation' of family members' motives, however unfortunate their consequences, can be helpful. Few parents, for example, deliberately harm their children. Their attempts to care for them, though, may fail for many reasons, some of these residing in their own life experiences and personality limitations. The actions of parents who yell at their children in a demeaning way, or beat them to the extent of causing serious injury, can be connoted as representing their attempts to train their children to behave well. These are unsuccessful, even harmful, attempts to be sure, but they may be the best choices available to certain parents at certain times. We may need to acknowledge this and help them make better choices.

Parents' histories, personalities, emotional states and current circumstances all place limitations on the choices they are able to make. Many parents who fail to provide for the basic needs of their children expect to be blamed or criticized. They may have a strong sense of guilt about what has happened. They do not expect to meet someone who positively connotes their intentions by saying that they obviously care a lot about their children, enough perhaps to go to extreme measures to bring their children's behaviour under control. Yet they need to experience the therapist as someone who is on their side, and wants to understand what has happened and how they can get out of the dilemma they are in.

By attributing good intentions to whatever the family members have done, therefore, we can establish ourselves as being there to help, not criticize. Once this has been achieved, we can proceed to explore alternative means of achieving the family's goals – means that are more likely to be successful and will not have destructive consequences. In other words we help the family broaden the range of behaviours available to them so that they have more choice. Once this is accomplished it can be surprising what some families prove able to do.

In dealing with task accomplishment problems it is important to break the therapy task down to manageable proportions. Every journey, however long, starts with the first step. The processes involved in task accomplishment – identifying the task, exploring alternative approaches, taking action, evaluating and adjusting – were set out in Chapter 5. In treatment it is sometimes possible to go through these processes directly with the family members, concluding with an agreement, even a written contract, that the family will take some action by the time of the next session. Much depends on the family's motivation, but even more important is the therapist/family relationship.

When trust has been established, therapy can follow the stages described by Epstein and Bishop (1981). The first two stages consist of identifying the problem and exploring alternative approaches. This should be a collaborative process, all present being encouraged to contribute suggestions and ideas. This should lead to an agreement with the family for them to take a certain course of action. This is the third stage. The agreed course of action may address the problems directly, though indirect approaches are sometimes more appropriate. At the next session the results are evaluated and any necessary adjustments are made. This is the fourth stage. The family may then be asked to do more work on the first problem. But if this is well on the way to being resolved another problem may then be examined. Again alternative approaches to dealing with this are explored. This leads to another task being set the family, and so on. Soon the family may set about dealing with other task accomplishment problems on its own initiative, as it acquires skills in this area.

This direct approach may not succeed, but it may be the first time the family members have given serious thought to how they might overcome their task accomplishment problems. Many prove to have resources they have not used, resources of which they may have been unaware.

While no one approach is uniformly successful in family therapy, if direct methods have not been tried previously it is usually best to start by using them. If they are not successful, any of the 'strategic' or other special approaches described in later chapters may be required.

Communication problems

Communications theory and its relevance to family therapy were discussed in Chapters 3 and 4. Communication problems exist in many families coming for therapy. We must take note of both the verbal and the non-verbal communications of the families we treat. We may find that there are discrepancies between the messages sent via each of these two channels. We must also consider the clarity, directness and sufficiency of communications, both verbal and non-verbal, and the availability and openness of those to whom communications are addressed.

Frances (10) and George (8) attended with their parents, Harry and Irene. Irene was a homemaker, while Harry had a job which took him away from home 4–5 months of the year, with individual trips lasting up to 6 weeks.

The presenting problems were George's severe temper tantrums and Irene's reported inability to control him, to the extent that she was fearful that he would do her serious physical harm. George had been referred to the emergency department because of a severe outbreak of violent behaviour at home a few days previously, while his father was away.

When the history of George's temper attacks was explored, Harry, who had returned home early because of George's admission to hospital, said they were a new phenomenon, of which he had just become aware. Frances, however, chipped in, saying that George had been losing his temper for at least 2 years, 'But my Mum doesn't tell my Dad because she's afraid he'll hit George, and he doesn't lose his temper when Dad's at home.' I turned to Irene, who confirmed that Frances' statement was true. I then asked Harry if he had been aware of what had been going on when he was away. He said he had not been. Irene then admitted that she had been afraid to tell Harry about George's behaviour at home, and also about behaviour problems the school had reported.

> During the remainder of the interview several other pieces of informa-
> tion emerged of which Harry, and in one case Irene, had been unaware.
> For example the children agreed that when George was worried about
> something the only person he would confide in about his worries was
> Frances. Neither parent had been aware of this, nor did they seem to
> realize how close the relationship between George and Frances was.
> Frances, it also emerged, confided freely in her mother, but neither child
> ever confided in Harry.

In this family the failure of communication, especially between the father and the other members, became obvious when it emerged that the father knew little of what went on in the family. It was also evident during the assessment interview itself. The information passing between Harry and the rest of the family was certainly not sufficient, although when the family members did speak to each other they did so with a good degree of clarity. There was however a tendency for communication to be indirect, with Frances acting as a sort of telephone exchange. She seemed to have freer communication with the remainder of the family than anyone else did, and she did not appear afraid to tell her father things which might upset him, or at least which the other two members of the family thought might.

This family was treated using direct methods. The members had never given much thought to the question of how information was communicated within the family, and when this was discussed they became interested. Initially work on the communication problem was carried out during the therapy sessions. At the very first session, when Irene's obvious failure to keep her husband informed about their son's behavioural problems emerged, there was progress towards resolving the difficulties. Harry did not react in the way Irene had feared he would. Instead of becoming angry and threatening, he expressed concern about the situation, and also regret that he had not been more involved in the family. The family 'myth', that father would become angry, perhaps even violent, if he was told what was going on, was exploded.

With the therapist's encouragement, the other family members proved willing to share with the father the important facts about what had been going on. A 'same-sex parenting programme' was also prescribed. Irene was put in charge of Frances, so that Frances was to come to her with any issues she wished to discuss, or requests she had to make, and similarly any-thing of significance that the parents wished to communicate to Frances was to be told to her by her mother. Harry's role was that of consultant to Irene, who was to consult him on matters concerning Frances on which she needed a second opinion. Harry could also offer input unasked, though the final decision on matters concerning Frances was to be Irene's.

When this had been explained to the parents and to Frances, and they had agreed to follow the prescribed plan, I turned to George. But before I could say anything George pointed to his father and said, but with a smile, 'So that leaves me with him.' 'Yes, it does,' I replied, and went on to explain that Harry's role in relation to George was to be exactly analogous to Irene's in relation to Frances. Harry accepted this readily, and George seemed quite delighted, though he could not bring himself actually to say so.

This quite direct intervention was designed to serve several purposes. It was aimed at altering family members' roles (an issue discussed later in this chapter), and it was intended to promote increased communication between Harry and his son, as well as between the parents, who would need to consult with each other on issues concerning their children. It was also a structural intervention, aiming to get Harry more involved in the family and to break down the boundary between him and the rest of the family.

Finally, during this session, I asked the parents to set aside 10 minutes before they went to bed each night to discuss how the same-sex parenting programme was going, and to ensure that they were keeping to the plan as agreed. This would also be an opportunity for them to exchange any information about the children which they had not been able to share earlier in the day.

This was a lot of work to do in a single therapy session, but I felt I had been able to establish good rapport with the family. All members seemed well motivated, even desperate, for help. In other cases it might have been necessary to spread the work done in this one session over several sessions. In the event the interventions were successful and only four therapy sessions were needed.

In the above family, communication, though insufficient, was usually clear when it occurred. In many families with problems, however, this is not so, and communication is either ambiguous or vague, or conflicting messages are given simultaneously. Sometimes the verbal message says one thing and the non-verbal another. It is easy to disqualify a verbal statement by one's tone of voice, body posture or actions. The 'double-bind' is a more extreme example of this kind of thing. Its main features, as described by Bateson et al. (1956), are:

- The presence of two persons.
- An oft-repeated experience.
- A 'primary negative injunction' to do, or not do, something with a threat of punishment if the order is not obeyed.
- A 'secondary injunction' which conflicts with the first at a more abstract level, often communicated non-verbally, again with threats of punishment.
- A situation from which the subject cannot escape.

To put it another way, we have two people who are in an intense relationship. Person A has a strongly felt need to understand the messages being communicated by person B. But person B is giving two orders of messages, one of which denies the other. But person A is unable to comment on or discuss the messages so as to come up with a suitable response. That is to say metacommunication, communication about the communication, is not possible. Once the individual has learned to perceive the universe in 'double-bind patterns', the complete set of conditions may not be needed and a part of it may be enough to provoke panic or rage.

Although the use of the double-bind was originally described as occurring in the families of patients suffering from schizophrenia, it soon became clear that it is widespread. It is perhaps best regarded as a special example of unclear communication, likely to occur more often in seriously dysfunctional families than in better functioning ones.

Direct treatment of families in which communication is unclear consists of raising questions about whether the communications family members offer each other are clear. Thus if family member A has said something to member B, the therapist might ask B, 'What was A trying to tell you?' or, 'Would you like to tell A what you thought she meant?' or, 'Perhaps you would like to check out with A what you thought she meant?'

As with everything else a therapist may do, this process is greatly facilitated if there is good rapport with the family members. The introduction of humour may help, though this should be used sparingly and respectfully, and the process of clarifying communication need not be a deadly serious one. The therapist should use his or her personality in a warm, empathic, kindly, but firm way, to insist that the family do as they are asked. The procedure must be repeated until a pattern of clear, direct communication has been achieved. Once A is communicating satisfactorily with B, the process can be reversed, and other family members can then be brought in, as necessary. When the process has got well under way during sessions, the family may be asked to practise it at home, usually for specific and initially short time periods.

Similar approaches may be used to deal with both insufficient communication and indirect communication. Family members are rehearsed until they learn to exchange information which is sufficient for the purpose in question, or until they have learned to address directly those people with whom they formerly communicated indirectly.

As well as teaching family members better communication skills, the above approach also draws their attention to the importance of communication. The value the therapist places on it can often heighten family members' awareness of the need to communicate clearly and in a straightforward way.

We can also help promote better communication by appropriate modelling. It is important that our own communications are sufficient, clear and direct. A model of frank, open communication, in a context of emotionally warm relationships, characterized by courtesy and respect, can be of real value to many families. It sometimes happens that after a few sessions family members begin to adopt some aspects of their therapist's style of communicating.

The process of examining, clarifying and modifying the communication occurring between family members can be applied to non-verbal as well as verbal communication. Analogic communication – the voice tones, facial expressions, body postures and other non-verbal behaviours – may be examined, clarified and changed during therapy. Thus the therapist may ask family member B what it was like being spoken to by A in a particular tone of voice. By asking such a question the therapist is disqualifying, at least for the moment, the digital meaning of the message and concentrating on its analogic qualities. Examples of other questions which might be put to family members are, 'What does it make you want to do when A talks to you like that?' or, 'How do you feel when A talks to you in that way?' A series of questions such as the following might be helpful:

To B: 'What is it like for you when A talks to you with that voice?'
To A: 'Did you know that B felt like that when you used that voice? Would you like to ask her to tell you a bit more about what it's like?'
To B: 'Tell A what you feel like doing when he speaks to you in that way.'
To A: 'Did you know that? Would you like to say the same thing in a different way?'

The next step might be to get the two people to practise talking in different tones of voice.

Similar approaches can be used with other forms of analogic communication, for example facial expression, gestures and body posture, failure to look at a person being spoken to, or sitting apart from or too close to another person. Communication can also occur through silence. It is impossible not to communicate, and we may have to address problems of silence, avoidance and the like. An interesting account of how improved communication can be taught to families is to be found in *Changing with Families* (Bandler et al., 1976).

Poorly defined and dysfunctional role patterns

Families are apt to develop problems if the various functions which have to be performed are not properly allocated to, or carried out by, appropriate family members. Role allocation and performance were discussed in Chapter 5.

Families containing children require at least two subsystems, or groupings of people: the parental subsystem and the child subsystem. The simplest situation is that of a one-parent family with a single child. In such a family the parent should take responsibility for the care of the child, by providing the basic necessities of life, and also by giving the child love, emotional security and the feeling of being a worthwhile person. The parent must also provide a sound role-model for living in the society of which parent and child are members.

Children's roles depend on their ages. Normally developing children become progressively less dependent on their parents as they get older. Depending on cultural norms, they should take increasing responsibility for instrumental tasks within the household, and by adolescence should play a substantial part in running it. Emotionally, too, children normally become more independent with increasing age. When adolescence ends, with emancipation from the family of origin, they should be relating to their parents more nearly as equals. Parents' roles change in a reciprocal way as their children mature. In two-parent families, and families with more than one child, role allocation is more complex than when there is only one parent and one child, though the same roles have to be performed. The parents also need to work together as a team, though their respective roles may well differ.

Role performance problems exist when appropriate roles are either not allocated or, if they are allocated, are not properly performed. In most families roles are mainly implicitly understood, though some may be deliberately discussed and consciously allocated. They also evolve as the family passes through its various developmental stages. Symptoms often develop in family members who are cast, because of the nature of the family system, into idiosyncratic roles.

The family scapegoat

This is probably the idiosyncratic role about which most has been written, though the term seems to be used less nowadays that it was in the earlier days of family therapy. It was first described, in relation to family functioning, by Vogel and Bell (1960). The term has biblical origins. The use of a scapegoat was one of the procedures laid down by Moses for use by the people of Israel. The priest was to lay his hands on the head of the goat and 'confess over it all the iniquities of the Israelites and all their acts of rebellion, that is all their sins'. Having laid the sins on the goat's head, the goat was to be sent into the wilderness, 'to carry all their iniquities upon itself into some barren waste' (New English Bible, 1970).

In the family therapy literature the term 'scapegoat' is used a little differently. The 'scapegoated' family member, often a child with symptoms, appears to act as the person on to whom all the family's problems are projected, but is usually maintained in the family system rather than being sent out into a 'barren waste'. (Sometimes, though, the scapegoat is placed in an institution, which presumably plays the role of the 'barren waste'.)

Some families seem to depend on having a 'bad' child or parent for their, often precarious, stability. The scapegoat's difficult behaviour may help keep the family together. A symptomatic child may be just about all the parents can agree about.

The parental child

The role of 'parental child' is another special, or idiosyncratic, one. It is sometimes appropriate to give older children some 'parental' functions in the care of younger children in the family, but if too much responsibility is given to a child, and especially if the delegation of authority is not explicit, the child may be unable to function as required and may develop symptoms. The parental child may be involved in 'parenting' younger children or in performing a similar role in caring for one, or occasionally even both parents. In extreme cases there is reversal of roles, the child looking after the parent, though this process may be camouflaged (Skynner, 1976, page 417).

Other special roles

These include the roles of martyr, 'family angel', sick member, handicapped member and disturbed or 'crazy' member. The martyr perpetually sacrifices his or her interests for the good of the family. The 'family angel' (Gross, 1979) performs a role analogous to that of the scapegoat, that of someone others can be agreed about, and may co-exist with a scapegoat.

Sometimes the adoption of special roles by one or more members enables the family to function without obvious problems, but this may be at considerable cost to those in the special roles. Not all special roles are undesirable, however, and we must take care to understand the function that each one has in any family we are treating. It is necessary also to discover whether the pattern of role performance is related to the problems for which the family is seeking help.

Treatment of role performance problems

Direct measures are sometimes effective. Once the problems have been identified, the therapist and family may be able to agree upon how family members' roles need to change. In doing this it can be helpful to start with the historical development of the dysfunctional roles. These may have had useful purposes at one time, but have outlived their usefulness, or have even become inimical to healthy family functioning. The therapist then negotiates with the family members for them, or some of them, to play different roles. An example is the 'same-sex parenting' procedure mentioned above. It is a way of enhancing, and making more appropriate, the roles of parents. It may be a useful intervention when there are one or more parental children, when there is enmeshment between parent(s) and child(ren), or when there are deficient behaviour control mechanisms. Kirschner and Kirschner (1986), in their description of 'optimal family process', commented as follows:

'The same-sex parent (SSP) tends to function as the primary programmer and disciplinarian. The SSP promotes maximum ego development by setting limits as well as progressively higher level goals and standards intrinsically suited to the child's unfolding skills and talents. The SSP uses rewards and discipline, education, inspiration, and modeling to help the child to attain these goals. The opposite-sex parent (OSP) functions primarily as the facilitator or mediator within the triangle . . . If the SSP disciplines a misbehaving child in an inappropriate fashion, the other-sex parent (OSP) takes responsibility for correcting the interaction . . . In a manner that creates a satisfactory rapprochement, the OSP is stable and loving and points out that the SSP still loves the child.' (Kirschner & Kirschner, 1986, page 35)

'Same-sex parenting' interventions are based on the above view, which is set out more comprehensively in the Kirschners' book, of 'optimal' family functioning. They involve putting the father in primary charge of the boys in the family, especially in the fields of discipline and 'programming' and the mother of the girls. 'Programming', as the Kirschners use the term, refers to the way children are helped to develop a particular view of themselves and the world. Programming can be targeted towards three areas: the definition of the self; the description of the world; and one's behaviours, attitudes and values.

In making a 'same-sex parenting' intervention the family is told that, except when the SSP is absent, and a major decision cannot wait until that parent returns, all decisions, advice, rewards, punishments and permissions concerning each child are to be made by the SSP. The OSP's role is that of consultant and adviser to the SSP. I usually explain the rationale for this procedure by pointing out that the parent concerned has had the experience of being a boy, or a girl, as the case may be. That parent is therefore in the best position to advise, assist and make important decisions about the welfare of the boys, or girls, in the family. The OSP supports both the child and the SSP, and may mediate between them when necessary, but always emphasizing that the SSP loves the child. Embedded in such instructions there is also the implication that parents are in charge of their children, and are responsible for making certain decisions concerning them. When parental roles have been unclear, interventions of this sort can bring greater clarity and definition to them, and lead to better parenting of the children.

Sometimes direct approaches to the treatment of role performance problems fail, and it is then necessary to use more indirect or strategic approaches. A useful one is the 'odd days–even days' type of intervention.

This, along with other indirect approaches, will be considered in Chapter 11.

Behaviour control problems

The behaviour of one or more family members is the presenting problem in many families seeking therapy. It is usually one or more of the children in the family who are presented as the identified patient or patients, but parents and other adults may also present behaviour which causes concern to others or to themselves. 'Conduct disorders' and their milder variant, 'oppositional deficient disorders', are the commonest child psychiatric disorders, although these terms do little more than describe certain patterns of behaviour. Both, however, refer to various forms of disobedient, anti-social and aggressive behaviour. Children to whom they are applied have failed to learn the types of socially acceptable behaviour expected in their families and/or the wider social environment. Conduct disorders usually start as behaviour control problems in the children's families (see *Basic Child Psychiatry*, Chapter 4 (Barker, 2004)).

Various types of behaviour control, namely rigid, flexible, laissez-faire and chaotic, were described in Chapter 5. Although in reality there is an infinite number of ways in which family systems may be organized, this is a useful framework for examining the control structure of families. Whether the parents work together is also an important factor in determining how successful their control of their children is.

The various aspects of family functioning we considered in Chapter 5 are closely inter-related. Behaviour control is related, for example, to role allocation and performance, and to the family members' affective involvement and their values and norms. We have seen how parents 'programme' their children to achieve a certain understanding of themselves and the world, a process that depends on parental roles, and the nature of family relationships.

If we take a structural view of family functioning, we may say that there need to be clear subsystem boundaries, with a well-defined parental system, adequately in touch with, but also distinct from, the child system. When these conditions do not exist, direct work to create them may be successful. Using the McMaster Model of therapy, this might involve contracting with particular family members to do certain things. For example the parents might be asked to work together to come to agreed limits to their children's behaviour, and then to communicate these to the children. They would then take specific steps to enforce these limits and, perhaps, to reward the children for keeping within them.

Control problems are not limited to children's behaviour, but may involve the family system as a whole. Task accomplishment depends in part on how well behavioural control operates, and role performance is also closely related. Sometimes direct discussion of the tasks that need to be performed, who is to perform them (role allocation and performance) and how the family system will be organized to see that roles are performed (behaviour control) may be undertaken as a single therapeutic process. By giving conscious thought to such issues, some families are able to make the necessary changes, with the therapist's help. This is 'first-order' change, but it may suffice. Often, however, it is not sufficient and less direct therapy methods, designed to produce 'second-order' change, may be needed.

Poorly functioning subsystems and boundary problems

Many family problems can be conceptualized as 'structural' ones, and statements about the 'structure' of a family system have implications for its communication patterns, the affective involvement of the family members, the behaviour control system and other aspects of its functioning. We need not be concerned, therefore, to decide whether there are, for example, either communication or structural problems. If there is one, there is likely to be the other. The structural therapist, however, tackles the therapeutic task using the structural model – which might, however, mean doing very similar things to what a therapist using another model, the McMaster one, for instance, would do.

Generally speaking, families require well-functioning spouse, parent and child subsystems (where there are children in the family). There should be clear, but not unduly rigid boundaries between the subsystems. In large families there may be more than one child subsystem, and there may also be a grandparental subsystem. The existence of a suitable hierarchy, as between generations, is something that Haley (1976) emphasizes. Yet there is no 'normal' or universally ideal family structure. The questions must always be, 'Does it work without anyone suffering or developing symptoms?' and, 'Does it provide for the healthy growth of the family and its members?' Thus giving a child parental power can, as we have seen, cause problems, but it can also be appropriate, at least in some measure, in large families. In many AIDS-devastated countries, including those in sub-Saharan Africa, there are families in which both parents have succumbed to AIDS, so that children, some as young as 10 or 11, are left heading families. It is remarkable how well some of these children cope.

In *structural therapy* the therapist works on the boundaries between systems and subsystems, promoting communication and emotional interchange where it is inadequate (as in disengaged relationships); and helping erect barriers, and create a necessary sense of separation, where there is undue enmeshment. The structural approach to therapy is described further in Chapter 12.

Suprasystem problems

The suprasystem, or 'ecological context', contributes to the difficulties some families experience. It is well known that middle-class families often choose to live in areas in which there are good schools and recreational facilities suited to their families' needs and tastes, together with an absence of serious problems of delinquency and social decay. Well-functioning suburban areas are preferred to declining inner-city areas. Such choices reflect awareness of the effects different neighbourhoods can have on families.

Satisfactory family functioning can be harder to maintain in some areas than in others. While in some poor areas there are helpful neighbourhood and extended support networks, in others this is not so. Families living in decaying areas with high crime rates, widespread drug abuse, prostitution and large numbers of alienated people and truants from school face great difficulties. In such situations the family needs to establish and maintain an adequate boundary between it and the surrounding environment. Therapy may need to focus on this particular aspect of family functioning.

Auerswald (1968) provided a description of the use of the 'ecological' approach to people's problems, illustrating it with a striking example. This was the case of a 12-year-old girl who had run away from home. The involvement and roles of the police, the mother, a sister, the girl's therapist at the local mental health clinic, the clinic psychiatrist, the school staff, the after-school group worker, the maternal grandparents, the Department of Welfare and the staff of the local adolescent ward are all described. The inadequacy of looking only at the girl, or her nuclear family, becomes very clear as one reads this account. The girl and her family were part of a complex suprasystem. Only if this were understood could rational treatment be planned and carried out.

The *treatment of suprasystem problems* consists of either strengthening the boundary between the family and the suprasystem, where the latter is having an adverse effect on the family; or working with the relevant parts of the suprasystem, which may include extended family, school staff, social agencies, other therapists, even employers. All this can only be done with the permission of the clients.

Delivering direct injunctions

'Direct injunctions', or instructions given to clients to change their behaviour in direct ways, are an important part of the treatment approaches discussed in this chapter. How families respond to them depends largely on how they are delivered. Good rapport with the family is an essential prerequisite, but attention to the following points increases further the likelihood of their being effective.

(1) Make the instructions as precise as possible. Thus rather than saying, 'Be kind to X', or 'Don't be rude to Y', say more precisely what the person concerned should do to be kind, or to avoid being rude.

(2) Use positive, rather than negative injunctions. It is better to give instructions for 'being polite' rather than for 'not being rude'.

(3) Enlist other family members, when available and when it is appropriate, to remind the subject(s), in a calm, non-critical and non-judgmental way, of the injunction.

(4) Use the force of your personality. Convey your enthusiasm for the plan of action you are putting forward, and your conviction that it will work. Another application of therapists' own personalities is the use of hypnosis, which seems sometimes to increase people's suggestibility, as well as helping convince themselves that they *can* do what they are being asked to do.

(5) Consider setting up a system of rewards or punishments, preferably rewards. This can be appropriate for children, but even parents, and other adults, can be told to reward themselves, perhaps by going out to dinner together, or perhaps just by exchanging a few words of approval or praise, for successful implementation of the treatment programme.

(6) Whenever possible tell clients to do something different rather than to stop doing something. The 'different' thing must be incompatible with the behaviour which you wish to discourage. Thus it is better to tell people who are talking rudely to others what they *should* be saying, rather than what they should *not* say.

(7) Tell clients to do things in a different sequence. This can be effective in disrupting established, dysfunctional patterns of behaviour, for example between spouses, or between parents and children.

Summary

Some of the more common family problems may be treated by direct methods of intervention. Such methods may be successfully applied to task accomplishment problems; communication problems; problems of role assignment and performance; behaviour control problems; 'structural problems' – that is those involving poorly functioning subsystem patterns; and suprasystem problems – those related to the nature and characteristics of the wider social environment of which the family is a part. Problems in several of these categories, or even in all of them, may co-exist.

The first step in the use of direct methods of treatment is the establishment of rapport and a trusting relationship with the family. The problem or problems are then made explicit, and a plan of action designed to overcome the problems is then suggested, or worked out with the family.

There are several ways in which the likelihood of direct injunctions being successful may be increased. Instructions should be precise, positive rather than negative, and delivered with conviction. Rewards for compliance may help. Family members may offer reminders to each other and altering the sequences of behaviours may be useful too.

Direct interventions involve 'first-order' change and this is not always sufficient, especially in the more seriously troubled families. In these cases other approaches are needed. These are often indirect and part of a strategic plan.

Chapter 11
Complex Problems and Second-order Change

The 'direct' interventions we have discussed in the previous chapter may be effective in the treatment of some family problems but they do not meet the needs of many more seriously troubled families. They promote 'first-order change', and sometimes more fundamental changes in family functioning are required. These are sometimes referred to as 'second-order' changes.

Second-order change involves alterations of perspective and a more fundamental change in the family system. The family's situation, or some aspects of it, must come to be looked at differently and understood in a new way. This is the process of 'reframing', the giving of a different meaning to behaviour, feelings or relationships. For example, in 'developmental reframing' (Coppersmith, 1981) the antisocial behaviour of an adolescent might be reframed as behaviour that is young for the individual's age. The young person is thus neither 'mad' nor 'bad', but is regarded as immature and needing to grow up. I have suggested that reframing may be part of the essence of psychotherapy (Barker, 1994).

The search for, and development of, effective ways of helping families with more complex problems has been a main focus of family therapists for the last several decades. Hoffman (2002) provides us with a personal account of some three decades of the development of family therapy techniques.

Therapies labelled 'strategic' and 'systemic' were among the first of the methods designed to bring about second-order change. The distinction between them is not always clear. MacKinnon (1983) reviewed some of the approaches to therapy which have been called 'strategic' – those developed at the Mental Research Institute (MRI) (Watzlawick, et al., 1974) and those developed by Haley (1976, 1980) and Madanes (1981) – and contrasted them with those of the Milan associates (Palazzoli, 1978; Palazzoli et al., 1978a), which have been labelled 'systemic'. She provides a valuable analysis of the main features of the therapy schools she discusses.

These three main approaches (MRI, Haley/Madanes and Milan) are different in several respects. The Milan therapists tend to be even more 'systemic' in their approach than the others considered, but this is probably more a matter of degree than anything more fundamental. All look at families as systems, and so can reasonably be called 'systemic', and all use strategies to help families change, and therefore could be called 'strategic'. But in a sense all therapy that has any aims at all might be called strategic, since the therapist is presumably using some strategy intended to help produce change. One thing that all three of these approaches have in common is the active role played by the therapists. Later developments have tended to downplay the role of the therapist as the primary generator of change. Instead, therapists have increasingly regarded themselves as catalysts or enablers whose function is to help families find their own solutions to the problems they face. We will consider these developments later.

The systemic viewpoint

Although it is hard to distinguish a specific school of 'systemic family therapy' – that of the Milan associates may be better called 'Milan systemic therapy' (Boscolo et al., 1987) – looking at families as systems is basic to many approaches to family therapy. This is where family therapy differs most from the many forms of individual therapy. Sometimes it is not just the immediate family system that must be considered, but the extended family. Grandparents, for example, can exercise a powerful influence on a family, even when they live at a great distance.

General systems theory and its application to family therapy were discussed in Chapter 3. The essence of the systemic approach is the belief that the family system is more than the sum of its parts, and that the system as a whole can be the focus of therapy. The symptoms of individual members of the family thus become manifestations of the way the family system is functioning. Family therapy must therefore address family system issues, rather than focusing on individual family members and their symptoms. Indeed doing the latter may make matters worse, since it can reinforce the idea that it is the behaviour of the 'identified patient' that is 'the problem', rather than the way the family system as whole is structured or is functioning.

Among the most systemic of all therapists were the Milan associates (Palazzoli et al., 1978a; Boscolo et al., 1987). In order to help maintain a systemic perspective therapists of this school tended to work as teams. One or more colleagues observe through a one-way screen, and offer input to the therapist. This may be done during sessions by telephone, or it may be achieved by having one or more 'intersession breaks' during which the whole team discusses the family system. There are usually also pre- and post-session discussions.

Perhaps the least systemic are behavioural family therapists, who tend to focus on the interactions between specific family members, working mainly with dyads or, at the most, triads. Between these two extremes therapists may be placed on a continuum, according to the extent to which they use a systemic approach to clinical problems.

Taking a systemic perspective is itself a form of reframing, at least in cases in which such a perspective has not been taken previously. Rather than seeing the problem as being the mother's depression, the father's alcoholism, the son's behaviour disorder or the daughter's anorexia, or whatever else may be the presenting symptom, it is conceptualized as lying in the family system. The symptoms of individual family members are rooted in the system as a whole.

The concept of 'coherence', or understanding the family as an 'organized coherent system' (Dell, 1982, and see also Chapter 3), is helpful. The family is regarded as a unit with certain properties. It will respond in certain ways to particular interventions, or 'perturbations', and the therapist's job is to find the perturbations which bring about the desired changes.

Whether the therapist makes the systemic view of the family's problems explicit during therapy session is a matter of technique. It is not always necessary to do so, though the systemic perspective is usually implicit in what the therapist does.

Support for a systems view, at least of children's behaviour, was provided by the Isle of Wight study of 10- and 11-year-old children (Rutter et al., 1970). In this large-scale epidemiological study rather little overlap was found between the group of children identified as disturbed at home, and those showing disturbance at school. Evidently children's behaviour depends to a great extent upon their social context. It is also common to find that children's behaviour differs according to which family members are present. Sometimes they are better behaved with one parent than with the other, or they may behave better, or worse, with grandparents.

A systemic approach and indirect methods of promoting change are often employed together. Direct methods can however be systemic if they are addressed to the family as a whole, and are designed to produce change in the way the family functions as a group. Conversely, indirect methods, such as paradoxical ones, can be applied to individuals. Victor Frankl, one of the pioneers of the use of paradox in psychotherapy, was not a family therapist and worked mainly with individual patients. (See, for example, his report of the treatment of a woman with an obsessive-compulsive disorder (Frankl, 1960).)

Strategic methods of therapy

The term *strategic* is generally used to describe therapy that uses a plan, which may be quite complex, to produce change, rather than a simple directive or mutually agreed task. As Cloe Madanes (1981, page 19) put it, 'The responsibility is on the therapist to plan a strategy for solving the client's problems.' Madanes considers that strategic therapy stems from the work of Milton Erickson. Many examples of his work are to be found in *Uncommon Therapy* (Haley, 1973) and in his own publications (Erickson 1980a,

1980b, 1980c, 1980d, 1980e). O'Hanlon and Hexum (1990) summarize Erickson's treatment of 316 patients and define the particular therapeutic approaches used in each.

Strategic methods of solving human problems are not new. 'Paradoxical intention', described by Frankl (1960) and referred to above, is an example of the use of a strategic plan in psychotherapy. Watzlawick et al. (1974, page xi) offered the following account of a strategic approach to solving a problem:

> When in 1334 the Duchess of Tyrol, Margareta Maultasch, encircled the castle of Hochosterwitz in the province of Carinthia, she knew only too well that the fortress, situated on an incredibly steep rock rising high above the valley floor, was impregnable to direct attack and would only yield to a long siege. In due course, the situation of the defenders became critical; they were down to their last ox and had only two bags of barley corn left. Margareta's situation was becoming equally pressing, albeit for different reasons: her troops were beginning to be unruly, there seemed to be no end to the siege in sight, and she had similarly urgent business elsewhere. At this point the commandant of the castle decided on a desperate course of action which to his men must have seemed sheer folly: he had the last ox slaughtered, had its abdominal cavity filled with the remaining barley, and ordered the carcass thrown down the steep cliff on to the meadow in front of the enemy camp. Upon receiving this scornful message from above, the discouraged duchess abandoned the siege and moved on.

This commandant would probably have made a good strategic therapist, since he apparently had a creative way of findings solutions to problems.

To Madanes (1981), strategic therapy is not a specific method to be applied to all cases but rather an approach which depends on devising a strategy for each clinical problem. The therapist takes responsibility for the therapy, clear goals are set and a strategy is developed, involving intervention in the client's social context, to deal with each problem. In many instances the social context concerned is the family, and strategic methods have been widely used as means of intervening in families.

There is an infinite number of possible therapeutic strategies, and the range of interventions available to us extends as far as the limits of our imagination and creativity. The following list of strategic techniques is not exhaustive, nor are the strategies mutually exclusive. Some of them, especially those described by the Milan group, would be called 'systemic' rather than 'strategic' by certain therapists. For our purposes, however, it is convenient to consider them all together:

- Reframing, including positive connotation
- The use of metaphorical communication, which may take various forms

- Giving paradoxical directives, including instructions to change either slowly or not at all
- Prescribing rituals and other tasks
- Declaring therapeutic impotence
- Prescribing interminable therapy
- Using humour
- Using a consultation group as a 'Greek chorus'
- Staging a debate
- Externalizing the problem
- 'Storied therapy'

This list is not exhaustive. Other strategic techniques are to be found in the literature, some of them in *Paradox and Counterparadox* (Palazzoli et al., 1978a).

Reframing and positive connotation

Reframing has been mentioned several times already. Any of the other devices listed above may be used to reframe situations, but reframing may also be done without using any of them. For instance, a child's non-compliant behaviour may be reframed as the parents' problem in controlling the child. This can be done during the course of conversation: when the parents have described the child's difficult behaviour, the therapist might comment, 'So you're having a hard time finding effective ways of handling Billy and getting his behaviour under control.' This kind of statement is hard to deny, though some parents may respond by saying they, and perhaps others, have tried 'everything' and 'nothing works'; the implication being that the child is 'impossible' and that the laws of learning theory have been suspended. Families may try to disqualify attempts to reframe situations in this way, but whatever the response, statements such as those above do offer a new perspective on the situation.

Other situations may be reframed during conversation as more serious, or less serious, than they have been considered, or as funny (when they have been considered serious), or surprising – or indeed anything they have not previously been considered to be by the clients.

Positive connotation is the ascribing of 'positive' or noble motives to the symptomatic behaviour of family members. It is thus a form of reframing, since usually the symptoms have previously been considered by all concerned to have 'negative' value, that is to be 'bad', or undesirable, behaviours. The value of positive connotation was set out by Palazzoli and her colleagues (1978a). Positive connotation, they stated, can be important, even essential, in the treatment of many of the more difficult families.

'It . . . became clear that access to the systemic model was possible only if we were to make a positive connotation of *both* the symptom of the identified patient and the symptomatic behaviours of the others, saying, for example that all the observable behaviours of the group as a whole appeared to be inspired by the common goal of preserving the cohesion of the family group. In this way, the therapists were able to put *all* the members of the group on the same level, thus avoiding involvement in any alliances or divisions into subgroups, which are the daily bread of such systems' malfunction. Dysfunctional families are in fact regularly, especially in moments of crisis, prone to such divisions and factional battles, which are characterized by the distribution of such stereotyped labels as 'bad', 'sick', 'weak', 'inefficient', 'carrier of hereditary or social taints, etc.' (Palazzoli et al., 1978a, page 56)

It is not the symptomatic behaviour itself which is positively connoted, but the intent behind it. Palazzoli and her colleagues (1978a) assumed that the intent is to maintain the homeostatic balance within the family, so that it does not 'fall apart'. Positive connotation is also an important preliminary to the prescription of a paradoxical injunction. It makes a lot more sense to prescribe a behaviour which has been connoted as having some value rather than one which has been called 'bad'.

The use of metaphor

Metaphor offers many possibilities for the indirect communication of ideas and for strategic intervention in families. Books which deal specifically with the use of this therapeutic device include those of Gordon (1978), Barker (1985, 1996) and Mills and Crowley (1986), but the use of metaphor is described by many other authors. Notable among these are Madanes (1981) and Erickson, who used this device extensively, both in therapy and in teaching his students. *My Voice Will Go With You* (Erickson, 1982) is a collection of Erickson's 'teaching tales' and makes fascinating and entertaining reading. In *A Teaching Seminar with Milton H. Erickson* (1980e) Erickson again makes extensive use of metaphor, seldom answering a question from a student other than by telling a story with a meaning that in some way addressed the issue raised.

Metaphorical devices that may be used in therapy can be classified as follows:

(1) Major stories designed to deal comprehensively with complex clinical situations (see Gordon, 1978).
(2) Anecdotes and short stories aimed at achieving specific, limited goals.
(3) Analogies, similes and brief metaphorical statements or phrases that illustrate or emphasize specific points.
(4) Relationship metaphors. A relationship metaphor uses one relationship, for example that between the therapist and one or more members of the family, as a metaphor for another relationship. Thus

the therapist might explore the reason why a family member is absent from a session by asking the family members who *are* present questions like, 'Did I last time say something tactless to your father?' Or, 'Did he feel left out of the discussion?' Or, 'Have I shown him insufficient concern?' Or, 'Did he feel in some way blamed for the family problems?' Or, 'How could I have made him feel more a part of the therapy process?' Such questions may cause family members to think about their own relationships with the missing family member. The discussion of the relationship between therapist and the father thus serves as a metaphor for that between other family members and the father.

(5) Tasks and rituals with metaphorical meanings. These may be carried out during therapy sessions, or they may be prescribed to be performed between sessions. An example of the former category is the 'couples choreography' described by Papp (1982). In this procedure couples are asked, first to close their eyes and have a 'dream' or 'fantasy' about their spouse. They are then asked to visualize themselves in the same fantasy. The fantasy is then enacted, under the therapist's guidance. The marital relationship is thus defined in metaphorical terms, and 'penetrates the confusing morass of verbiage that often sidetracks both couple and therapist . . . and reveals the ulterior level of the relationship' (Papp, 1982, page 455). An extensive discussion of the types and uses of therapeutic rituals has been provided by Imber-Black et al. (1988).

(6) Metaphorical objects. These are objects used during therapy to represent something other than what they actually are. Angelo (1981) described the use of an envelope containing a blank sheet of paper to represent a family 'secret', that is an issue the family members were having difficulty dealing with, namely the fact that the son was adopted. By this means the family was able to talk about what was 'in the envelope' without specifying its nature. This enabled that particular block in the therapy process to be overcome.

(7) Artistic metaphors. These are artistic productions, such as drawings, paintings, clay models or structures built with 'Lego', which are used to represent a feeling state, experience or something else which may be significant in the treatment process.

The therapeutic use of artistic metaphors was pioneered by Richard Crowley and Joyce Mills, and the creative way they have employed them is described in *Therapeutic Metaphors for Children and the Child Within* (Mills & Crowley, 1986). The essence of this technique is that clients who say, for example, that they are angry, or sad, or in pain, are asked to draw their pain, or to draw what 'angry' looks like. They can then draw the same thing getting better. The drawing thus becomes a metaphor for feelings, which people often have difficulty expressing in words. Artistic metaphors may be used to reframe a subject's experience in another sensory modality. The technique can be used during family therapy, or in individual work with children or adults.

The above classification of metaphors is taken from *Using Metaphors in Psychotherapy* (Barker, 1985), which provides a fuller discussion of metaphorical methods of therapy and many examples. Further discussion of the use of metaphor is to be found in *Psychotherapeutic Metaphors: A Guide to Theory & Practice* (Barker, 1996).

The use of paradox

Paradoxical injunctions are directions or suggestions that family members continue their symptomatic behaviour. They may be useful when direct injunctions have failed. They hand responsibility for the symptom over to the family. They may be used with families that take a confrontative position with the therapist. There is seldom much to be gained from engaging in a symmetrical dispute with clients. When such a situation exists or threatens to develop, a paradoxical approach may prove fruitful.

Frankl (1960) developed the technique of replacing efforts to extinguish symptoms by intentional, even exaggerated, efforts by the subject to carry out the symptomatic behaviour. He called this 'paradoxical intention'. Paradoxical techniques have also been described, with examples, by Watzlawick et al. (1974), Fisch et al. (1982), Barker (1981b) and Weeks and L'Abate (1982), among others. In *Paradox and Counterparadox* (Palazzoli et al., 1978a) the Milan associates described a variety of paradoxical interventions they used with the families they had treated. 'Symptom prescription' is closely related to paradoxical injunction and is the term O'Hanlon and Hexum (1990) use to describe much of Erickson's use of paradoxical methods.

Paradoxical methods are usually employed when direct methods have failed. Weeks and L'Abate (1982) recommend their use 'when a family and/or any of its subsystems is in a developmental crisis' (page 58). They also describe some 'dysfunctional transactions where paradoxical intervention appears especially appropriate' (page 60). These are:

(1)   Expressive fighting and bickering: members of a system relate to one another overtly by fighting. Weeks and L'Abate suggest that therapists who attempt to deal with such families in a straightforward way will find themselves at odds with them.

(2)   Unwillingness to cooperate with each other and complete assignments. This is a more passive and subtle way of expressing hostility than that found in families in the previous category. Such families may express verbal compliance with one another, but defeat each other non-verbally. There is often one marital partner who is more verbal

and articulate than the other and who defeats the other by continuous complaints and diatribes. On the other hand the second partner is more skilled non-verbally and achieves defeat of the first by non-verbal means.

(3) Continuation of the same patterns in spite of all types of intervention, as is seen in the 'rigidly resistant' family.

(4) 'Divide and conquer', the term used by Weeks and L'Abate for the situation, often seen in families in which there are teenagers skilled at separating the parents, and exploiting any polarization there may be in the marriage.

(5) Using disqualifying communications, such as self-contradictions, inconsistencies, subject switching, metaphor (which can be used by clients to avoid defining or facing issues directly) and making cryptic statements.

As with other strategic techniques, the use of paradox presupposes that a desired outcome has been agreed upon by therapist and family. The family should also be actively engaged in the therapy process before these techniques are employed.

Weeks and L'Abate (1982, Chapter 5) put forward 'basic principles' for using paradoxical methods. These are applicable to individuals as well as to couples and families.

Principle one. New symptoms are positively relabelled, reframed or connoted. The value of reframing and positive connotation, as means of using symptoms to positive effect has been discussed above.

Principle two. The symptom is linked to the other members of the family. Family therapy is based on understanding the relationship context of clients' symptoms, and positively connoting the intent behind symptoms is often an effective way of putting symptoms in such a context.

Principle three. Reverse the symptom's vector. This procedure aims to put those concerned in charge of the symptom. In the case of individuals it involves the intentional enactment of the symptom, and sometimes also its deliberate amplification. In working with families, reversing the vector may be achieved either by having other members help the symptom-bearer have the symptom, or by having the other members play a paradoxical role. As an example of the latter process L'Abate and Weeks (1982) discuss the case of a single-parent family in which a daughter is acting out and taking charge. To reverse the vector, the mother might be told to assume the role of child, giving up her position of authority and pretending to be a helpless child. Such measures place the people concerned in charge of the symptom or symptoms, which is the first step towards bringing about change.

Principle four. Prescribe and sequence paradoxical interventions over time in order to bind off the reappearance of the symptom. Weeks and L'Abate (1982) suggest that a series of interventions over a period of time is usually needed, rather than a single one. A sequence of interventions which these authors recommend as often effective is:

(1)   Positive relabelling, reframing, or connotation
(2)   Symptom prescription
(3)   Predicting a relapse
(4)   Prescribing a relapse

Prescribing a relapse, in families which respond 'negatively' to injunctions, is of course a way of preventing relapse.

Principle five. The paradoxical prescription must force the client(s) to act on the task in some way. Good rapport is a basic requirement for ensuring that therapeutic prescriptions are carried out, but in addition they may be ritualized, for example by prescribing them in a fixed sequence, or by laying down that whenever event X occurs the client is to have the symptom. Paradoxical prescriptions can also be put in writing.

Haley (1976, pages 72–75) suggested eight steps in giving paradoxical directives:

(1)   A relationship must be established with the client(s). This should be defined as one directed to producing change.
(2)   The problem must be clearly defined.
(3)   Clear goals must be set. The therapist must understand precisely the changes the directive is designed to bring about.
(4)   A plan must be offered. It is helpful to offer some rationale for the paradoxical directive. This may be that it is necessary to continue with the symptom, or even increase its intensity, because to abandon it would be 'too risky' or 'too difficult for the rest of the family'. For example, a 13-year-old boy and his stepmother were told that it was essential that they express their hostile feelings towards each other, since 'bottling them up' would create too much tension in them both. At the same time a specific 15-minute time each day was agreed for the expression of these feelings.
(5)   Anyone who is an authority on the problems must be disqualified. One way is to suggest that the person would be upset if the symptom disappeared. Another is to praise that person's self-sacrifice but suggest another area of the subject's life where self-sacrifice would be more important. In the case above, the stepmother initially raised objections to the plan, saying that she did not believe in children and their parents insulting each other. It was, she said, against the principles she lived by. Her views were commended as praiseworthy, and the therapist said that he too did not believe in this sort of thing. He realized that it seemed crazy to encourage undesired behaviour, but it was important for him to know how the experiment would work out, in order to plan further treatment. He complimented the stepmother on her willingness to consider compromising her principles for this purpose, whereupon she agreed to take part in the suggested plan of action.
(6)   The paradoxical directive is given. In the case of the boy and the stepmother, they were to meet at a set time every day when each would

say what he or she disliked in the other, and how the other person had irritated or annoyed him or her during the previous 24 hours. They could be as frank and insulting as they chose. Such matters were only to be discussed at that time, however. If the son and stepmother were tempted to discuss them at other times they were to postpone doing so until the set time.

(7)   The response is observed and the therapist continues to encourage the undesired behaviour, especially if the behaviour shows signs of improving. The therapist's pleasure at this turn of events should be hidden, and doubt expressed that the improvement will continue. In the case mentioned above there was a rapid improvement, but the therapist warned that it might not continue.

(8)   The therapist should not accept credit for change as it occurs. Puzzlement is often better, combined with scepticism that the changes that have occurred are real and will continue.

There is often an element of challenge in paradoxical directives.

A family came to me with complaints about the antisocial behaviour of their 13-year-old son, but actually talked about little except their 19-year-old unmarried daughter, Tina, and her son, aged $1\frac{1}{2}$. Father, mother, son, and 17-year-old daughter all complained about Tina's behaviour who, characteristically, had refused to come to the family interview. They said that she took no part in caring for her son; consistently failed to contribute from her wages the sum she had agreed to pay for her keep and that of her son; was dirty, lazy, self-centred and a liar; and was prone to take things belonging to other family members without asking. She often 'borrowed', and damaged, her sister's clothes and other property. She seemed to be in control of the household.

As an infant Tina had had a kidney removed for cancer. Her parents had expected that she would die and had apparently indulged her greatly when she was younger. However the cancer did not recur and she was now in good physical health.

I discussed the situation with the family. The parents were aware of the need to achieve control of their wayward daughter, but had tried 'everything' without any success. It seemed that the daughter used the family's apartment as a sort of free hotel. I pointed out that she would undoubtedly continue to do this if allowed, and that the only alternative would be to make staying in the household conditional upon certain specific behaviours, such as paying her 'rent', doing her share of caring for her son and of the household chores, and acting as a constructive adult member of the family. If these conditions were not met she would have to be asked to leave and live elsewhere. Changing the locks or seeking the help of the police to remove her might even be necessary.

Having spelt this out, I then said I believed this course of action would be impossible for the parents. Their concern and love for their daughter was too great. It would be better, and less distressing, for them to accept continuation of the present situation. So I advised against this plan, though not until after I had spelled it out in detail. The parents, led by the father, immediately said no, they *would* take control of their daughter. She was quite capable of taking care of herself and had done so when she first left home $2\frac{1}{2}$ years previously. She was earning enough to rent her own apartment. The present situation had gone on long enough, they said. I expressed doubts about whether the parents could bring themselves to offer this choice to their daughter, at least if they were sincere in their intention to tell her to leave the home if she didn't shape up.

The parents left expressing their intention to carry through with the plan, and they did so. The daughter decided to leave and found her own accommodation. She continued in her job, became financially self-supporting, and signed over guardianship of her son to her parents, a situation with which all concerned seemed well satisfied.

A simple, and often effective, example of the use of paradox is 'symptom prescription'. The case, mentioned above, of the mother and son who were told to meet together for 15 minutes daily is an example of this process. Another was described by Hare-Mustin (1975). This was the case of a 4-year-old with temper tantrums which occurred frequently and unpredictably. The therapist negotiated with the child and his family where the tantrums should occur, picking a safe place at home. If the boy started to have a tantrum he was to be taken to that place, the 'tantrum place'. By the next session a week later Tommy had had only one tantrum, so the therapist then said it was necessary to decide what time the tantrums should take place. The period 5.00–7.00 p.m. was agreed upon. As expected it proved hard for the child to have tantrums to order and they soon ceased.

It is also possible to prescribe that a symptom occur during a therapy session. In most cases the symptoms are not produced under these circumstances. This was so, for example, in the case of William, aged 8, and described at greater length elsewhere (Barker, 1985, pages 30–32).

William had severe tantrums which had failed to improve despite several previous attempts at therapy. In the course of a family interview I asked him to have a tantrum, so that I could see exactly what his tantrums were like. He declined to do so, despite some pressure from me. I therefore asked the parents to have a cassette recorder ready in the home at all times, so that the tantrums could be recorded and played back to me at the next session. This proved an effective way of eliminating the problem. The cassette recorder functioned as a metaphorical object and represented me, the therapist. William was now supposed to have tantrums, so that I could be given recordings of them. His tendency to respond negatively to what he was told to do, however, led him to abandon having them.

How and why do paradoxical directives work? It seems that an important factor is the taking over of the symptom by the therapist who, instead of attempting to stop it, is perceived by the client(s) as encouraging it, at least in certain circumstances. This is a new situation for the individual or family, and it evokes a new response. When it is a family that is being treated it disturbs the family's homeostatic processes, so that some change in their way of functioning becomes necessary. O'Hanlon and Hexum's (1990) account of Erickson's work contains many elegant examples of the use of symptom prescription.

It is worth noting that in the case of the rebellious 19-year-old recounted above, I implicitly reframed the family situation. I was presented, after the son had been used as an 'admission ticket', with a rebellious teenage girl as the problem and was, it seemed, expected to do 'something' about it, even though the parents had already tried 'everything'. To enter into treating the family on this basis is a recipe for failure. So I reframed things so that the issue became the parents' problem. This was realistic. The daughter was quite happy living in her free hotel, and from her point of view there was no need to make any changes. She did not even deign to come with the family to see me. If there was to be change the rest of the family had to make a move and it was through a paradoxical intervention that they were enabled to do so. Note, too, that the problem was that of overcoming a developmental hurdle – that of letting the daughter leave the nest and become an independent person in society – a situation in which paradoxical methods seem to have particular application.

Rituals and tasks

The setting of tasks and the performance of rituals are used by many family therapists as devices to promote change. Wolin and Bennett (1984) have pointed out that rituals are 'a powerful component of family life', and are 'central to the identity of the family'. Providing new rituals, or altering pre-existing ones, can therefore be powerful change-promoting devices. The ritualizing of tasks set as part of a strategic (or other) therapy plan, can also help ensure that the tasks are performed.

Wolin and Bennett (1984) divided family rituals into family celebrations (weddings, baptisms, bar mitzvahs, religious celebrations and so forth); family traditions (ritualized activities specific to the family, such as summer vacations, visits to extended family members, family reunions, birthday and other parties and so on); and patterned family interactions, often not consciously planned (such as regular dinnertimes, bedtime routines for children, customary treatment of guests and weekend leisure activities). The modification, or prescribing, of rituals in any of these categories may be used to promote change in families. Otto van der Hart, in his book *Rituals in Psychotherapy* (1983), describes how rituals may be used, both in psychotherapy and in other situations.

In *Rituals in Families and Family Therapy*, Imber-Black (1988) defines 'five themes' which can 'orient the therapist's decision-making' when therapeutic rituals are to be designed and used. The themes are:

(1)   Membership
(2)   Healing
(3)   Identity
(4)   Belief expression and negotiation
(5)   Celebration

Imber-Black gives examples of all the above, and in other chapters contributors discuss the use of rituals in a variety of clinical situations. Whiting (1988) contributes helpful guidelines to designing therapeutic rituals. Anyone planning the use of therapeutic rituals would do well to study this book.

Discussing the therapeutic use of rituals in family therapy, Sutcliffe et al. (1985) list the following purposes they can serve:

- Supporting competence
- Increasing skills
- Differentiating roles
- Establishing hierarchies
- Influencing expectations
- Altering communication patterns
- Developing support systems
- Challenging stereotypes
- Introducing rewards
- Promoting proximity or challenging enmeshment

Tasks, whether ritualized or not, may be used as a form of direct therapy as, for example, when parents are told to get together to decide on rules for their children's behaviour, or on the rewards to be given the children when they conform to the rules. In strategic therapy however tasks usually have a hidden meaning, as well as a more obvious one.

Rituals are often employed as components of strategic plans, which may also involve one or more other strategic devices or concepts. For example, the case of the boy with temper tantrums mentioned in the preceding section (Hare-Mustin, 1975) involved the ritualization of the symptom, as well as the use of paradox. Not only was the child told to have tantrums, but these were to occur at a particular time and place.

Rituals have long been used to assist people in moving from one developmental stage to another. van der Hart (1983) discusses the 'rituals of transition', that are features of the lives of many primitive tribal communities. They include initiation rites for women, marriage rituals and birth rituals. In western society, as Wolin and Bennett (1984) point out, we too have marriage ceremonies, funerals, house-warming parties, retirement parties, birthdays and so forth. The Jewish bar mitzvah is, however, one of the few currently practised rites marking the assumption of a more adult role in society. It seems our adolescents therefore often stage their own rites of transition, which tend to take the form of wild parties and the rather conspicuous rejection of the 'child' role which they have previously played. In some other societies, however, formal puberty rites have great importance.

According to Wallace (1966, page 203), 'rites of passage are a type of ritual which educates participants for, announces publicly, and initiates a new relationship'. Similarly therapeutic rituals can educate people for, announce and initiate new relationships, which therapy often aims to promote.

van der Hart (1983) offers examples of rituals dealing with detoxification, healing in various forms, including exorcizing illness, saying goodbye, bereavement, transitions, spoiled children and separation, among other things. Most rituals have a symbolic or metaphorical meaning. The following, reproduced from *Using Metaphors in Psychotherapy* (Barker, 1985), is one such.

Fay had lived in a common-law relationship with George for 18 months. The relationship was a stormy one and Fay was ambivalent about it. When she eventually decided to leave George she and her two sons nevertheless mourned his loss a great deal. Fay complained that she couldn't sleep at night, thought constantly about George, was unable to concentrate and felt lonely. At interview she also appeared depressed. It seemed important that she discard the unhappy associations and memories, as she came to terms with the separation. Had she not resolved her feelings she might have been tempted to seek reconciliation with George, as she had done with men with whom she had previously lived.

Fay still had a number of items in the house which reminded her of George. Some were things which had belonged to him but he had left behind, while others were things he had given her.

After exploring Fay's feelings and situation carefully with her, the therapist gave her the following task. She was to go through everything in the house that had belonged to George and decide whether it was worth keeping or whether it was something that would be better got rid of. The two classes of things were to be placed in different boxes. Fay was then to take the box of things that were not worth keeping, make a fire in the backyard and burn the box and its contents. As she did so she was to feel free to weep as much as she felt like doing.

The other box now contained all those things of George's that Fay valued. These were to be packed up carefully and Fay was to dig a hole in her backyard and bury them. This was a symbolic act of preserving the good things about George and the happy times they had spent together.

Fay carried out the task as directed. When she returned to the therapist, however, she reported that she had been unable to weep at the burial because 'so much trash was not worth wasting tears over'. She also reported that she was now feeling a lot better and was once again getting a good night's sleep. She no longer appeared depressed and seemed to be making good progress in the business of mourning and coming to terms with the loss of George.

Fay was faced with the problem of making a transition in her life, and quite an abrupt one too. The ritual actions prescribed were designed to have appropriate metaphorical meanings and to assist her in making the transition. They did indeed appear to be helpful to her.

Rituals can be used at any stage in the therapy process, including termination. When finishing treatment it can be helpful to give clients something to take away with them, as a continuing resource. Imber-Black (1988, page 82) describes how she did this with a family in which there was a 12-year-old girl with an eating problem. Two metaphorical objects were offered the family at a 'celebration' dinner. These were to be used in a ritualistic way. Among the very few foods the girl would eat were french fried potatoes. She had also been seeing a dietician who urged her to eat kiwi fruit, something she hated.

At the final therapy session the therapist handed the family a potato and a kiwi fruit. She asked them to freeze them 'with the understanding that, in the future, when any member of the family felt that a family discussion was needed, the thawing out of the potato and the kiwi fruit would signal the call for such a meeting'. The two objects symbolized the process the family had been going through, and the ritual was designed to help them recall and again make use of the problem-solving skills they had learned during therapy. The ritual may also have been helpful because it gave the family time to reflect on the situation while the contents of the bowl thawed, rather than reacting precipitately.

Palazzoli et al. (1978a) coined the term 'ritualized prescription' and applied it to 'odd days and even days' tasks. They used this strategy with certain families in which children are the identified patients. Its essence is that one parent, let us say the father, makes all the decisions about the 'problem' child on even days, that is Tuesdays, Thursdays and Saturdays; while the mother does the same thing on odd days, that is Mondays, Wednesdays and Fridays. On Sundays everyone is to behave spontaneously. Each parent, when it is his or her turn to be in charge, has absolute discretion to make decisions about the identified patient. The other parent acts as if not there, as far as such decisions are concerned, and the parent who is in charge must note in writing any infringement of this rule by the other one.

There is more to most strategic therapy devices than simply the carrying out of the task. Indeed they can be effective even though the tasks or rituals are not carried out at all. Thus the 'odd days-even days' prescription carries a number of important messages, which are implicit in the task. One is that *someone* has to be in charge of the children and make the key decisions concerning them, a point that is not directly stated and might be disputed by some families if it were. ('They're old enough to look after themselves' might be the response.) Another is that both parents need to share the responsibility of caring for, and making decisions relating to, the children. The setting of the task makes these points even if the ritual is never carried out. The ritual may also suggest that the parents need to have different roles, or that one may be a more effective, or more appropriate, disciplinarian in certain circumstances. Finally, there is an implied contrast between 'spontaneous' and controlled behaviour, and the opportunity is provided to observe, on Sundays, how far family members have progressed in internalizing the lessons they have learned in therapy, and thus behaving 'spontaneously' in an acceptable fashion.

Declaring therapeutic impotence

Chapter 16 of *Paradox and Counterparadox* (Palazzoli et al., 1978a) is entitled 'The therapists declare their impotence without blaming anyone.' This strategic manoeuvre, which is really another example of the use of paradox, can be effective when the family and the therapist have become locked in a symmetrical relationship. In such a situation every intervention the therapist attempts to make is in some way blocked or disqualified, so that the strength of the symmetrical conflict steadily increases. The Milan associates described the delivery of this intervention as follows:

> 'We say that in spite of the willing collaboration of the family, which has done everything possible to facilitate our understanding, we find ourselves confused and incapable of forming clear ideas, of helping them, and that the team has in no way clarified our ideas. The attitude of the therapists should be neither indifferent nor overdramatic but simply that of those who dislike acknowledging their incapacity in doing what has been asked of them. In saying this, we attentively observe the feedbacks of the various members of the family. We leave a pause of "suspense", fix the date for the family's next session, and collect our fee.' (Palazzoli et al., 1978a, page 148)

The timing of this intervention is important. Palazzoli and her colleagues emphasized that it should not be done too soon. They suggest that the right time is when the 'angry obstinacy of the therapists' (the Milan group usually worked as a team, so we will use the plural), together with the family's reinforcing of its disqualifications of the therapists, indicate escalation of the symmetrical battle. The intervention is designed to put an end to the battle, and is another example of the use of the 'one-down' position in therapy. It also avoids the therapists appearing as the initiators of change. If they did seem to be playing that role, in a family such as we are discussing, the family would tend to regard them as hostile, and would continue to defend its position.

This device has the effect of creating a complementary relationship between therapists and family. It might seem to be one in which the therapists are giving over control to the family, but in reality they are taking control. There is also a paradox in the contrast between the declaration of impotence on the one hand, and the collection of a fee and the making of a further appointment on the other. At a certain level the intervention involves an invitation to the family to come up with something new, and challenges them to prove that the implication in the intervention, namely that their case is hopeless, is wrong.

Prescribing interminable therapy

Yet another strategic device is the prescription of interminable therapy. Its purpose is similar to that of declaring therapeutic impotence. The symptoms, or the family problem, are labelled as chronic and unlikely to change quickly. Such a prescription might be indicated when efforts to get the family to change quickly, or perhaps to change at all, have failed. In effect, the family is told it will have to attend indefinitely at prescribed intervals. This intervention, too, incorporates a paradoxical element.

The use of humour

It can often help to see the funny side of things. This applies to family therapy as much as to many other of life's activities. Sutcliffe et al. (1985), in an article entitled 'New directions for family therapy: rubbish removal as a task of choice', pointed out that 'family therapists, if they take families seriously, need to be able to laugh and joke with them'. The article reframes the disposal of rubbish (in North America we would call it garbage) as a worthwhile, indeed valuable activity, and one which we should not feel guilty about asking our children to perform. Nor need we be reluctant to perform it ourselves, for it may be just what we, as therapists, need to do.

Frankl (1960) encouraged his patients to laugh at their symptoms, and Erickson also advocated the use of humour.

> 'In teaching, in therapy, you are very careful to use humour, because your patients bring in enough grief, and they don't need all that grief and sorrow. You better get them into a more pleasant frame of mind right away.' (Erickson, 1980e, page 71)

The use of humour is a very personal thing and depends, perhaps more than any other therapy device, on the therapist's personality, and on non-verbal communications as well as verbal ones. The aim, usually, is to laugh *with*, not *at*, the family. Doing this can both help establish and maintain rapport, and assist in reframing things. For example, children's behaviour, which may have been arousing their parents' severe disapproval, can sometimes be shown to have a funny side: another example of reframing.

Humour is a double-edged therapeutic weapon. Its use presupposes some understanding of the family's sense of humour. Without this our jokes may fall flat or, more serious, remarks which are intended as jokes may be taken seriously. Yet despite these possible disadvantages, humour is a valuable therapeutic tool and skill in its use is well worth developing.

The 'Greek chorus'

The 'Greek chorus' (Papp, 1980) is a 'consultation group' which watches the session through a one-way observation screen and sends a series of messages into the therapy room. Papp (1980) lists some of the types of message sent:

- Support messages. These simply praise or support certain aspects of the family.
- Public opinion polls. These take, and report to the family, the odds on the family changing. They can thus present families with challenges.
- Messages designed to surprise and confuse. Surprise and confusion can be important elements in promoting change, and these messages are intended to arouse the family's curiosity, stir up their imagination, or provoke them into revealing hidden information.
- Messages disagreeing with the therapist's expressed opinion. Therapeutic 'splits' can help promote change; usually the therapist in the room advocates change, while the 'Greek chorus' advises against it at the present time, or against the proposed speed of change. This is a process similar to that described in the case history included in the section on the use of paradox (pages 142–143), though in that case the therapist offered both alternatives himself.
- Messages offering advice from outside the circle of therapist and family. These can reframe situations, and bring psychological pressures to bear on families in various ways.

While a consultation group can usually be helpful, it is especially so when complex paradoxical and other strategic devices are used. It is costly in terms of staff time, but this may be considered worthwhile for severely disturbed families, resistant to other interventions, and also as a method of speeding up therapy. Moreover the Greek chorus may consist mainly, even entirely, of students, and thus be a valuable learning experience for them.

The debate

The debate as a strategic therapy device was described by Sheinberg (1985). It is a development of the use of the Greek chorus. The consultation group, or 'strategic team', comes out from behind the one-way screen and stages a debate in the presence of the family. The debate concerns 'a dilemma that is a strategically constructed isomorph of the family situation. From this position, therapists have the option of changing levels between themselves and the family, asking the family to help solve the therapists' dilemma so that they can be free to help the family' (Sheinberg, 1985, page 259).

The family members are able to observe the therapists' struggles to resolve their difficulties from a 'meta', or outside, position. From this different perspective they may be able to find new solutions to their own dilemma. This procedure has some similarities to the use of the 'reflecting team' (Andersen, 1991; Hoffman, 2002, Chapter 9).

Externalizing problems

White and Epston (1990), in *Narrative Means to Therapeutic Ends*, described a number of original means of helping families achieve change. Among these is the 'externalization' of problems. The therapist encourages family members to objectify and, sometimes, personify the problems. Thus people, or families, are redefined as being under the influence of 'anger', 'aggression', or 'hopelessness' or, as in the case of a child with encopresis, 'Sneaky Poo'. In one case reported in White and Epston (1990, pages 51–52) a child's sleep problem was redefined as 'insecurity'. Therapy then became a matter of assisting the family in overcoming the effects of insecurity on the family.

This process reframes problems. From being seen as inherent in particular family members, or in certain relationships, a problem can become 'a separate entity and thus external to the person or relationship that was ascribed as the problem' (White & Epston, 1990, page 38). In other words, 'the problem becomes the problem'.

According to White and Epston (1990, page 39), externalizing problems:

(1) Decreases unproductive conflict between persons, including those disputes over who is responsible for the problem.
(2) Undermines the sense of failure that has developed for many persons in response to the continuing existence of the problem despite their attempts to resolve it.
(3) Paves the way for persons to cooperate with each other, to unite in a struggle against the problem, and to escape its influence in their lives and relationships.

(4)   Opens up new possibilities for persons to take action to retrieve their lives and relationships from the problem and its influence.

(5)   Frees people to take a lighter, more effective, and less stressed approach to 'deadly serious' problems.

(6)   Presents options for dialogue, rather than monologue, about the problem.

Those considering using this approach are advised to study White and Epston's book.

A storied approach

The above is the title of another section of the book by White and Epston (1990). Quoting Bruner (1976), these authors point out that there are 'two modes of . . . thought, each providing distinctive ways of ordering experience, of constructing reality . . . A good story and a well-formed argument are different natural kinds.'

We have seen earlier how metaphor, which may be presented in narrative form, can be therapeutically effective. White and Epston however suggest that narrative may be used in a more direct way. The flavour of their method is caught in the following letter to a child who would not come to a first family session.

Dear Jane,

I'm writing because we didn't get to meet each other last Wednesday at 5 pm.

My name is Mary. I've worked at the Leslie Centre for four years. I have a daughter a little younger than you.

When your mother phoned to say your family wouldn't be coming in, she said you were feeling badly with acne that had flared up. I can understand how you felt – I sometimes get a rash on my face and neck myself.

It's hard writing to you when I don't even know what you look like. If you send me a photo, I'll send you one.

Well it's pretty clear that things are going wrong in your family. Growing up is very hard these days – I'm sure it's harder than it used to be. It sounds like you're failing to get to school sometimes and failing to get on with your life. That would sure make anyone feel miserable.

When I meet with your mother and father next time, I would think that you'll probably have another attack of acne – and I do know what it's like to face people when you're not at your best – I do it quite often.

So I'll understand if you don't feel like coming and facing into your future. But, on the other hand, I'd feel really badly talking behind your back with your mother and father.

I've been thinking of this dilemma quite a bit and I've come up with some ideas. I wonder what you think about them:

> (1) Could you get a friend to represent you at the session – a bit like a lawyer – who could come in your place and speak for you?
>
> (2) If that's not a good idea, what about you let your mother or father choose a friend of theirs to represent you?
>
> (3) If that's not a good idea, what about you go on 'stand by' at the telephone while your parents are here? Then I can call you if I get the impression that your parents have forgotten what it's like to be your age. I can ask for a few ideas about how it feels for you.
>
> Sounds like you've got your parents pretty worried about you.
>
> If you really want to show your parents this letter it doesn't really matter. But I'd prefer you didn't.
>
> I'm planning to meet with your mother and father on Wednesday, April 3rd, at 5:30 p.m. I suppose you might come or you might not or you might try one of those other ideas. It's up to you, I guess.
>
> Well, bye for now,
> > Yours sincerely
> > Mary

White and Epston's (1990) book contains many other examples of letters written to family members in all sorts of clinical situations. There are also specimen certificates and diplomas. These include:

- Monster-tamer and Fear-catcher Certificate
- Breaking the Grip of Sneaky Poo Certificate
- Certificate of Concentration
- Escape from Tantrums Certificate
- Diploma of Special Knowledge.

'King Tiger'

In a paper entitled 'King Tiger and the roaring tummies: a novel way of helping young children and their families change', Wood (1988) describes what he refers to as 'the work of a good friend and colleague, King Tiger'. King Tiger, Wood explains, was created to assist him in promoting and maintaining change in young children and their families. This therapeutic intervention makes use of the 'special gift' young children possess, namely their ability to imagine, create and fantasize. Wood (1988) points out that the likes of Father Christmas (Santa Claus to North American readers), the Easter Bunny and the Tooth Fairy bring not only wonder but material wealth as well. 'King Tiger was created in the tradition of another branch of heroes; those heroes that can become living metaphors of strength, endurance, courage and persistence.' These include Superman, Wonderwoman, Batman, ET and The Saint.

Wood (1988) has found King Tiger to be most effective with children between the ages of 4 and 9. Rapport must be established before King

Tiger is introduced, with a touch of mystery, suspense or surprise, to the family. King Tiger writes letters to the children concerned. He also responds to the children's letters. His letters are hand printed by Wood on coloured paper on which there is a drawing of a tiger. The letters are written directly to the child, while at the same time communicating indirectly with other family members. They 'enable the therapeutic influence or leverage to be more fully extended into the child's and family's private world at home'.

Wood (1988) has found King Tiger letters to be useful in highlighting 'news of a difference' (see Bateson, 1980) regarding changes occurring in the family. King Tiger can highlight any initial success on the part of the child. He can also communicate metaphorically with child and family, for example using the 'my friend John' technique of Erickson (1980e) – this being the use of anecdotes concerning similar situations of which King Tiger has had experience. Reframing and the recalling of old memories are other functions King Tiger can perform.

This is a creative and useful strategic technique. Those planning to use it should consult Wood's (1988) paper for further details of how to do so.

Non-traditional approaches to the treatment of complex family problems

The 1990s saw a move away from approaches in which therapists took on the responsibility of assessing families presenting for help, and then devising methods of helping them make the changes considered to be needed. Atwood (1997), in her book *Challenging Family Therapy Situations: Perspectives in Social Construction*, describes the movement from therapist-centred approaches such as the strategic and structural methods discussed above, to those based on the 'social construction' principles.

In Chapter 1 of the above-mentioned book Atwood summarizes the basic assumptions of both structural and strategic therapies. In both, the therapist is an expert who works to promote change in the family using any of the methods outlined above, or in the previous chapter. Referring to structural therapy, for example, Atwood writes (page 6):

'. . . the therapist is generally a diagnostician and assessor who acts upon the family to "fix" their fusion, disengagement, rigidity, overprotection, conflict avoidance, symetricality, complementarity, hurts, wounds, dysfunctional patterns, communication problems or whatever else is considered to need attention.'

Traditional family therapists adhere to a 'first order cybernetics stance' and 'tend to fit families into or compare them to a normative template' (page 6). This assumes that there is such a thing as a 'normal' family and therapy's task is to restore the family to normality. But, as we have seen in Chapter 2, the concept of the 'normal family' is elusive, although each therapist may have his or her own ideas about this.

Atwood (1997) summarizes the assumptions made by traditional family therapies as:

- There are multiple interpretations of one objective reality
- Models of normalcy should be adhered to
- The role of the therapist is to be an expert
- The therapist is a therapeutic tool, a lever intending to create change in the system
- The therapist is very visible
- There are multiple aspects of self
- Pathology is located in the system
- Change is an either/or process
- A client is dependent upon the therapist to fix future problems

The 'post-modern' approach preferred by Atwood (1997, page 36) involves a 'second-order therapeutic stance'. She summarizes this as follows:

'... the therapist becomes part of the system and, as such, acts in collaboration with the client to co-create new stories, new possibilities, new ways of seeing and being. Together they work, fostering awareness and growth that will affect both. Their agreement is nothing more than to come together for a time, one human being to another, to work together by talking to each other about their realities. Ultimately, through trust and mutual respect, they will "see" with expanded vision ... There is no therapist/client dependency; both therapist and client are equal and they are both equally dependent, for all things are dependent on all other things in perfect balance ...'

The post-modern approach advocated by Anderson is discussed in Chapter 4. Anderson supports the use of *conversational questions* (Anderson and Goolishian, 1988; Goolishian and Anderson, 1990). Such questions, Anderson points out (1997, page 145), invite clients to talk *with* the therapist; they invite the client into a shared inquiry. This is the essence of the post-modern approach.

What approach should the novice family therapist take?

The variety of available therapeutic approaches can certainly be confusing to the therapist coming fresh to this field. Possible ways of tackling the challenge of selecting the best approach to take in a particular case are discussed in Chapter 16.

Summary

Family therapists aim to bring about change by working to alter the functioning of the family system. For most, the psychopathology of the individual members is not the main focus, though this may also be taken into account. Taking a 'family systems' view is a form of 'reframing', in that it changes the focus from the 'problems' of individual family members to the family.

Systemic therapy addresses the family system as a whole. 'Direct' methods of promoting change, discussed in the previous chapter, are sometimes effective. They should generally be tried first. If they fail to bring about the desired changes, approaches such as those outlined in this chapter may be tried. These may be indirect or strategic.

The strategic therapist devises a strategy, or plan, that is intended to bring about the changes desired. If the strategy is not effective, the therapist will nevertheless have acquired some new information about the family. This will assist in the planning of another intervention. This process may need to be repeated several times.

Reframing, and positive connotation, the ascribing of 'positive' intent to symptomatic behaviours, are basic strategic manoeuvres which aim to give new meaning to the actions and attitudes of family members. Other strategic devices include metaphorical communication; the use of paradox; giving families ritualized tasks to perform; declaring therapeutic impotence; prescribing interminable therapy; using humour to give situations different meanings or values; employing a 'Greek chorus' to comment from behind the one-way screen; and staging a debate by members of the therapy team in the presence of the family.

White and Epston (1990) introduced the concept of 'externalizing' problems and they also described the use of narrative approaches they call 'storied therapy'. A related approach is the 'King Tiger' intervention described by Wood (1988).

More recently a 'post-modern' school of therapy has been developed. In this, therapist and client are equals. They work together collaboratively, their objective being to come up with new perspectives on clients' situations out of which solutions may emerge.

The therapeutic procedures described in this chapter and the preceding ones are not mutually exclusive, nor is the list exhaustive. The range of possible strategies is restricted only by the limits of the imagination and creativity of the therapist.

Chapter 12
Other Therapeutic Approaches

There is probably no limit to the ways in which therapists might intervene to change the functioning of families. This chapter will outline a few that have not so far been mentioned. The trend, during the last couple of decades, has been to enable families to find within themselves the resources with which to overcome their problems and achieve their goals.

Family sculpting

'Sculpture' as a family therapy technique was developed by Frederick Duhl and his colleagues (1973). The essential feature of family sculpting is the placing of family members in positions and postures that represent aspects of their relationships and interactions with each other. Any aspect of family functioning may be sculpted, for example closeness or power.

Family sculpting requires a *sculptor*, whose view of the family it is that is revealed in the sculpture; a *monitor*, namely the therapist, who guides and supports the sculptor and the others involved in the process; and the *actors*, usually the family members, who portray the sculptor's system. There may also be an *audience*, but usually the family members and the therapist both play the other roles mentioned and comprise the audience.

Walrond-Skinner (1976) included in her description of the family sculpting process, drawings of the sculptures created by the different family members in a particular case. She recommended the technique as useful for involving young children in therapy, since for them non-verbal methods of expression are more natural. It can also be a useful diagnostic procedure and a substitute for asking a family to describe their problems. Families can be asked to describe the changes they want to see by sculpting their idealized family. Walrond-Skinner also considered sculpting as a useful way of helping family members get in touch with their feelings. Another use is in overcoming families' resistance to therapy, and it can be something to do 'when the therapist just feels stuck'.

Once the sculptor has been chosen the other members of the family are asked to stand up and then move to whatever position and posture the sculptor directs. The therapist must make it clear what everyone is to do, and initially some encouragement may be needed. The rules of the procedure have to be clearly defined, especially the one that the actors must do whatever the sculptor says. Once this has been accepted, so that the sculptor is not overcome by the family's power struggles, the therapist can begin to observe what happens and comment upon or interpret it. It may be helpful to emphasize from time to time that this is just one view of the family, and that the other members will be able to express their points of view in the same way later.

Once the tableau is completed, which may not be until after much discussion and comment, the therapist may ask the sculptor also to enter it, in an appropriate position and posture. Both the process of sculpting, and the finished tableau, may be used to assist in restructuring the family, or for some other purpose, such as clarifying or changing communication, feelings or roles. Sculpting can be an adjunct to other treatment approaches.

Role playing

Role playing is another 'action technique' which can be useful when verbal approaches prove ineffective. It can be especially valuable in families that intellectualize, that is discuss things on a cognitive level and produce intellectual ideas and explanations, rather than real change. Having such families act out scenes or events from their lives can facilitate change. For example, a family might be asked to act out what happens when father returns home from work, or when it is time for the children to go to bed, if these appear to be times when the family experiences difficulty. If family members are hesitant or reluctant about role playing, the therapist may start with a simple, non-threatening scene, but if rapport has been well established, obtaining agreement to what is suggested usually does not present difficulty.

Like sculpting, role playing brings something of the reality of family life into the therapy session, and gives the therapist material with which to work. This can be particularly helpful when the family is inhibited in the therapy room and so does not behave 'naturally', in the way it does in other situations.

Videotape replay

Alger (1969, 1973) was a pioneer of videotape replay, the playing back to families of tapes of their therapy sessions. Whole therapy sessions may be played back, or selected portions may be used. Videotape replay enables family members to see what is going on in the family 'from the outside', as it were. They can observe not only what they are saying, but also their tones of voice, facial expressions, body postures and other non-verbal behaviour.

For families with a strong conscious desire to change, videotape replay can be an effective way of defining and getting members to understand how they may be able to change. In other families it can promote understanding of the need to change. The effects of seeing and hearing oneself and one's family on tape can be salutary.

A family in which the children were anxious to know how the videotaping process worked was taken, following a therapy session, into the viewing room in which the recording equipment was installed. Part of the tape was played back for them to see. This was not intended as a therapeutic move, except insofar as it provided a model of openness about the process. Having watched a few minutes of tape, however, the 4-year-old son commented, apparently in all innocence, 'Why do you talk all the time, Daddy?' The segment of tape had indeed included a lot of talking by the father, who tended to be a bombastic, controlling and very talkative person. This remark, said openly in front of the family, therapist and technician, seemed to strike a chord in the father. He returned to the next session more aware of his role in the family, and open to making changes.

The relatively inexpensive television equipment nowadays available makes the use of videotape replay in therapists' offices a practical and economic proposition. Serial recordings may be used to document progress. It may sometimes be helpful to use split-screen techniques, slow motion, fast motion and still framing. Split-screen techniques can be used to show people side by side when they are really sitting apart. This can draw attention to how they react to each other.

The uses of videotape we have discussed serve to draw family members' attention to how the family functions generally, and particularly to the interactions between its various members. Videotape replay may therefore fit best into a direct therapeutic plan, though indirect and strategic uses of videotape replay are also possible.

Network therapy

Network therapy (Speck & Rueveni, 1969; Speck & Attneave, 1971), in its classical form, is probably used rather rarely. It consists of getting the family's complete 'network' together. The network consists of the kinship system, the family's friends and other significant people. This may mean that as many as 30 or 40 people are assembled to work on the problem. It is claimed that by having all significant people present, progress in therapy may be possible where it otherwise would not be. One advantage of the procedure is that blame cannot be placed on absent family members because all are present. Another is the addition of the voices and opinions of healthier, better functioning people to the therapy process.

Rueveni (1975) described the use of four network sessions in the treatment of a couple who presented with conflicts in their relationship, with major disagreement about their 16-year-old son. Network therapy was started when the crisis continued despite more conventional therapy. In addition to the family members, six of the son's friends came to the first session. Rueveni (1975) described the considerable improvements in the family situation that were achieved in four sessions. Network meetings, without the therapist, continued for 3 months after the last of the four sessions. The author believed that the breakthrough that occurred as a result of network sessions was possible 'because of the intensity of the involvement and caring on the part of those network activists who maintained a continuous support'. Each of the three 'nuclear' family members was henceforth able to rely on other family members for advice, suggestions and support when needed. The process is thus, in part, a way of mobilizing the extended family supports which so many contemporary families lack.

Gatti and Coleman (1976) described what they called *community network therapy*. Their approach arose out of school consultation work in a small New England town. Using structural family therapy techniques as their basic approach, they also established and maintained continuing contact with all the 'important extra-familial people and institutions' to which they could gain access. They report contacts with extended family, neighbours and friends; responsible people from schools, public welfare, the housing authority, employment agencies and courts; interested members of private groups such as charitable, church and children's organizations; and such professional groups as doctors, lawyers and ministers of religion. Gatti and Coleman considered themselves also to be a part of the wider community network, and their paper contains a number of interesting ideas about how to involve, work with and help families get into contact with those people in the community who may be of help to them.

Network therapy is a means of tackling the problems in the supra-systems of families. There is a limit to the effectiveness of therapy which stops short at the boundary of the nuclear family. Many therapists recognize this, and Minuchin (1974, page 130), in his classical account of the structural approach, made it clear that the therapist should review 'the family life context, analysing the sources of support and stress in the family's ecology'. Family boundaries are not impermeable, and what happens outside them can help or hinder family functioning.

An important part of a school-age child's ecological context is the school, and the school/family relationship often requires the therapist's attention. In a sense, a child's behaviour and adjustment in school can be regarded as a function of the family situation: if the parents wish the child to behave well in school, then it is reasonable to consider it as a family problem when the child is not so behaving. But while children's failure to behave or perform satisfactorily in school sometimes seems to be related to the situation at home, in many cases it does not. There can be systems problems in school classes or even in entire schools (Rutter et al., 1979).

When a schoolchild is the identified patient, the school is the part of family's suprasystem, or network, to which attention most often needs to be given during therapy. There are various ways of involving schools in the therapy process. One or more meetings of family, or at least the parents and the child concerned, and the relevant school staff, may be useful. It is important that all the key members of the school staff are present. These normally include the child's own teacher or teachers, the person who has the authority in the school, usually the principal but perhaps a vice-principal, and the guidance teacher, school counsellor or school psychologist, if these people are involved. Aponte (1976) discussed the purposes of family/school interviews and their conduct and provided an illustrative case report. He recommended that, when referral comes from the school because of problems there, the first interview should be at the school, and should include family and school staff.

Multiple family therapy

Multiple family therapy, or multi-family therapy, apparently had its origin in 1951 when, as Peter Laqueur (1973) explained much later, he started bringing family members together to explain to them the insulin therapy that was being carried out in a psychiatric hospital. According to Laqueur the term *multiple family therapy* was coined by Carl Wells in 1963. Wells was co-author of a later paper (Laqueur et al., 1979).

In multiple family therapy the therapist, or more often co-therapists, meet with several (usually four or five) identified patients, together with their families: parents, siblings, spouses, children. Laqueur's groups were open-ended, that is members could join and leave during the life of the group. Videotape and playback facilities are useful. As described by Laqueur (1976), opening exercises included asking the mothers in the group to say what they thought of themselves and how they rated themselves as mothers and wives. The fathers were then asked to describe themselves and rate how they performed their roles. Next the children might be asked to divide themselves into a 'good' and a 'bad' group, and then to state briefly their problems with their families.

Nowadays many therapists would probably conduct multiple family therapy groups rather differently, depending on their theoretical orientation. A helpful review of 'multiple family therapy systems' is that of Anna Benningfield (1980).

Vector therapy

We owe the concept of vector therapy to the work of John Howells, formerly Director of the Institute of Family Psychiatry, in Ipswich, England.
Vector therapy is designed to effect 'a change in the emotional forces
within the life space to bring improvement to the individual or family
within the life space' (Howells, 1968, page 102). Vector therapy aims to
alter either the magnitude or the direction of the relevant emotional forces.
These may be within the individual, outside the individual and within the
family, outside the family and within the community, or outside individual,
family and community, but within the culture.

Vector therapy involves such procedures as advising family members
to seek work outside the home, sending a child to boarding school, and
the use of various individuals, agencies and institutions in the family's
suprasystem. When it deals with forces outside the family, vector therapy
seems to be another way of conceptualizing therapy with a family's
suprasystem. In other words it is then a form of network therapy.

The concept of vector therapy has not gained wide acceptance among
family therapists generally. Howells preferred the term 'family psychiatry'
to 'family therapy', and perhaps vector therapy is more a 'family psychiatry' than a 'family therapy' procedure. Yet the therapist struggling to
promote change in a family that seems stuck in its way of functioning does
well to bear in mind the possibility of altering the emotional forces bearing
upon the family from outside.

Multiple impact therapy

Multiple impact therapy was developed by Robert MacGregor (1962) at
the University of Texas Medical Branch Hospitals at Galveston. The Youth
Development Project, a research project treating adolescents referred
from correctional services, found itself dealing with families in crisis who
often lived long distances from the clinic. The team therefore developed a
plan which involved the intensive treatment of entire families for 2 or $2\frac{1}{2}$
days, while they slept overnight in a neighbouring motel. A team of therapists of various disciplines would meet with the family on their arrival at
the unit. This initial team–family conference was the beginning of a therapy
process which would continue intensively for 2 days.

What happened after the initial conference varied from family to family,
but typically each family member was seen individually by a team member,
and subsequently in overlapping sessions in which, for example, the
therapist who had been seeing the teenage identified patient might join
another therapist during the course of that therapist's interview with the
teenager's parents. The parents' therapist would then summarize the

session so far, with perhaps some interpretation of what had happened, and then the session would continue.

At mid-day the team would confer and further and varied interviews would be held in the afternoon, the day ending with another team–family conference. The procedure, though with more variability, would continue the next day and it ended with a final conference with the family. If satisfactory progress had not been made the team might arrange a further half-day of treatment the next day. A follow-up visit was a requirement and in one quarter of the cases that MacGregor (1962) reported, a further day's treatment was arranged after about 2 months. Community resources such as local treatment agencies, teachers and ministers, were used extensively in the follow-up period.

The treatment and its results were documented by MacGregor et al. (1964). Multiple impact therapy has not been widely practised, perhaps because of the practical difficulties associated with admitting whole families, or accommodating them nearby, and assembling a team to work intensively with them. It may be particularly valuable when families live at great distances from clinics, but as family therapists become more numerous this applies to fewer families.

Interventive interviewing

The process of interviewing families can itself produce change. The interviewer's questions, statements and non-verbal communications carry messages which are apt to have their effect on those being interviewed. Consider the difference between the questions, 'What are the problems for which you have come?' and, 'What are the changes you want us to help you achieve?' The first question is problem orientated; the second is change orientated and carries the implicit message that change will occur.

A pitfall awaiting all who interview people with problems is that of getting too deeply involved in the discussion of supposed causes. It is rarely possible to ascribe definitively a 'cause' for any human problem, if only because the causes are usually multiple and interact with each other in complex ways. When we are dealing with families, the supposed 'cause' is often believed by the family to lie in one particular member. This is usually a gross oversimplification at best or downright wrong at worst.

Tomm (1987a, 1987b, 1988) discusses the role of 'interventive interviewing'. The term 'refers to an orientation in which everything an interviewer does and says, and does not do and say, is thought of as an intervention that could be therapeutic, nontherapeutic, or countertherapeutic' (Tomm, 1987a, page 4). And again, 'every question asked by a therapist may be seen to embody some intent and to arise from certain assumptions' (Tomm, 1988).

This means that the therapist must have a strategy. This will determine what he or she does and says at each moment during the interview. Tomm (1987a, page 6) defines 'strategizing' as 'the therapist's (or team's) cognitive activity in evaluating the effects of past actions, constructing new plans of action, anticipating the possible consequences of various alternatives, and deciding how to proceed at any particular moment in order to maximize therapeutic utility'.

In the three papers Tomm focuses on the kind of questions to ask, while acknowledging that the strategy will include other behaviours. He defines four types of questions which he calls lineal, circular, strategic and reflexive:

- Lineal questions are mainly 'investigative'. Questions such as 'Who did what, where? and when?' or 'Have you gained or lost weight lately?' are lineal.
- Circular questioning was discussed in Chapter 6. Tomm (1988) considers circular questions to be 'predominantly exploratory'. The 'guiding presuppositions are interactional and systemic'. Examples are, 'What does A do when B appears worried?' or, 'What does C do when D has a temper tantrum?'. . . 'Who gets most upset?' and so forth. These questions are designed to reveal 'patterns that connect'.
- Strategic questions are designed to influence. Examples, from Tomm (1988), are 'How come you're not willing to try harder to get him up?' 'Is this habit of making excuses something new?' and, 'When are you going to take charge of your life and start looking for a job?'
- Reflexive question have predominantly a facilitative intent. The types of reflexive questions Tomm (1987b) distinguishes are future-orientated questions, observer-perspective questions, unexpected context-change questions, embedded-suggestion questions, normative-comparison questions, distinction-clarifying questions, questions introducing comparisons and process-interruption questions.

Tomm's (1987b) paper contains examples of all the above and suggests how these questions may be used to promote change. Many of these questions leave open the question of what the family should do. This contrasts with the strategic and systemic therapies in which, for the most part, the therapist is trying to offer the family some input that will help bring about the changes the family desires.

Social construction theory

In discussing social construction theory, Atwood (1997, page 13) refers to the work of Berger and Luckman (1966) in their book on the origin of social realities. This is:

'. . . a process by which individuals who repeatedly confront a task or situation relevant to their lives develop habitual ways of dealing with it. People first recognize the recurrent nature of a situation; then they develop roles or functions for cooperating individuals to perform in connection with the task involved.' (page 13)

So it is that routines develop to deal with particular situations. These may become institutionalized and in due course they can become 'full-fledged social constructions'. Social constructions that have survived over time may be called institutions and come to be considered 'normal and/or natural'. Atwood (1997, page 15) cites the 'fallacy' that:

'the often-made assumption that the nuclear family, with father as bread-winner and wife and children as economic dependents, is the normal and best way of life and that all other family forms are suspect. If problems appear to be associated with aspects of family life, the solution proposed is often to reinforce the dominant nuclear family form, rather than explore new forms, which might be more effective, in light of the recent social and economic changes.'

Behavioural approaches

The special techniques mentioned above, other than the use of social construction theory, are probably not widely used today, though they are of historical interest and may still be helpful when other approaches are unsuccessful. However, behavioural methods have an established place in the treatment of troubled families. Most, perhaps all, the changes that occur in families during therapy might be understood in terms of learning theory, as it was outlined in Chapter 3, but it is also possible to use the behavioural concepts and methods outlined in Chapters 3 and 4 as the main basis of a treatment approach.

Behavioural methods are most readily applied to the modification of interactions involving two or at the most three people. Their use with larger family systems presents greater challenges. Nevertheless the rules of learning theory apply to the transactions occurring between family members, and between therapist and family, as much as they do to any other human interactions. Thus paying attention to a symptom often tends to reinforce or strengthen it, as when it has been serving the function of obtaining attention for the individual concerned. Ignoring a symptom, for example tantrum behaviour, often leads to its disappearance, perhaps after some initial increase. Turning attention to another behaviour, or to a different topic, for example talking about the extended family, may also reduce the attention given to the presenting problem. This may lead, in time, to the partial or complete extinction of the problem behaviour.

Another factor that should always be considered is the model which the therapist presents to the family. Our communication styles, ways of relating and non-verbal behaviours generally are all apt to have their effects on the behaviours of the families we see. Not only does the therapist's behaviour inevitably affect the responses of family members, but the behaviours of family members affect each other. Changes in family systems can therefore be brought about if members of the family respond to instructions as to how they should interact. This is 'first-order' change, and in many more seriously disturbed families this is insufficient. Sometimes, though, it can be effective.

Sylvia was a 21-year-old single parent. Her 3-year-old son, Tom, had twice been removed from her care for short periods by the child welfare authorities, because of her alcoholism and the effects it had on the care she gave him. She had then entered a detoxification centre and started attending Alcoholics Anonymous meetings. When she presented for therapy she was no longer drinking and her son had been returned to her. He now displayed severe behaviour problems. He had long been in the habit of disregarding, or defying, his mother's inconsistent shouted injunctions and threats – threats that were rarely followed by action.

Sylvia herself had had an unstable childhood. Her mother also had a drinking problem and had been married six times. As a child Sylvia had been cared for by a variety of relatives, and she spent several short periods in foster homes which, she told her therapist, she hated. She ran away from home at 15 and lived an unstable life for several years, drinking excessively, using street drugs and living with a series of physically abusive young men, who themselves abused drugs and alcohol.

Sylvia had never experienced stable, consistent, loving care and discipline as a child. Consequently she had no suitable internal model of parenthood. Yet she had made good progress in many areas of her life. She no longer used alcohol and drugs, nor did she now seem to need to associate with abusive men as she had done previously.

Therapy with Sylvia and Tom used a behavioural model. It was designed first to help Sylvia realize that shouting at children, and especially uttering idle threats, is unhelpful. Instead she was given specific instructions about what to do in response to certain of Tom's behaviours.

One behaviour was dealt with at a time, starting with the behaviour Sylvia considered most important: Tom's habit of running recklessly out into the road in front of the house. A detailed plan for dealing with this problem was developed. This was done in discussion with Sylvia, since it is important that whatever behavioural management is prescribed be tailored to the specific situation, resources and personalities involved. Tom was only to be allowed out of the house to play at times when Sylvia could observe his activities and had nothing else to distract her. As soon as he stepped on to the roadway, Sylvia was to bring him into the house and sit him on a chair for 5 minutes. If he yelled or protested actively in any other way the five minutes did not start until he had settled down. When

Tom was playing safely in the area his mother permitted him to use, she was to give him intermittent approving attention.

The above programme was successful, and within a week of its implementation, in summer weather when Tom could play outside every day, he had ceased running on to the roadway. Then other troublesome behaviours were dealt with in a similar fashion, though as Sylvia's confidence in her ability to parent her son developed, she was soon devising her own behavioural approaches.

As well as dealing with one specific behavioural problem, treatment plans such as the above offer families a model of healthier functioning, and a way of dealing with other problems. As in Sylvia's case, once family members have used behavioural interventions successfully for one or two problems they are usually able to devise ways of dealing with other problems without the help of the therapist.

Behavioural interventions such as the one used with Sylvia and Tom can also be understood in structural terms. Implicit in the intervention was the principle that parents should be in charge of their children and have a right, indeed a duty, to set limits on the children's behaviours and to enforce these in appropriate ways. This can lead to the creations of a more functional hierarchy within the family.

Early in the history of family therapy, Alexander and Parsons (1973) carried out a controlled study of behavioural intervention in the families of delinquent teenagers. A carefully planned procedure was developed to:

(1) Assess the family behaviours maintaining the delinquent behaviour.
(2) Modify family communication patterns to bring about greater clarity and precision, increased reciprocity and the presentation of alternative solutions.
(3) Institute a pattern of contingency contracting in the family to modify the maladaptive patterns and institute more adaptive behaviours.

These authors also studied three comparison groups, two receiving other forms of family intervention and one receiving no treatment. Certain changes in the families undergoing the 'short-term behavioural family programme', as the treatment was called, were hypothesized. These were less silence, more equality of speech and greater frequency of positive interruption, that is asking for clarification of unclear messages and providing feedback on messages received. Another hypothesis was that there would be less recidivism in the experimental group than in the comparison groups.

A treatment programme designed to extinguish in a systematic way maladaptive interaction patterns and substitute reciprocity was devised. Families were randomly assigned to this treatment or to one of the comparison groups. The latter received client-centred family group treatment, a psychodynamic family programme or no treatment. Statistically significant differences were found between the results in the first group and those of the other groups. These were in the directions hypothesized. Significantly better recidivism rates at 6- and 18-month follow-up were also demonstrated. The rates were:

- 'Short term behavioural family programme' – 26%
- 'Client-centred' treatment group – 47%
- 'Psychodynamic' group – 73%
- No treatment group – 50%

This was an important study. Precise therapeutic goals were set, and the treatment procedures were carefully defined. Recurrent delinquency was reduced in youths from families which showed the changes in interaction which the therapists aimed to achieve. On the other hand it was not reduced in the families in which interaction patterns did not change.

Also important is the work of Patterson and his colleagues which we reviewed in Chapter 3. *Intervening in Adolescent Problem Behaviour: A Family-Centered Approach* (Dishion & Kavanagh, 2003) describes in detail a systematic behavioural method for use with the families of adolescents with disruptive behaviour disorders.

Recently the principles of cognitive-behavioural therapy have been applied to families. The basic premise of this, as enunciated by Epstein et al. (1988, page 5) is that:

> '. . . in their complex interactions with one another the members of a family in most instances actively interpret and evaluate each other's behaviours, and that their emotional and behavioural responses to one another are influenced by these interpretations and evaluations.'

These authors go on to quote Barton and Alexander (1981) who proposed that family members' behaviours towards each other will change only if their views of themselves and each other change. Barton and Alexander (1981), who proposed a system of *functional family therapy*, proceeded on the assumption that in disturbed families members tend to attribute the problems to negative traits, such as laziness or mental illness, in other members. Such attributions impede therapeutic change since they suggest the inevitability of the *status quo*. The therapist therefore needs to offer alternative attributions in such cases.

The promotion or facilitation of cognitive change is probably central to a variety of family therapy approaches which do not claim to be 'cognitive-behavioural therapy'. Structural therapy redefines the family's problems in terms of its 'structure' and the boundaries between its subsystems and the suprasystem; and 'strategic' interventions usually aim to achieve some reframing of the family's situation or way of functioning, that is, a cognitive shift.

Cognitive-Behavioural Therapy with Families (Epstein et al., 1988) contains chapters reviewing the uses of cognitive-behavioural approaches in a range of family problems including child abuse, physical aggression in marriage, problems of remarried families, conduct disorders of children and adolescents, addictions, suicidal behaviour and adult sexual dysfunctions. Behavioural methods may be particularly applicable in marital therapy, since one is dealing with a system of only two persons and the therapist. Their application in this work is discussed in Chapter 14.

Family therapy and schizophrenia

As we saw in Chapter 1, many of the pioneers of family therapy devoted much of their attention to the investigation and treatment of the families of people suffering from schizophrenia. But since those early days the attention of most family therapists has shifted to the clinical problems of a much wider range of troubled families. To quote McFarlane (1983b, page 1):

'During the 25 years that family therapy has been developing, there has been, until very recently, a nearly linear decline in interest in the family treatment of schizophrenia. Reports of treatment techniques and even research studies have dwindled in the family literature, while most family therapists have become increasingly reluctant to treat the families of schizophrenic patients . . . Drug therapy is still the mainstay in dealing with schizophrenic psychoses, while research on this baffling condition has become almost completely oriented toward its biological aspects.'

McFarlane suggests that 'conventional' family therapy has not provided enough in the way of results to warrant its continued use, and that the evidence for a family 'cause' for schizophrenia is lacking. On the other hand there is good evidence of genetic and biological components, and drug therapy is apparently more effective than conventional family therapy. Children whose parents suffer from schizophrenia who are placed early for adoption in non-schizophrenic families still develop schizophrenia at rates higher than the population rate, sometimes as high as those reared by their schizophrenia-afflicted parents. Adoptive relatives of those with schizophrenia do not have elevated rates of schizophrenia, but the biological relatives of the adoptees do have higher rates; and children of normal parents fostered into homes in which a parental figure became schizophrenic do not show an increased rate of schizophrenia. Twin studies have found that the concordance rate for schizophrenia is three times greater in monozygous (MZ) twins that in dizygous twins, and 30 times the general population rate. Nevertheless, more than half the MZ pairs are discordant for schizophrenia, despite the fact that they have identical genes. Genetics are therefore not the whole cause, and there is room also for social, including family factors.

What, then, are these social factors and what can the family therapist do about them? Jacob (1975) and Goldstein and Rodnick (1975) concluded that there was no good evidence for the concept of a 'schizophrenic family', but that there was evidence that 'communication deviance' (CD) and 'expressed emotion' (EE) were relevant concepts in these families. Since then evidence has been accumulating that social, and particularly family, factors *are* important, at least in determining whether patients with schizophrenia relapse after discharge from hospital, but perhaps also in contributing to the onset of the condition. These developments have led to new approaches to the treatment of these families:

(1)   They seem to have major therapeutic effects on the schizophrenic process, beyond those achievable with drug therapy.
(2)   They all, except for the systemic variety, start from a major expansion of family systems theory that also takes extra-family factors into account.

Expressed emotion and its relevance were the subject of a series of studies in Britain by staff of the Medical Research Council's Social Psychiatry Unit. The findings of these studies were summarized, reviewed and discussed in *Expressed Emotion in Families* (Leff & Vaughn, 1985). They are of particular interest, both because of the sound research methods used, and because the findings have been confirmed in replications of the work done. This research has been approached more from a sociological perspective than from a 'family therapy' one, so that the investigators have not set out with a commitment to family therapy as a treatment for the disorders concerned.

These studies have shown that certain characteristics of the families to which patients with schizophrenia discharged from hospital return, have significant effects on the patients' relapse rates. Expressed emotion was measured using scales developed over a period of years (Leff & Vaughn, 1985). Five scales were developed: two involve 'a recognition of particular comments ("critical" and "positive") and consist of a count of all such comments occurring at any point in the interview' (Leff & Vaughn, 1985, page 37). The other three, emotional overinvolvement, hostility and warmth, involve the recognition of particular kinds of comments. The interviewer then makes a judgment of the degree to which the emotion concerned was shown. In all cases the information was obtained in the course of interviews with relatives, usually spouses or parents.

These studies showed that high scores on the EE scales were associated with high rates of relapse in patients with schizophrenia discharged from hospital. The best results occurred when there was both the regular use of anti-psychotic drugs and low expressed emotion in the relatives. The

British workers also investigated a group of 'depressed neurotic' patients, with a view to discovering how specific their findings were for schizophrenia. They found that the depressed neurotic patients were even more vulnerable to critical comments by relatives, but that face-to-face contact between patients and relatives did not relate to relapse, as it did in the schizophrenic group. Low face-to-face contact appeared to protect schizophrenic patients in 'high-EE' homes, but it had no such function for depressives. The researchers concluded:

> 'We interpret this as an indication of a poor relationship between a patient and a relative that predates the illness. We consider it likely that low contact and high criticism are both indicators of a poor marriage (virtually all these relatives were spouses) and that the poor quality of the marriage predicts relapse of depression.' (Leff & Vaughn, 1985, page 93)

It seems that high EE may predispose to relapse in schizophrenia, but there is no clear evidence that it is a significant causal factor.

Communication deviance (CD), on the other hand, may play at least a small role in the aetiology of the condition. Singer et al. (1978) and Wynne (1981) developed instruments for measuring CD, and found it to be present in the parents' communication with each other, as well as in communication involving the patient. CD consists of various forms of vague, ambiguous, wandering, illogical and idiosyncratic language, similar in some respects to schizophrenic thought disorder but less severe. These abnormal speech patterns may be present in the parents years before the onset of the schizophrenic disorder in their offspring, and they are similar in type to those that develop in the offspring. They may therefore play a part in the aetiology of the disorder, along with genetic and biological factors.

If 'conventional' family therapy is not effective, what can family therapy offer? This question was addressed in *Family Therapy in Schizophrenia* (McFarlane, 1983a), in which various possible ways of intervening were discussed. Hatfield (1983), for example, suggested that what families want of their therapists is often different from what therapists wish to provide. Families, Hatfield (1983, page 63) says, 'are turning to mental health professionals for assistance in becoming more effective care givers for their disturbed relatives and in coping with the many problems that develop'. Yet professionals seemed to Hatfield to be reluctant to give this kind of help. Other chapters in the book discuss crisis intervention, psychoeducational programmes for families, behavioural interventions, multiple family therapy, supportive group counselling for relatives and the coordination of family therapy with other therapies.

Leff et al. (1983), from the MRC Social Psychiatry Unit, described a trial of an intervention programme designed to reduce EE in the families of patients in which there was a high risk of relapse. All the patients received medication, but in addition the experimental group also received a programme of social treatment. This had two components. One was an educational programme, designed to help relatives understand the nature of schizophrenia and its symptoms; the other was a relatives' group. The idea of the group was that those relatives falling into the 'low-EE' group and living with patients with schizophrenia admitted to hospital (who comprised almost half of the total), would help teach the necessary coping skills to the 'high-EE' relatives. In addition to these generally applied measures, specific measures were applied in particular cases, for example conjoint marital therapy or attempts (usually unsuccessful) to move the patient out of the family to another living setting.

The results of this small-scale treatment trial – there were 12 families in the experimental group and 12 in the control group – were encouraging. The researchers found that it was possible to reduce the critical comments in the experimental group, while there was little change in the control group. In many of the experimental families there was also a significant reduction in the social contact between patients and relatives, a change which seldom occurred in the control families. Leff et al. (1983) also reported a significantly lower relapse rate in the experimental group, compared with the control group.

In summary, evidence is lacking that family factors, in themselves, cause schizophrenia, but they may contribute to its development in genetically prone individuals. They may also play a part in precipitating relapse in schizophrenics who have improved during treatment in hospital. There is apparently a connection between the degree of 'expressed emotion' in the family and relapse. In addition 'communication deviance' (CD) may play some part in causing a predisposed person to develop schizophrenia. How far it is possible to lessen the chances of this happening by reducing the CD in the family remains unclear. Other systemic interventions may also be helpful to these families, but family therapy should not normally be the sole therapy. It seems to be most effective when combined with the use of antipsychotic drugs.

Summary

The interview process itself can be a powerful instrument of change. 'Action techniques' such as family sculpting and role playing, and videotape replay of sessions, or parts of sessions, can bring something of the reality of a family's functioning into the therapy room when this is proving difficult.

Other techniques which may be helpful in some clinical situations include network therapy, treatment which includes the wider family and social network; multiple family therapy, the treatment of several families together; vector therapy, which aims to alter the emotional forces bearing upon the family; and multiple impact therapy, which consists of an intensive 2- or

$2\frac{1}{2}$-day process during which a variety of therapeutic inputs are offered the family and its various subsystems, by a team of therapists.

Concepts derived from behaviour therapy are helpful in the treatment of families. Being aware of, and using, the principles of learning theory can increase the effectiveness of many other forms of family therapy.

Conventional family therapy techniques have proved largely ineffective in the treatment of schizophrenia. This condition appears to have multiple causes, and while social, particularly family, factors are among these, treatment of them alone is not adequate. There is good evidence that high 'expressed emotion' in patients' families predisposes to relapse, and 'communication deviance' may contribute to the development of schizophrenia in genetically predisposed individuals. Both may be appropriate targets for therapeutic intervention.

Chapter 13
A Method of Therapy

Every family therapist needs a way of approaching therapy. Most use concepts derived from several schools of family therapy. It is not necessary to adopt, in complete form, any of the therapy models we have discussed so far, nor any other specific model. It *is* important, though, to have a coherent approach and to subscribe to a theory of how change may be brought about in families.

This chapter describes a model of therapy I have found useful. It is derived from various sources. It is not put forward as necessarily the best way of doing therapy, but rather as an example of how a method may be derived from several sources. Therapy is often carried out by a team and when I find myself working as a team member I usually adopt the team's therapeutic approach. Clearly one can only work with a reflecting team when one has available a suitable team of therapists with whom to work.

How therapists work, and the methods they use, depend partly upon their personalities, partly upon who has taught them, and largely upon what they find works for them. The personalities of some therapists are better suited to the use of certain types of therapy than to others. For example, some feel comfortable with the use of humour, while for others this is difficult. The therapist's type of practice is another relevant variable. What is effective for many middle- and upper-income families functioning well in instrumental ways, may not be helpful to some families in different socioeconomic circumstances, and *vice versa*.

Most therapists, and surely all who have not reached a state of professional stagnation, are constantly developing their skills and refining the therapy techniques they use. One of the more remarkable things about family therapy has been the variety of approaches that has been used and the pace of development of new therapy methods. Lynn Hoffman's (2002) book is a beautifully written account of how her approach to therapy developed over the course of some three decades. What must be said, though, is that research into the relative effectiveness of the different methods has lagged behind the pace of development of new therapeutic approaches.

So how should you, the therapist starting out in this field, proceed? Much will inevitably depend on the training you have received. You should by this time have acquired a philosophical approach, adopted a theory of change and developed a way of working with families. You will then want to continue incorporating new ideas and approaches as you learn of them. The techniques you add later may include some of those mentioned in this book. Others you will learn elsewhere, or acquire in the course of your clinical experience with families and in working with colleagues. The method that follows is offered as a beginning, a foundation upon which you may build.

The relationship between assessment and treatment

While experienced therapists may choose not to spend much time and effort on formal assessment, the beginning therapist should at the very least ascertain what it is that the family wants to achieve by coming for treatment. I prefer to explore the changes sought, rather than asking for a list of the problems the family believes it has. I do my best to discover how the family functions and I explore its strengths and areas of successful functioning.

As we have seen, and Tomm (1987a) has pointed out, anything the therapist says or does may be either therapeutic or countertherapeutic (or non-therapeutic). Many therapeutic interventions also result in the therapist acquiring new knowledge about the family. At the very least they tell you whether or not the particular intervention brings about the desired changes. This knowledge may lead you to modify your understanding of the family and your treatment plan.

Sometimes a family's problems, or some of them, quickly emerge, even within the first few minutes of their first session. The family members may also quickly make clear the changes they seek. For example there may be a concern that communication, or the control of members' behaviour, are not the way they would like them to be. If communication is something the family would like to see improve, the therapist might choose, even in the first session, to try to promote more effective communication between the family members. This would be both a diagnostic and a therapeutic procedure. It would test the hypothesis that verbal communication between the family members concerned was poor; and it would reveal whether the particular approach to improving communication was effective.

Despite the above considerations, I believe it is good practice, at least for the beginning therapist, both to carry out an assessment as set out earlier and to establish clear therapeutic goals, as discussed in Chapter 7. By the time these processes have been completed there may already have been changes in the family. These may occur as the members review their situation in conversation with the therapist, and think about family issues, perhaps from new points of view.

Treatment by stages

Once I have established rapport and reached agreement with the family on the objectives of therapy, I usually employ direct methods before considering the use of more complex, indirect and strategic interventions. The main exceptions are some families that have had much previous unsuccessful therapy, and those that adopt an oppositional stance from the start. Most families newly presenting for therapy are, however, keen to receive any input that may help them resolve their problems or help them function better. If a family fails to respond satisfactorily to direct interventions, I proceed to use one or more of the other approaches discussed earlier.

The importance of *the establishment of rapport* can hardly be exaggerated. It enables the process of 'joining' the family (Minuchin, 1974), referred to as 'bonding' by Kirschner and Kirschner (1986), to occur. How to build rapport has been discussed in Chapter 6. If adequate rapport has not been established it is hard even to assess families properly, let alone treat them.

Once you have good rapport with the family members, you can proceed with therapy. A systematic scheme was described by Epstein and Bishop (1981). These authors distinguished 'macro stages' from 'micro moves'. The 'macro' stages are:

(1)   Assessment
(2)   Contracting
(3)   Treatment
(4)   Closure

Each macro stage is composed of four steps. The assessment stage comprises:

(1)   Orientation. The therapist explains to the family members what he or she proposes to do, and seeks their agreement.
(2)   Data gathering. This is the process of learning about the family's history, structure and organization, as discussed in Chapters 5 and 6.
(3)   Problem description. This comprises more data gathering, but the focus now is on the problems with which the family presents.
(4)   Clarification and agreement of a problem list. Epstein and Bishop (1981) believe that therapy should not start without a full knowledge of the family's problems and strengths, and they like to commit this to writing.

The above is essentially just a way of ordering the process we discussed in Chapter 6. I find it a useful approach, but usually put more emphasis on *desired changes* than on *problems*. While these are closely related, I prefer to speak of changes sought rather than problems perceived, because this helps define therapy as a change-producing process. Whether to use written problem and strength lists, rather than agreeing them verbally, is a matter of the therapist's style and preference.

What Epstein and Bishop (1981) describe as their *contracting* macro stage, corresponds roughly to the process described in Chapter 7, on the establishment of treatment objectives. They list the following steps:

(1) Orientation. As in the orientation to the previous stage, the therapist tells the family what is to happen.
(2) Outlining options. The therapist tells the family about the treatment that is being offered. The family members must then decide whether to enter therapy, work on their own or not pursue treatment.
(3) Negotiating expectations. These are the expectations family members have of each other and of the therapist, and the therapist's expectations of them.
(4) Contract signing. Epstein and Bishop require all concerned to sign a written contract listing the problems, what would be a satisfactory outcome and the negotiated treatment conditions, including the frequency and approximate number of sessions.

I do not usually make a written contract, but find contracts to be useful with certain disorganized families, and some that fail to honour verbal contracts. Such contracts are a means both of clarifying what should happen between sessions, and of emphasizing the importance the therapist attributes to this and to the therapy process generally.

The third of the macro stages identified by Epstein and Bishop (1980), is divided into the following four steps:

(1) Orientation
(2) Clarifying priorities
(3) Setting tasks
(4) Task evaluation

This is a good model for use when direct, as opposed to strategic, therapy methods, are to be employed, though it need not be confined to direct methods. The setting of tasks is a major feature of Epstein and Bishop's 'problem-centered' approach, but many other therapists also set their clients tasks to perform between or during sessions.

The final macro stage described by Epstein and Bishop (1981) is that of *closure*. It is dealt with in Chapter 15.

Epstein and Bishop's scheme is a good example of a planned approach to therapy, based on the use of a particular model of family functioning – the McMaster Model. This, and the related Process Model, were summarized in Chapter 5. They are quite similar and are closely related also to the structural model which complements them in some respects. Together, they provide the material needed for effective therapy for many family problems.

(I should point out here that my first family therapy supervisor, and the person who taught me the basics of therapy with families, was Duane Bishop, Epstein's co-author. This has no doubt left me with a permanent bias towards using their approach.)

Direct treatment approaches

Direct injunctions, or directives, are a central feature of direct therapy methods. They are sometimes called *behavioural prescriptions*, for example by Watzlawick and his colleagues (1974), though these authors use the term to describe mainly paradoxical directives. In many cases, however, it is not necessary to use paradoxical methods. Families that are strongly motivated to change often willingly follow the instructions or directives of the therapist.

It appears that even Milton Erickson, who was a past master at indirect and strategic methods, used direct methods 80% of the time (Hammond, 1984). It is in more severely disturbed families, including some containing psychotic members, that direct injunctions tend to be resisted, ignored or even defied. The beginning family therapist should first practise giving direct injunctions, becoming comfortable in doing this before starting to use paradoxical ones, if indeed he or she chooses to take this path.

Direct interventions for some common family problems were discussed in Chapter 10. Whether they are successful depends not only on the existence of adequate rapport, but also on how the directives are delivered. Haley (1976, Chapter 2) provided a good account of how to do this, acknowledging his debt to Erickson. Haley (1976, page 51) also pointed out that it is hard not to give directives, even when we do not wish to do so. Directives are not necessarily framed as orders. Thus if a person says two things and a companion responds to one but not to the other, this is effectively a directive by the companion, even though at first sight it may not look like one. The companion is expressing interest in the one thing rather than the other, indicating a desire to hear more about that subject than about the other one.

We also give directives in non-verbal ways. These include showing interest or boredom in our faces; turning our back on, or facing, a speaker; using particular tones of voice; and taking care or showing enthusiasm, or its lack, in responding to a request. Thus a therapist may not wish to give a man advice on whether to quit his job or divorce his wife. Yet simply not giving an opinion verbally does not prevent the therapist's opinion being expressed. It is likely that the therapist's views will be communicated, at least in some measure, through such channels as voice tone, facial expression or posture.

The giving of directives is not a one-way process. Just as therapists influence clients in many subtle ways, so also do clients influence therapists, by responding differentially to the therapist's statements and actions. It is hard for therapists to be fully aware of these processes as they occur, but an assumption on which therapy is based is that therapists have more understanding of these processes than their clients have. The planned use of the self in the giving of directives, both verbal and non-verbal, is moreover an important part of most, perhaps all, family therapy.

According to Haley (1976, page 49), there are three purposes which directives may serve. The first is the straightforward one of causing people to change their behaviour by telling them to do things differently. The second purpose is to increase the involvement of therapist and those being treated. When directives concern tasks to be carried out between sessions, they help maintain the relationship with the therapist during the period until the next session. This applies whether or not the tasks are performed, since the family is either complying with or defying the therapist's wishes.

There is also a diagnostic purpose to the use of directives. Whether, and how, a task is performed provides useful information, particularly about a family's willingness and ability to change. Thus a task may be done as instructed, not done at all, half done, attempted and failed, or altered. Even talking about a proposed task often reveals useful information, for example about the family's mealtime behaviour, if the task is one that is to be done at mealtimes.

How should direct injunctions be given? We have three alternatives:

(1) Telling people to stop doing something
(2) Telling people to do something different
(3) Telling people to do things in a different sequence

Telling people to stop doing something may not be effective. In many cases our clients already want to stop doing whatever it is, and simply having the therapist tell them to stop does not help. There are however ways of increasing the effectiveness of direct injunctions:

- Making the instructions as precise as possible. This may involve repetition and having the family members repeat back, in detail, what they are to do.
- Enlisting other family members to remind those concerned of what has to be done.
- Using the force of the therapist's personality. How effective this is will depend on the quality of rapport that has been established.
- Setting up a system of rewards or punishments. Rewards are generally to be preferred to punishments.

Telling people to do something different is often more effective than telling them to stop doing something. Thus rather than telling parents to stop arguing about how to handle their child's behaviour, the therapist might tell them to list the possible ways of dealing with certain troublesome behaviours. These could then be discussed and a joint plan of action agreed. If it seems unlikely that the parents will be able to reach agreement on a joint plan, they could be asked to return with their list of possible courses of action for discussion and, if possible, agreement at the next therapy session. With some families it may be necessary for the whole process to be carried out during therapy sessions with the therapist's active help, at least for the first few issues tackled.

Procedures such as the above can have more value than that of simply resolving particular problems. They can help couples learn to communicate and discuss issues, and then to resolve them by the use of compromise and the rational consideration of alternatives.

Telling people to do things in different sequence can lead to changes in set, problematic patterns of behaviour. A good example is an instruction given by Milton Erickson, and reported by Haley (1973, page 225).

A husband and wife had run a restaurant business for many years, but were constantly quarrelling about how it should be managed. Although the wife said the husband should manage it, he protested that she would not allow him to do so. She insisted on nagging him about the buying, the book-keeping, even when the floor needed scrubbing.

Erickson discovered that they opened the restaurant at 7.00 am, both partners carried keys and the wife would open the restaurant door while her husband parked the car. Erickson's behavioural prescription to the wife was to see that her husband arrived at least half an hour before she did. He thus carried the keys, opened the door, unlocked everything and started setting up the restaurant for the day. By the time the wife arrived, the husband had got things going and was managing satisfactorily. She stayed at home, washed the breakfast dishes and did some housework before she left. Gradually she found she could be later and later, and that her husband could still run the restaurant. By this simple intervention, Erickson unbalanced the game the couple had been playing by changing the rules, and set in train a sequence of events which led to the resolution of their problems.

Motivating people to follow directives can be a challenge. In addition to choosing from the above three ways of giving direct injunctions, there are other points to consider. It is necessary to persuade the family that carrying out a directive will lead to a result they want. In other words, there must be something in it for them. This is easier when the family are agreed on the changes they want. When they disagree, the therapist's efforts are usually best directed to devising tasks that will help the family members reach agreement. Such tasks must offer the prospect of some advantage accruing to everyone concerned. Another option is to start with small non-threatening tasks and work up to more complex ones.

Another way to motivate families is to rehearse with them the various ways in which they have tried to solve their problems. They can be asked to list everything they have tried, and what resulted in each case. As they realize that everything tried so far has failed, they may become more responsive to the therapist's suggestions. On the other hand, if they state that things have been improving recently, the therapist may present directives building on this, to add to the improvement the family has achieved by its own efforts.

As well as promoting motivation by the above means, the therapist should be sensitive to what is acceptable to the family. Some families respond better to the challenge of what is presented as a big task, while others prefer the less threatening idea of a small one. Some respond better than others to the weight of the therapist's professional authority as an expert.

You will often find it best to offer directives for use during sessions, before you offer them for use between sessions. Remember that almost everything you do or say during any session with a family has directive properties. Selective attention given to different things can itself be a powerful factor in bringing about change.

Assigning tasks

We have seen that family therapists often assign tasks as part of the treatment of family problems. This is a major feature of the 'problem-centered' approach of Epstein and Bishop (1981). Tasks may be assigned to be carried out during therapy sessions or between them, or both. Ultimately, though, the family must practise new ways of functioning outside the therapy sessions.

Provided the changes the family seeks have been carefully defined, the tasks set by the therapist should be more successful than the family's own past attempts to overcome their problems. Families can seldom take an objective view of their problems, but the therapist can help them to do so. In many families the problems turn out not to be what was initially thought. In other words some reframing takes place. The following case illustrates this.

> Mr and Mrs C. complained of the behaviour of their 8-year-old son, David. They said he lied, stole money and other items from family members, generally defied his parents' authority, and had tantrums when confronted about his behaviour. They had tried many ways of dealing with these problems, but had difficulty agreeing on what approach to take.
>
> Mr C. preferred to be the 'heavy,' imposing severe prolonged sanctions, like early bedtimes, or no television, for a month; while Mrs C. thought he was too harsh in his punishments. She sometimes managed to persuade her husband to modify the sanctions he had imposed on David, and also

tended to make concessions when he wasn't present. For instance she might let David watch a few cartoons on television when he arrived home from school, even though his father had said he should not be watching any TV.

Exploration of the family revealed longstanding marital tensions. The parents came from very different families of origin, and their marriage had been precipitated by Mrs C.'s pregnancy with David. Before that she had been far from sure she wanted to marry Mr C. The therapist hypothesized that David's difficult behaviour was a secondary problem, related to the tensions between the parents. It was these tensions that seemed to be behind the parents' failure to agree on how to deal with David. By behaving badly David also gave his parents something other than their own marital problems on which to focus their attention.

When the time came for therapist and family to agree on a problem list, and the changes desired by the family, the therapist suggested that the parents' disagreements regarding David should come high on the list. During the discussion of this 'problem', namely the parents' disagreements, the original 'presenting problem' became reframed. Now the top priority was to enable the parents to find means of agreeing on how to handle David and his problem behaviours. His behaviour *per se* became a secondary issue.

The initial tasks set the family addressed parenting issues. They were designed to help Mr and Mrs C. communicate better, and learn to problem solve in a cooperative way. The difficulties they had in functioning as an effective parental couple were closely related to their marital problems. These too were included in the problem list, and in due course became a focus of therapy.

The C. family did well. David's behaviour ceased to be a problem, and indeed it was not long before the presenting symptoms were forgotten, as the underlying issues were tackled and resolved. Left to themselves, however, the parents would probably have continued their futile (because they were disunited) attempts to control their son.

The 'C.' family had a number of problems. The most obvious concerned behaviour control. Not only were the parents' efforts to control their son ineffective, but neither could control what the other did in dealing with David. But there were other, perhaps more fundamental, problems. Communication between the parents was poor. Many important issues were not discussed, and sometimes communication was through David, rather than direct. The affective involvement of the parents was also less than optimal. Indeed it appeared that Mrs C. was emotionally closer to her son than she was to her husband.

There are other ways in which the 'C.' family's problems can be conceptualized. The structural therapist might see the essence of their problem as being the lack of a clear boundary between parents and son. The parents appeared relatively disengaged emotionally from each other, while there was an unhealthy degree of enmeshment between mother and son. The structural therapist would endeavour to establish a clearer boundary between parents and child, while opening up that between the parents. Represented graphically as recommended by Minuchin (1974, Chapter 3 and 5), the structure looks like this:

```
     .                                            F M
     .
M  .  Son      needed to become changed to:       - - - - -
     .                                            Son
    __
     F
```

The diagram on the left represents a subsystem pattern in which there is a diffuse boundary (shown by a vertical dotted line) between mother and son, and a coalition (shown by the horizontal bracket) between mother and son on the one hand, and father on the other. The diagram on the right shows a parental subsystem consisting of mother and father working together, separated from the son by a clear boundary.

The above change in the family structure would probably represent quite well the objectives of a therapist using the 'problem-centered systems therapy' of Epstein and Bishop (1981). Such a therapist would not however conceptualize the process in quite the same way. But the tasks set the family would probably be aimed at getting the parents to work together in a united way in dealing with their son, and at improving the communication of both information and feelings between them.

Structural, and other, therapists often use the power of their personalities to help alter the structure of the family system. In this case the structural therapist might for part of a session join with father, supporting him in the view that the sanctions he imposes should not be undermined or ignored by mother. This procedure would have to be balanced by supporting mother in her desire that the sanctions imposed on her son should not be too severe or prolonged. The opening up of the boundary between the parents could be promoted by addressing the parents collectively as a couple during sessions, having them sit together apart from their son, or even seeing them on their own without the son present at all. These actions might help create an appropriate boundary between the parents and their son. Tasks set the family between sessions would have similar aims. Implicit in all the therapist's words and actions should be the assumption that parents are in charge of their children, and have both a duty and a right to teach them society's ways and the limits to behaviour that are acceptable.

Haley (1976), employing his 'problem-solving' approach, would probably concentrate on the confused hierarchy in the 'C.' family. It was not clear who was in charge, and there was a lack of a properly functioning parental subsystem. The therapist takes charge of the family for a while, and puts the parents in charge of the children.

Direct treatment approaches to common family problems were discussed in Chapter 10. These are the basis for the setting of tasks in this phase of treatment.

The 'problem-centered systems' approach, structural therapy and Haley's 'problem-solving' therapy are all relatively direct, though not necessarily easy, methods of resolving family problems. Each requires the therapist to assess the family situation, and conceptualize it according to the relevant model of family functioning. This may involve redefining the problem, or even reframing it, although the distinction between redefining and reframing is slight. In the case of the 'C.' family the problem was redefined as being the parents' inability, in the past, to agree on a common approach to David's problems, and generally to work together as a parental pair. This in turn was related to longstanding marital conflict.

Some therapists might say that the problem was reframed, rather than redefined, but this is really a matter of semantics. Reframing is not an all-or-none process. A more drastic reframing would have been to tell the family, for example, that it appeared to the therapist that David was doing an excellent job in drawing attention to the problems between the parents, and that he should be congratulated because his behaviour had had the effect of bringing the family to therapy. For many families, however, this would probably be unacceptable.

Reframing and strategic therapy

Therapy methods which have come to be labelled 'strategic' usually involve a greater degree of reframing than was used with the 'C.' family, but the borderline is vague. Reframing is however 'fundamental to strategic therapy' (Coyne, 1985).

We must now consider what the therapist should do when direct injunctions prove ineffective. Such injunctions fail either because they are not obeyed, or because the changes the family seeks do not occur even though they are obeyed. Sometimes there is improvement in one area of family functioning, but this is accompanied by deterioration in another. It is important to remember, however, that giving direct injunctions can be successful even though the instructions are not carried out. This is usually because the content of the injunction, or the nature of the task, serves to reframe the situation. Thus setting a task that is concerned with communication in the family, may draw attention to the family's communications problems and cause the family members to think differently about them. This might lead to change. Sometimes it proves difficult to persist in the same pattern of behaviour once attention has been drawn to it.

The failure of direct approaches is a signal to consider indirect, or strategic, ones.

The therapeutic use of reframing

If therapy addressed to the unreframed problem has failed, it is usually best to consider next how the problem, or the family's situation generally, may be reframed. To quote Coyne again:

> 'The reframing of problem behaviour is a basic tool of strategic thera-pists. This class of therapeutic interventions involves shifting the per-spective within which a client experiences a situation in a way that fits the "facts" of the situation at least as well, but that changes its entire meaning.' (Coyne, 1985, page 337)

Developmental reframing (Coppersmith, 1981) is a relatively simple form of reframing. It usually involves labelling behaviour which has been regarded as in some way disturbed as 'young' or 'immature'. Coppersmith's (1981) three clinical examples were entitled, respectively, 'He's not bad, he's just young'; 'She's not mad, she's just young'; and 'They do not need to divorce, they're just young'. Talking of behaviour as immature can give it a meaning different to what it had before. The teenage terror, who seems out of control and perhaps has temper tantrums like a toddler's, is spoken of as being just a young child who has yet to grow up. It can be difficult for teenagers to continue to behave in the same way once their behaviours have been reframed in this way. At the same time the parents may be encouraged to treat the young person as a child several years younger. This will probably mean less responsibility and fewer privileges than hitherto. The latter become dependent on age-appropriate behaviour, and temper tantrums are not age-appropriate in the teenage years.

Other therapeutic strategies

Strategic therapy has been discussed in Chapter 11, and the various tech-niques described there should be considered when direct methods fail. Several may be used simultaneously or in succession. Nowadays several other approaches are available including 'narrative' methods and other 'post-modern' approaches as outlined elsewhere in this book.

Working with a team

The therapeutic methods discussed so far in this chapter are for the most part suitable for use by therapists working on their own, but in planning and delivering strategic interventions the use of a consultation team is usually helpful. In addition to assisting the therapist in devising interven-tions, the team can act as a 'Greek chorus', as described by Papp (1980), or a 'reflecting team'. The beginning therapist in particular is wise to seek help from colleagues, preferably having them watch sessions 'live'. Even one observing colleague can help greatly. In family therapy training centres live supervision is usually the routine, but it is valuable whatever the circumstances and however great the experience of the therapist.

Having several therapists involved simultaneously in a single case may sound like an expensive proposition, but it is not necessarily so. It may greatly speed treatment, or even lead to the successful treatment of families which otherwise might fail to respond, even to prolonged therapy.

Summary

Every family therapist needs a coherent theory of change, and a systematic way of tackling families' treatment needs. We must each of us pick out, from the available information, that which is most helpful to us in assisting families to make the changes they seek. As an example of how available knowledge may be used, this chapter has described an approach to family therapy which employs techniques from different schools of family therapy.

The establishment of rapport is the essential first step in helping any family. Treatment commences following assessment and the establishment of agreed objectives. Assessment is also an ongoing process, and strict separation of assessment and treatment is impossible.

Direct methods of therapy are used first, unless they have already been given a fair trial and have failed, or the family appears to have oppositional attitudes such as would make it unlikely to respond to direct injunctions.

When direct methods prove unsuccessful, indirect ones are indicated. These involve reframing the problems and/or the changes the family seeks. The family is usually offered a more radically different way of looking at things than the redefining of problems which is often necessary with direct methods. Any of the strategic therapy techniques described in Chapter 11, or the other special techniques discussed in Chapter 12, may be needed at this stage.

In dealing with complex family problems the use of a consultation team is valuable. This applies also to the use of some of the more recently developed narrative approaches and other 'post-modern' methods.

Chapter 14
Marital and Sex Therapies

The treatment of marital problems is an aspect of family therapy. As Kirschner and Kirschner (1986, page 25) put it, 'a healthy marital interaction is the key to optimal family process'. According to these authors, there is a natural drive towards a healing marital relationship. This 'not only replicates, but also transcends the transactional gestalts that the spouses experienced in their families of origin'.

The marital relationship is also the basis of the parental one. It is hard for a couple to work effectively together as a parental couple if they are not happy as a marital pair. Many problems that manifest themselves in the behaviours of individual family members, whether parents or children, can be related to marital tensions. In families in which there are no children, marital therapy and family therapy are the same thing.

A couple's sexual relationship is an important part of their total relationship. Sometimes sexual problems are but one aspect of a wider set of problems. When this is so, the sexual difficulties may disappear as the marital relationship improves in the course of marital or family therapy. In other cases the sexual difficulties may be the primary problem, or even a separate one, and therapy directed specifically to them may be required. The treatment of sexual disorders has, however, become a specialized field, and will not be discussed in detail here.

The development of marital/couple therapy

The term 'couple therapy' has, in recent years, increasingly replaced 'marital therapy'. This is because many couples living together in an intimate relationship, and raising children, choose not to be legally married. While there are some subtle differences between the married and the 'common-law' state, the therapeutic challenges when partners, whether married or not, present for help with their relationship are similar. I shall therefore usually use the term 'couple therapy' to cover both types of relationship.

The development of marital, or couple, therapy has parallelled that of therapies for larger family groups. When psychodynamic theories held near-exclusive sway, marital problems were seen as being consequences of the intrapsychic difficulties of the partners. Treatment therefore tended to concentrate on individual therapy with one or both partners. This is, theoretically at least, a valid approach. When there is marital conflict, the individuals concerned may indeed have unresolved intrapsychic conflicts that are interfering with their marital relationship. If these intrapsychic problems can be resolved, improvement in the marital relationship may result.

Unfortunately individual therapy often proves difficult, may need to extend over a long period and may not be effective. Quicker, and often better, results are often achieved when the marital partners are seen together. Much the same could be said about family therapy. In theory at least, family problems could be dealt with by providing treatment for individual family members. It seems, however, that when the presenting problems are interactional, work with the whole family is usually required to achieve the best results.

An important development was the publication of *Marital Tensions* by Henry Dicks (1967). Although Dicks viewed marital problems primarily from a psychodynamic viewpoint, he looked also at the interactional processes occurring between marital partners. He recommended conjoint treatment of marital couples, but emphasized intrapsychic processes and mental mechanisms, and also the use of the transference relationship, in helping the partners gain an understanding of themselves and their problems in relating to each other.

It has been generally held that individual treatment for marital problems tends to yield poor results when compared with conjoint marital therapy. This was the conclusion reached by Gurman and Kniskern (1978, 1981) who reviewed the available research data. This view was challenged by Wells and Giannetti (1986a) who stated that 'from the highly inadequate evidence available, no conclusions can be reached concerning either the absolute or relative effectiveness of [individual marital therapy]'. There was a commentary in *Family Process* on the article by Gurman and Kniskern (1986) entitled 'Individual marital therapy – have reports of your death been somewhat exaggerated?' and a 'rejoinder' headed 'Whither marital therapy?' by Wells and Giannetti (1986b). While this issue has never been resolved to the satisfaction of all, the current consensus seems to be that conjoint therapy is to be preferred.

Why might conjoint marital therapy be more effective? Consideration of the factors which lead people to marry may provide an answer. Couples usually marry, or enter into some other form of intimate relationship, because each of them sees something attractive in the other, and at some level feels the other partner would meet her or his needs. Individual therapy aims to change the partners and may remove some of those characteristics each found attractive in the other. Someone who has undergone effective therapy is no longer the same person the partner married. If there have not been reciprocal, or in some way compatible, changes in the other partner, the basis of the relationship may have been removed. This is may be why, when an alcoholic partner in a marriage stops drinking, the marriage sometimes breaks up. The non-alcoholic partner may have felt a sense of superiority over the one who drank, something that no longer applies when the former alcoholic is no longer drinking. Crafoord (1980, page 72) put the situation well, describing the situation when the husband is the alcoholic:

> 'There is an extreme polarization of the role distribution between man and wife in the family, an inequality which makes it impossible for the man to get rid of the role as the "family bastard" if the wife would not lose her role as the "angel". If she is very dependent on being an angel, she has an interest in keeping the husband as a "bastard".'

So in situations such as the above, treatment of the apparent problem, the husband and his excessive drinking, could upset the balance in the family. The wife might have married her husband in order to feel, at an unconscious level, the superior partner in the relationship. This, in turn, might have been a reaction to her own deep-seated feelings of insecurity. In conjoint marital therapy, however, it is the relationship that is the primary focus of therapy. Changes in the individual partners occur as the relationship changes and *vice versa*. Individual and relationship changes are part of one and the same process.

As family therapy developed, and therapists increasingly found that looking at family problems interactionally, and from a 'systems' perspective, often yielded better results than the more traditional methods, similar approaches were adopted for marital therapy. The marital *system* became the focus of therapy, rather than the marital *partners*.

Behaviour therapy techniques can readily be applied in the treatment of dyads, though they are less easily adapted to larger groups. This has led to their extensive use in marital therapy. It is usually easy, once a behavioural analysis has been carried out, to discover how each marital partner, by responding differentially, is reinforcing or extinguishing particular behaviours in the other. From this information, behaviour modification programmes can be developed.

Current approaches to marital/couple therapy

Couples therapy, as I will henceforth call it, often requires its own special approaches, although most of the treatment methods for families discussed in previous chapters can be used as well for marital problems as for problems in larger family groups. The McMaster Model of Family Functioning, for example, can be applied to couples, who may have problem-solving difficulties, communication problems, role definition problems, difficulties with affective responsiveness and affective involvement, and behaviour control problems. Such problems can be tackled using the various treatment approaches discussed in Chapter 10.

Any of the therapeutic approaches mentioned in Chapters 11 and 12 may also be used with marital couples. As with larger family groups, it is usually best to use direct methods first, unless they have already had a fair trial. Then, if the desired results have not been achieved, indirect strategies may be employed.

Behavioural couple therapy

Behavioural methods have come to be used extensively in work with couples. The interactions between the partners must be analysed before therapy can start. Behaviourally orientated therapists believe that marital conflict is related to the rate of reinforcement of various behaviours directed by the partners towards one another, and by the proportions of reinforcement and of punishment that are delivered.

Reinforcement is defined as any response that is followed by an increase in a behaviour. *Punishment* is any response that is followed by a decrease in a behaviour. These processes can each be applied to desired or to undesired behaviours. The behavioural approach does not concern itself primarily with the origins of the present behaviours. These can vary from biological and temperamental factors, through childhood rearing patterns and other childhood experiences, to deficits in problem-solving or other skills. The therapist is concerned with what is *maintaining* the undesired behaviours, regardless of their origins which are, in any event, often hard to determine, especially when the problems have been present for a long time.

In this form of treatment, as in any other, the therapist must first establish rapport. The rapport-building techniques discussed earlier in this book are as important in behavioural therapy as in any other. The therapist's interest in helping, concern for the couple and belief that change for the better is possible, should be made clear from the start. The marital partners are usually assessed and treated as a couple, though many therapists see the partners individually in the course of the assessment. If one partner is seen, however, it is usually wise to afford the other the same attention.

It is important to assess the couple's objectives and motivation for change. Not all couples coming for help want to repair their marital relationship. Some want to end it. They may come in order to demonstrate that the situation is hopeless, or for help in ending the relationship in as constructive a way and with as little harm to all concerned as possible.

An early account of behavioural methods of marital therapy is to be found in the book *Marital Therapy: Strategies Based on Social Learning and Behavior Exchange Principles* by Neil Jacobson and Gayla Margolin (1979). A basic principle is to increase the 'positive' exchanges between the couple (see also Chapter 17). Highly specific agreements are usually worked out with the clients. Each partner agrees to do certain things in relation to the other, the process of behaviour exchange (BE). These agreements may be committed to writing so that they can be regularly reviewed by all concerned. This helps reduce uncertainty about what actually has been agreed. While different interpretations of written agreements are possible, they are less likely than with verbal ones.

The more flexible the couple, and the less well established and chronic their problems, the more likely it is that a straightforward approach, which identifies the behaviours to be changed, and then deals directly with them by prescribing changes in the partners' behaviours, will be effective. Jacobson and Margolin (1979, Chapter 6) offered various clinical examples.

Skill deficits and performance deficits

When developing any behavioural treatment programme, it is important to consider how far the problems to be tackled are due to skill deficits or to performance deficits. (See Murdoch and Barker (1991) for a fuller discussion of this.) Do the couple have the necessary communication, problem-solving or other skills needed? If one or both of the partners does not have the requisite skills, these must be taught.

In other cases, the couple have in their behavioural repertoire the needed skills but, for whatever reason, they are not using them. Therapeutic failure is likely if the distinction between performance and skill deficits is not taken into account.

If problem-solving difficulties need to be tackled, the therapist should keep in mind some general principles of learning theory. These include the pin-pointing of target behaviours, the use of specific behaviour management strategies, for example 'shaping', and the use of positive, rather than aversive, approaches to learning. Shaping is the gradual changing of behaviour by rewarding each step, even if it is only small, towards the behavioural goal.

Behavioural communication training comprises three processes. The first is the provision by the therapist of *feedback*, that is information about clients' current communication patterns, and how these fail to serve their intended purposes. The second step is the provision of *instructions*: the therapist suggests alternative communication patterns which appear likely to be more effective. Then, during *behavioural rehearsal*, the clients practise the new communication patterns. The therapist continues to give feedback, and further instructions may be needed as treatment progresses. The three processes may thus continue together.

This form of communication training is similar to that used by therapists of other schools, but behavioural therapists tend to make the process more precise and specific. Role playing, and role reversal, in which the partners swap their usual roles, can be helpful when addressing these problems.

Communication training may address various aspects of the interactions between marital partners. It may aim to help the partners respond more empathically to each other; to improve their listening skills; to increase their validation of each other; or to develop their skills in expressing feelings in appropriate ways, both angry feelings and positive, loving ones. *Validation* is the process whereby people affirm the legitimacy and reasonableness of others' opinions, suggestions or actions, even though they may disagree with them.

A widely used technique, which can be helpful also in other forms of family therapy, is *contingency contracting*. A contingency contract is an agreement in writing between the people concerned, specifying a change in the relationship (usually a well-defined behavioural change), and containing specific contingencies for compliance with the contract. ('Contingency' is a technical term for the consequences that follow an event or action.)

Contingency contracting, as Jacobson and Margolin (1979) point out, is the last stage in problem solving. It presupposes that a solution to a problem between the couple has been found, and is a means by which the marital partners contract to put the solution into effect. If a couple already have adequate problem-solving skills but cannot make suitable agreements to apply them to their relationship, contracting skills may be taught without teaching problem solving.

Contingency contracts are of two types, the 'quid pro quo' contract, so named by Weiss et al. (1974), and the 'parallel' contract, which the same authors recommend as an alternative. In the first type there is a direct, simultaneous exchange of behaviours by the couple. In parallel contracts two independent change agreements are made. Although there is no specific exchange of behaviours, these are nevertheless accurately described as contingency contracts because specific rewards are agreed for compliance.

While behavioural marital therapy often yields good results in the short term these tend not to be maintained in the longer term. This was subsequently acknowledged by Neil Jacobson who wrote that 'traditional behavior therapy is not enough' in the book *Acceptance and Change in Couple Therapy* (Jacobson & Christensen, 1996, page 5). So what needed to be added? These authors had come to the conclusion that communication/problem-solving training (CPT) was required. CPT is the antithesis of BE:

> 'Presenting problems are de-emphasized. Short-term changes in the ratio of positive to negative behaviours are ignored. Instead couples are taught to be their own therapists through the training in communication and conflict resolution skills. The theory of change is that if couples can be taught to solve their own problems, then they can function on their own in the future, after therapy is over, when problems recur, as they inevitably do.' (page 4)

The combination of BE and CPT has been studied in a randomized clinical trial. This combination of treatments was found to be more effective than either BE alone or CPT alone. Couples in all three treatments did better than a waiting list control group. BE was more successful than the other treatments in changing the ratio of positive to negative behaviours at home, but BE couples relapsed at a high rate. CPT alone was more successful than BE in improving communication and conflict resolution skills. But BE and CPT combined yielded the best and most long-lasting results (Jacobson, 1984; Jacobson & Follette, 1985; Jacobson et al., 1986, 1987; Jacobson & Christensen, 1996, page 5).

Jacobson and Christensen (1996) also discuss, indeed emphasize, the importance of *acceptance* in determining the outcome of couple therapy. They point out that 'traditional behaviour therapy places great emphasis on accommodation, compromise and collaboration' (page 10). They go on to assert:

'When couples enter therapy with the ability and willingness to adopt these stances, therapy proceeds quite smoothly – or at least works eventually. However, when a couple cannot or will not compromise, accommodate or collaborate ... traditional behaviour therapy has little to offer them.' (page 10)

Some couples come to therapy with what Jacobson and Christensen describe as 'incompatibilities, irreconcilable differences, and unsolvable problems', but nevertheless some of them want to work things out. These authors mention the 'serenity prayer' used by Alcoholics Anonymous and other '12-Step' fellowships:

God, grant me the serenity to accept the things I cannot change,
Courage to change the things I can,
And the wisdom to know the difference.

Applied to couples in conflict, this may mean accepting things about one's partner that one would wish changed but that cannot be changed, either by oneself or by the therapist. Many marital and other relationships are entered into on the basis of unrealistic romantic expectations. But living together and, even more so, raising a family, are challenging tasks, requiring accommodation and compromise. Acceptance of things that are not entirely as one would wish is necessary for success. It is also necessary for therapy, particularly traditional behaviour therapy, to be successful.

Many couples presenting for therapy have long been trying to change each other. But the attempts by one partner to get the other to change have not been successful. If they had, the couple would not be seeking therapy. Indeed they often make things worse. What is needed, as the couple enter treatment, is acceptance of the situation that exists, including the 'incompatibilities, irreconcilable differences, and unsolvable problems'. If these are accepted while work proceeds on BE and CPT, change may nevertheless occur.

The balance of Jacobson and Christensen's book *Acceptance & Change in Couple Therapy: A Therapist's Guide to Transforming Relationships* (1996) is devoted to a description of 'integrative couple therapy' (ICT). It is not possible to describe details of the process of ICT here. It is clear though that its development was an important step in the ongoing evolution of couple therapy.

Further developments in couple therapy

The development of couple therapy has proceeded apace since the publication of the above book. Susan Johnson and Jay Lebow (2000) reviewed the previous decades' progress in an article entitled 'The "coming of age" of couple therapy'. They identified as 'key trends' over the last decade:

- Couple therapy becoming firmly established as the accepted treatment of choice for couple problems.
- The blossoming of the science of relationships.
- Strong evidence supporting the effectiveness of couple therapy both for relationship problems and [disorders listed in the *Diagnostic and Statistical Manual of the American Psychiatric Association*].
- Greater understanding of the ramifications of gender.
- New respect for the diversity of family forms.
- Increased accent on the role of emotion.
- The influence of post-modernism.
- Greater recognition of couple violence.
- The move towards integration across models of treatment.

Johnson and Lebow identified, as the main models of couple therapy in use at the end of the decade of the 1990s, cognitive-behavioural, narrative, solution-focused and emotionally focused, with feminist, Bowenian, psychodynamic and integrative models also flourishing. However they identified, as the methods with the 'strongest research base and support', behavioural marital therapy (BMT) (Baucom et al., 1998); and emotionally focused therapy (Johnson et al., 1999). It is thus clear that at the end of the decade a wide variety of approaches to couple therapy were in use, as they are to this day, without a clear consensus as to which method is to be preferred for which type of problem.

Johnson (2003), in an article entitled 'The revolution in couple therapy: a practitioner-scientist perspective', offered 'an overview of the expanding field of couple therapy', focusing on what the author considered to be 'new and even revolutionary in this field'. She focused on four areas of growth:

(1) The continuing research into the nature of clinical problems, leading to better understanding of the nature of relationship.

(2) Research into the process of change in therapy.
(3) The application of couples therapy as an effective treatment for individual disorders.
(4) Greater integration of general research from clinical psychology, human development, and social psychology so that this informs, guides and evaluates interventions of couple and family therapists.

Other approaches to couple therapy

Short-Term Couple Therapy (Donovan, 1999) is an edited book with sections on 'psychodynamic methods'; 'the systemic approach'; 'collaborative models'; and 'the postmodern schools'. It is clear from the diverse therapy approaches described that a wide variety of approaches to the treatment of couples is available. The editor, in the opening chapter, discusses the 'principles of brief treatment' (Donovan, 1999, pages 1–9). He lists six 'guidelines' for such treatment:

(1) Find the focus
(2) Maintain flexibility
(3) Build affective intensity
(4) Encourage the alliance
(5) Arrange an emotionally affirming experience
(6) Plan the treatment

Donovan's chapter expands on each of these guidelines, and in the remaining 14 chapters a total of 23 contributors describe a variety of treatment approaches.

Emotionally focused couple therapy (EFT) owes much to attachment theory. When attachment needs are not met, in the context of a couple's relationship, distress of a degree that leads the couple to seek help may result. Johnson (1999) asserts that this is 'an effective short-term approach to modifying distressed couples' constricted interaction patterns and emotional responses and fostering the development of a secure emotional bond' (page 13). She claims that EFT is 'one of the best empirically validated approaches to changing distressed relationships'.

According to attachment theory, fear, anger and sadness arise when an attachment figure is perceived as inaccessible or unresponsive. In a healthy couple or other relationship the partners feel that they can count on each other to be there when they need them. When this is not the case, distress results and this may escalate as efforts by one or both partners to have their attachment needs met fail. According to Johnson (1999, pages 16–17):

> 'Attachment theory provides a map for adult intimate relationships. It outlines needs for contact, comfort, security, and closeness as the features that define this landscape.'

Johnson goes on to write that the attachment theory (page 17):

> 'Stresses the significance of experiences of deprivation and loss of trust and connection. It directs the process of therapy toward the creation of the accessibility and responsiveness that foster safe emotional engagement. Such engagement encourages partners to express their attachment needs.'

Johnson (1999, pages 13–42) provides a fuller description of EFT, including the nine steps involved in using this approach with distressed couples. Research reported by Baucom and colleagues (1998) supports the effectiveness of EFT when used with distressed couples.

Brief Couples Therapy (Chaim et al., 2003) has as its subtitle *Group and Individual Couple Treatment for Addiction and Related Mental Health Concerns*. It is a manual presenting a step-by-step programme for the treatment of couples. It is intended as a tool for 'therapists and counselors working in substance abuse settings who would like to augment their practice by seeing couples'. It consists of eight sessions and uses an 'integrative model' drawing from various schools of family therapy.

Divorce therapy and mediation

Family therapists are increasingly being consulted by couples who are in the process of separating or becoming divorced. While some therapists specialize in this work, this is a field with which all who work with troubled families should be familiar. Sometimes marital partners decide to separate after entering therapy. It may only become clear that their marital goals are incompatible once they start exploring their difficulties, and the sort of marriage each wants.

Divorce is an increasingly common feature of the family life cycle. How it occurs, and its consequences, vary greatly. Much depends on the length of the marriage, whether there are children and, if so, how old they are. However, relationships between spouses rarely end with divorce, particularly when there are children of the marriage. The therapist may have much to offer couples during and after the divorce process, using any of the techniques mentioned in previous chapters, especially when there are problems with the children of the marriage.

Children of divorced parents are at risk in various ways. They may feel responsible for the divorce, and therefore be burdened with feelings of guilt; their lifestyle may have been greatly changed, perhaps because of the poorer economic situation of the parent caring for them; they may have had to move house, neighbourhood or school; and they may be used as pawns in a continuing game between the parents. It is important that the parents do not put each other down in conversation with the children. Nor should one seek the children's support in criticizing and finding fault with the other. Nevertheless these things happen only too frequently. Divorced couples may for years continue feeling anger, bitterness and resentment towards each other. Therapy can sometimes help in resolving these continuing problems.

Kressel et al. (1980) proposed a 'typology of divorcing couples', although their data were derived from a study of only 14 couples. They identified four patterns in the process by which the couples reached the divorce decision. This classification was based on 'three complex and highly intercorrelated dimensions':

(1)   Degree of ambivalence
(2)   Frequency and openness of communication
(3)   Level and overtness of conflict

The four patterns were labelled *enmeshed*, *autistic*, *direct* and *disengaged*. The enmeshed pattern was characterized by high levels of conflict, communication and ambivalence about the divorce decision. In the autistic type of divorce decision making, communication and overt conflict about the possibility of divorce were almost absent, though there was a high degree of ambivalence. The 'direct-conflict' pattern was characterized by high levels of overt conflict (but less intense than in the enmeshed pattern), and frequent and open communication between the parties about the possibility of divorce. Ambivalence was initially high, but moderated during a period of a year or more of 'working through'. The 'disengaged-conflict' pattern was distinguished by low ambivalence, and communication and conflict which were nearly as low as in the autistic pattern.

Although this was a small study, confined to a particular socioeconomic group – all the husbands were in professional or managerial positions – it appeared that task-orientated mediation worked best for the couples in the 'direct' and 'disengaged' groups. In the 'enmeshed' and 'autistic' types it was less successful. In addition the post-divorce adjustment in these groups was poor, worse than in the other two groups.

'Divorce mediation', sometimes known as 'family mediation', is increasingly being sought by divorcing couples, as an alternative to adversarial legal processes. In the USA there are both a Family Mediation Association and an Academy of Family Mediators. In 1982 the president of the latter organization reviewed the status of family mediation, and the training needed to practise it (Haynes, 1982). There have also been many other publications on divorce and divorce mediation (for example, Coogler, 1978; Haynes, 1981; Irving, 1980, 1981; Kaslow, 1984; Lowery, 1984; Marlow, 1985a, 1985b; Bogolub, 1995; Ellis, 2000; Lebow; 2005). Although agreements reached in the course of mediaton usually have to be confirmed by the court, Marlow (1985b) contends that, 'divorce mediation represents a rejection of a legal model of divorce and a substitution of a mental health model'. He identified 12 steps in the process of mediation:

(1) Referral
(2) Intake/orientation
(3) Budget development
(4) Reconciliation of budgetary needs
(5) Identification of assets
(6) Identification of parenting goals
(7) Clarification of issues
(8) Rank ordering of issues
(9) Identification of options
(10) Bargaining
(11) Drafting the memorandum of understanding
(12) Consultation with lawyer(s)

It will be clear from the above list of steps that this process requires more than an understanding of family dynamics, and of communications and other theories of human behaviour. Haynes (1982) points out that knowledge of bargaining and negotiation, in which lawyers are usually expert, are also necessary. Family therapists should therefore undergo some additional training if they are to undertake this work effectively. *Family Mediation and Collaborative Practice Handbook* (Landau et al., 2005) provides a comprehensive account of current practice in the field of family mediation.

Sex therapy

Sexual difficulties may exist as part of a wider marital problem. They are sometimes found to be a central feature of a marital problem but they may also be secondary to marital conflict arising from other causes. They may also be but one feature of a larger set of systems problems. In some cases the marital partners' sexual difficulties cease to exist with resolution of the larger family systems problems. In other cases they do not and treatment directed specifically at the sexual dysfunction is necessary. A detailed discussion of sex therapy is beyond the scope of this book, but a brief look at the history of the treatment of sexual disorders is in order.

Sex therapy, like much other psychotherapy, used to be based principally on psychodynamic theories. These looked at sexual problems in terms of the psychopathology of the individuals concerned, rather than examining the processes going on between the partners with the troubled relationship. But, much as family therapists have concerned themselves with interpersonal, rather than intrapersonal, processes, sex therapy nowadays considers interactional phenomena. It has also become clear that many sexual problems can be successfully treated using direct approaches.

An important event in the development of sex therapy was the publication of *Human Sexual Response* (Masters & Johnson, 1966). These authors reported a careful study of human sexual behaviour. This led to the development of therapy methods based on the understanding of sexual behaviour they had achieved. Masters' and Johnson's approach was primarily a behavioural one, rather than one based on the uncovering and resolution of intrapsychic conflict. It was described in *Human Sexual Inadequacy* (Masters & Johnson, 1970). These two books became standard works of reference, and are the basis for much modern sex therapy.

In 1974 Helen Singer Kaplan's *The New Sex Therapy* appeared. Building on the work of Masters and Johnson, it examined the anatomy and physiology of the sexual response and then looked at the various factors which may affect sexual performance. These include physical illness, age, drugs, intrapsychic causes, relationship difficulties and faulty learning experiences. Kaplan recommended an assessment along these lines of both members of the couple, leading to the development of a plan directed to the specific cause or causes of the problem.

Kaplan (1979) took her understanding of sexual disorders further in *Disorders of Sexual Desire*. In this book she was careful to distinguish the many different types of sexual problems, and she also pointed out the error of the old ways of looking at them:

> 'The psychoanalytic establishment, consistent with the prevailing monistic concept, had – erroneously, I believe – regarded all sexually troubled patients as variants of the same psychopathological population. Thus fetishists, asexuals, those with disturbances of romantic attachments, the sexually phobic, patients with gender disturbances, impotence, anorgasmia, vaginismus, and so on were considered together. The second error was the belief that the cause of sexual difficulties was specific and profound. It was thought that all sexual problems were produced by specific and serious unconscious conflicts about sex which were acquired during particular developmental phases in early childhood. Thus, all sexually inadequate patients were believed to be in need of psychoanalytically oriented treatment which has the capability of resolving such unconscious conflicts.' (Kaplan, 1979, page 4)

Kaplan asserted that therapy was formerly impeded by a failure on the part of therapists to realize that sexual response is not an entity, but consists of a series of phases. Masters and Johnson (1966) divided the sexual response into four stages: excitement, plateau, orgasm and resolution. Kaplan (1979) however suggested that a 'triphasic' model best fits the facts. The three phases she recognizes are:

(1) The desire phase
(2) The excitement phase
(3) Orgasm

Masters and Johnson's 'excitement' and 'plateau' stages correspond to Kaplan's 'excitement' phase, and their 'orgasm' phase to Kaplan's phase of the same name. Resolution is simply the termination of sexual arousal. Masters and Johnson did not describe a 'desire' stage.

Kaplan (1979) described separate treatment approaches for sexual problems, according to which of the three phases is involved. Problems of the orgasm phase include premature, retarded or absent ejaculation in the male and inhibition of orgasm in the female. Inhibition of the excitement phase produces impotence in the male and a failure to become excited and to produce adequate vaginal lubrication in the female. Desire phase problems are characterized by low libido. In both sexes this is manifest in reduced or absent desire for intercourse. It is possible for problems to exist in two or in all three phases simultaneously. Generally speaking treatment of orgasm phase difficulties has the highest success rate, and that of desire phase problems the lowest.

Kaplan's approach is generally directive and behavioural, but when this proves ineffective she looks at psychodynamic factors which may be responsible for resistance to treatment. This, she believes, is the main importance of a psychodynamic understanding of the case. She pays less attention to the symbolic meaning of the symptoms and their historical origins.

Further information on sex therapy is available in the books that have been mentioned. *Principles and Practice of Sex Therapy* (Leiblum & Pervin, 1989) also provides a wide-ranging look at the field. A concise account of current sex therapy practice is that of McCarthy & Bodnar (2005). Sex therapy has also spawned its own journals, for example the *Archives of Sexual Behaviour*, *The Journal of Sex and Marital Therapy* and *The Journal of Sex Research*. Advances in this fast-growing field are reported in these journals, often in preference to family therapy journals or other publications in the mental health field.

Summary

Marital therapy is an aspect of family therapy. Sometimes a marital problem is at the heart of a problem which presents as dysfunction in the wider family system. Marital therapy has increasingly concentrated on the interactional processes occurring between the marital pair, rather than on the partners' intrapsychic processes.

Any of the therapy methods which have been described for use in larger family groups may be applied to marital couples, but the last two decades have also seen the development of methods designed specifically for use with couples. Behavioural methods are particularly well suited for use with dyads such as marital pairs. They seem to be especially valuable when there is open strife, and much 'negative' interchange between the partners. They can promote the substitution of 'positive' exchanges for the negative ones.

Behavioural approaches and emotionally focused therapy, which uses concepts derived from attachment theory, appear to be the methods with the best empirical support. However many other approaches are currently in use.

There may be also psychodynamic aspects of the relationship which need to be addressed in therapy, but individual treatment of one partner, independent of help for the other, tends to lead to a poor result. Various self-help programmes for couples with marital problems are also available.

With the rising frequency of divorce, therapists are increasingly being consulted by couples who want help during this process, both in preventing any more psychological harm than necessary befalling family members, and in mediating disputes about the custody of children, and about financial and other issues. This has led to the development of specialist 'family mediators'.

Problems of sexual dysfunction are often present when there are other marital and family problems, though they may also occur in the absence of other serious problems. Sex therapy, too, has become a largely separate field of study and clinical practice, but all therapists need to be aware of what it has to offer.

Chapter 15
Terminating Treatment and Dealing with Treatment Interruptions

Treacher (1989) refers to termination as 'a neglected topic', and it is true that the literature tells us more about how to start and continue family therapy than about how to end it. The way termination is handled is nevertheless important. Lankton and Lankton (1983, page 345) pointed out that:

'The termination of a therapy session, as well as the termination of the entire therapy relationship, has special meaning to clients ... the therapist orients clients away from dependence on therapy to the interdependence of their social network. But individual coping styles and mechanisms for frustration tolerance will determine just how clients consciously anticipate their adjustment.'

Treatment contracts

Some of the purposes of making formal contracts with families were discussed in Chapter 9. When a specific time-limited or session-limited contract exists, the family can prepare for termination from the start. Having a time limit can also motivate families by providing a sense of urgency. 'If we don't get these issues sorted out by the fifth (or tenth, or whatever) session,' they may say to themselves, 'we shan't be able to achieve a solution to our problems.' A time-limited contract also helps families see therapy as a discrete process extending over a certain period of time, following which they will be able to continue their lives without needing the help of a therapist.

There can be some flexibility about contracts. The frequency of sessions may be decreased as changes in the family occur, and the intensity of the problems lessens. Some therapists foreshadow, at the outset, the possibility of negotiating a further contract at the end of the initial one. While there are advantages in a flexible approach, and in keeping options open, early talk about renewing time-limited contracts tends to remove much of the point of setting them up. I prefer not to mention the possibility of renewing any contracts I negotiate when they are first made. Some families, however, raise the issue, and in that case I tell them I am sometimes willing to do this.

When is a time-limited contract indicated? Firm data on which to base an answer are lacking. Some therapists use such contracts and others do not, but no scientific study of the respective results seems to have been carried out.

The number of sessions recommended does not seem necessarily to be related to the severity of the family problem. For example the Milan group (Palazzoli et al., 1978a), reported that they used ten-session contracts for the very severely disturbed families they treated. Occasionally they renewed the contracts for a further ten sessions, but in most cases they did not. The Brief Therapy Centre of the Mental Research Institute in Palo Alto also worked on the basis of limited-session contracts. The 97 cases reported by Watzlawick et al. (1974, page 115), comprising identified patients with a wider range of problems than those treated by the Milan group, were seen for an average of 7 hours each.

If you have previously agreed a contract specifying when therapy is to end, you should have a contingency plan ready in case the family asks for an extension. The choice lies between negotiating another contract, perhaps for a small number of further sessions; assuring the family they do not need any more treatment; or suggesting some other treatment. The latter could be something quite different, for example individual therapy for a family member, involvement in a therapeutic group or self-help organization, non-time-limited family therapy (such as the 'interminable' treatment mentioned in Chapter 11), or referral to another therapist or agency.

Sometimes a family's request for further treatment once the initial contract has come to an end can be the occasion to get therapy on to a new footing. If treatment has failed to achieve the hoped-for results, a new approach, perhaps with new conditions, may be employed.

Open contracts

The alternative to a time-limited contract is an open one: one which does not specify the length of the treatment, nor the number of times the family will be seen. In *Family Therapy: Full Length Case Studies* (Papp, 1977), there are accounts of the treatment of 11 families by eminent family therapists. In none of them was there mention of the setting up by the therapist of a contract for a fixed number of sessions. This is despite the presence among the authors of two therapists (Weakland and Fisch) associated with the Brief Therapy Centre in Palo Alto, and also of Papp herself, describing a family seen in the brief therapy project of the Ackerman Institute. This book, and the family therapy literature generally, suggest that open contracts are more commonly used than closed ones.

When the therapy contract is an open one, the management of the termination process is even more important. With closed contracts, families know from the start when treatment will end, and can prepare themselves for this. With open contracts this is not so, and at some point the subject of termination must be raised and related issues discussed.

Indications for ending treatment

The termination of family therapy may be initiated either by the therapist or by the family.

Termination on the initiative of the therapist

Termination on the initiative of the therapist may be indicated under any of the following circumstances:

(1) When the objectives set at the start of treatment have been met. Assessing whether or not this has happened is greatly helped if clear goals and objectives were agreed at the outset.

When it appears that the desired state has been achieved, or is being approached, I review with the family the changes that have taken place during treatment. If the family members feel things have changed, I ask them to examine the changes that have occurred. What exactly has changed? What specific things are different, compared with the situation at the start of therapy? Do these changes amount to the achievement of the goals set when therapy began, or at later stages?

Termination is often better accomplished when the family members are able to see the extent of the changes that have occurred, and when they realize that their problem-solving skills have improved. Tomm and Wright (1979) suggested that a paradoxical question such as 'What would each of you have to do to bring the problem back?' helps the family understand better what has happened during treatment.

(2) When there has been a change in the family's functioning such that further treatment is not necessary, even though the objectives originally specified have not been fully met. In other words, the family now has the resources it needs to deal with any remaining problems. Outside help is no longer required.

There may have been structural changes in the family, or improvement in the family's problem-solving skills. These may now enable it to cope with problems which previously defeated it. For example there might have been an improvement in the effectiveness of the parental couple's ability to work together in caring for their children. So, although their children's behaviour might still present problems, the parents are now able to handle them appropriately. If treatment is to be terminated in these circumstances, it is important that the changes that have occurred are labelled, explained and agreed by the family members, even though the means whereby they have been achieved may not be made explicit.

(3) If therapy has proved ineffective, despite having had a fair trial. This may be an indication for stopping therapy, at least of the type that has been used so far. A possible source of failure, as Watzlawick et al. (1974, pages 111–112) pointed out, is the setting of unrealistic or inappropriate goals. It is unrealistic to suppose that every family can achieve all the changes its members might desire, and sometimes there is a lack of agreement among the members about what they really want, though this may initially be camouflaged. Coleman and Gurman (1985) list as some of the causes of failure:

- Inadequate understanding and analysis of the circumstances surrounding the referral, particularly with regard to the assessment of the problem.
- Insufficient goal setting, particularly with regard to who sets the goals.
- Conflictual goals that affect therapy outcome.
- Overlooking the role of the presenting problem.

Coleman and Gurman's (1985) analysis of therapeutic failures confirmed the importance of the initial assessment of family problems, and of defining and agreeing therapeutic objectives, as set out in earlier chapters of this book.

(4) Loss or lack of family motivation. This is really an aspect of therapeutic failure, but issues of motivation merit separate consideration. If therapy appears to be failing to achieve its objectives I find myself wondering whether the family wants to change, or whether perhaps some members do while others do not. This is a delicate issue, for it is always possible for the therapist to blame a family's lack of motivation for the failure of therapy. Yet we must also consider the therapist's limitations or lack of the necessary skills, or the choice of the wrong therapeutic approach for the family concerned.

Sometimes a family's apparently weak motivation, or fear of change, may be part and parcel of the problem that brought it to therapy in the first place. We should therefore be cautious about blaming failure on the family's motivation. Part of our job is to motivate the families we see to do what they need to, to achieve their objectives. When I find myself wondering about my own part in the failure of the therapy, or the family's lack of motivation, I usually feel that the time has come to ask for consultation from a colleague.

There are various ways of motivating families. An optimistic attitude on the therapist's part, combined with mention of how things will be when (not if!) therapy is successfully concluded, and the embedding in conversation of statements that look forward to that situation, are useful.

In more difficult families a strategic approach may be needed. Metaphorical methods may succeed where direct ones do not. A number of examples are to be found in *Using Metaphors in Psychotherapy* (Barker,

1985, particularly pages 94–101). Stories about people who have come to a crossroads, or a fork in the highway, may be useful. The excitement, challenge or happy outcome of taking a new direction may be stressed, and may serve as a metaphor for the adventure of entering therapy. Imber-Black (1988, page 81) refers to 'celebration rituals to end therapy' and, as we saw earlier, she also describes (on page 82) a ritual prescribed at a closing dinner session, the identified patient being one with an eating disorder.

For those who believe that discontinuous change is not possible, Milton Erickson's story of Joe, the chronic and apparently incorrigible criminal whose life became suddenly and dramatically transformed, can be used. (It is to be found in Erickson, 1980e, pages 211–216, and is summarized in Barker, 1985, pages 55–56.)

(5) Tomm and Wright (1979) suggested that when continuing treatment does not appear to be cost-effective, it may be wise to consider termination. Sometimes progress is very slow, despite all the therapist's efforts. In that case it may be best for the therapist to clarify his or her limitations and initiate termination.

Termination on the initiative of the family

Termination on the initiative of the family may occur in various ways. The desire of the family to stop therapy may be manifest in failure to attend sessions, but there are often warning signs that this may be about to happen. These include failed appointments, last-minute cancellations, late arrival for sessions and the absence from sessions of family members who are supposed to be present. The content of sessions may also provide hints about what is happening, as when family members express dissatisfaction with the course of therapy, or begin complaining about the practical difficulties of attending, the loss of time at work, or the children's lost schooling.

Treacher (1989) suggested that when therapy has been 'strategic', clients should just drift away, perhaps in the above manner. She points out that in strategic therapy the objective of the therapist is to have clients change their behaviour without attributing the changes to any of the therapist's interventions. She says:

> 'It is therefore not surprising that this type of model has little to say about termination and is also very cautious about undertaking follow-ups.' (Treacher, 1989, page 138)

Tomm and Wright (1979) recommended that whenever initiatives such as those above become apparent, the therapist should take certain steps. These include considering what problems remain and what goals have not been achieved; assessing why the family is inclining towards termination; and looking especially for any evidence that there is serious danger of deterioration if treatment stops at the current stage. The therapist may take any of the following steps:

(1) Exploring with the family their motives for wishing to end treatment.
(2) Reviewing with the family the present state of their problems and, if appropriate, renegotiating the therapy contract. It may be helpful for the therapist to point out the benefits which therapy may still offer.
(3) Actively encouraging the family to remain in treatment, should there be reason to believe that deterioration is likely if treatment ceases at its current stage. It can be helpful to seek out the support of any people, inside or outside the family, who are likely to benefit if therapy continues. It may be necessary for the therapist to bring to the notice of such people the benefits that are likely to accrue.
(4) Accepting the family's wish to end treatment, and indicating respect for their right to make that decision. This is appropriate when there is evidence that termination is inevitable, and the therapist's wish to continue is stronger than the family's. In such circumstances the chances of further change occurring as a result of therapy are slight.

How to terminate treatment

Treacher (1989), noting that there is little about termination in the literature on structural therapy, proposed that, at the point of termination, the following questions should be asked by the structural therapist.

(1) What has happened to the presenting problem? Has it disappeared, or been reduced to a level which is now considered acceptable, or been reframed so that it is no longer seen as a problem?
(2) What structural changes have taken place; that is, have family relationships changed in demonstrable ways?
(3) What changes have taken place in individual and family beliefs, particularly those concerned with the problems discussed in therapy?

Treacher (1989) also described a way of operationalizing these questions. A problem area is explored in detail to establish what changes have occurred. The family is then asked what it will do if, for example, Johnny starts stealing (instead of Phil who has now stopped).

Lebow (1995) listed ten tasks that should be addressed in terminating family therapy:

(1) Tracking progress in therapy to determine the appropriateness of ending it.
(2) Reviewing the course of treatment as it proceeds.
(3) Emphasizing the gains made and the clients' role in these gains.
(4) Abstracting what has been learned from treatment and how it may be applied later.

(5)   'Internalizing' the therapist, who may become an internalized family member.
(6)   Relating the ending of therapy to other endings in life.
(7)   Saying goodbye with an opportunity to express gratitude and exchange feelings.
(8)   Discussing the conditions for returning to therapy, for example for 'booster' sessions.
(9)   Referring when continuation, for example in a self-help group, is indicated.
(10) Defining post-treatment availability.

My own practice is based on a modification of the model of Epstein and Bishop (1981). They identified four steps in the closure process:

(1)   Orientation
(2)   Summarizing what has happened during treatment
(3)   Discussing long-term goals
(4)   Follow-up (which is optional)

During the *orientation* stage I explain why I am raising the question of termination. This may be because the objectives appear to have been met, because the contracted number of sessions has been, or is about to be, completed, or, less often, because there has been little or no progress.

The summary of what has happened during therapy provides an opportunity for all concerned to review the progress that has been made, and the present situation in the family. I go back to my notes on the initial sessions and review the problems that were identified then, enquiring about the status of each.

I next ask the family to discuss their *long-term goals*. I like to present treatment as part of a continuing process of family growth and development. This goes hand in hand with the growth and development of the individual family members. I aim to help the family identify challenges it may face in the future, and discuss how it may use its strengths and psychological resources to meet such challenges. It can be helpful also to identify the outside resources that are available: extended family, friends, social and other agencies, the family doctor, professional workers in the mental health field, school counsellors and so on. *Follow-up*, the final stage, is considered below.

During the closure process I take as optimistic a view as possible of the situation, and the family's prospects. I do this even if closure is due to the family's unwillingness to continue to attend, rather than because the goals of therapy have been attained. I emphasize the family's strengths, the changes they have made and the effort they have put into achieving these changes. Even if the changes have been small, it is worth pointing them out. It may also be helpful to mention that family therapy is not the only means by which families make changes. Indeed most families, most of the time, are making changes, meeting challenges and surmounting developmental hurdles, without the help of therapists.

I believe it is important to affirm families as treatment is terminated. I like to express confidence in their ability to continue to make necessary changes. I aim to give a message such as, 'You've done well during treatment, and I believe you know what you have to do in the future, and how to set about making any further changes you want.' It is not usually a good idea for us as therapists to take credit for the changes families make, however clever we may think we are. Emphasis on the work the family has done is to be preferred.

Termination tasks and rituals

It can be helpful, when therapy sessions end, to leave the family with resources they can continue to use. These can consist of straightforward tasks, like arranging family meetings at regular intervals, or when major decisions have to be made. Another possibility is to prescribe symbolic or metaphorical tasks, perhaps of a ritualistic nature. These tasks or rituals will often build on processes started during therapy. They can be a means whereby the therapist can remain psychologically with the family, even though the sessions have ended. They are similar to post-hypnotic suggestions. Indeed Ritterman (1983, page 316), in *Using Hypnosis in Family Therapy*, describes the deliberate use of post-hypnotic suggestions in work with a client who was having difficulty dealing with issues concerned with the death of her husband. Erickson, too, made frequent use of post-hypnotic suggestion, as implied in the title of the book *My Voice Will Go With You* (edited by Rosen, 1982). The title is taken from one of the 'teaching tales' in the book.

Termination metaphors (Barker, 1985, pages 184–185) can keep alive, at the unconscious level, something of what has happened during treatment. A termination ritual was described briefly when the use of rituals was discussed in Chapter 11.

Emotional and psychological aspects of termination

The ending of therapy may be a time of great emotional significance to family members. It may, consciously or unconsciously, remind them of previous separations or losses. Inexpertly managed, it can appear to clients as a rejection but, just as the death of a loved one can be the occasion to celebrate that person's life and achievements, so can the ending of treatment be an occasion to celebrate what has been achieved. Nevertheless the therapist should always be on the look-out for signs that termination is proving difficult for the family, or for some of its members. The Lanktons put it well:

'The business of other unfinished "goodbyes" may be revived. These may have nothing to do with the expressed purpose of the therapy but nevertheless be stimulated by the parallel situation. For example the death of a friend from college may have had nothing to do with the marital therapy sought by the client. Yet, at termination, the client or therapist may find the need for adequate adjustment to this past situation stimulated by the end of the session or the therapy. This is often typified by negative emotions, tensions, "dead" spots, internal dialogues with deceased loved ones, unexplainable preoccupations, or unexpected delayed stress reactions from involvement in, for instance, the Vietnam War.' (Lankton & Lankton, 1983, pages 345–346)

Fenell and Weinhold (1989, pages 82–83) also point out that 'when a termination date is set, frequently many conflicts and defenses begin to emerge'. They emphasize the need to identify the gains made during therapy and the need to help each family member reduce his or her anxiety about separation. They point out that some couples or families try to prolong therapy rather than deal with their feelings of loss. They suggest that tapering off sessions or periodic follow-up sessions can help resolve such issues.

Similar reactions, I have found, may occur in response to my being late for or cancelling an appointment with a family. Punctuality and reliability on the part of the therapist are important (and not only in family therapy). When lateness or cancellations are unavoidable, the family should be told the reasons at the earliest opportunity, and the therapist should be prepared to deal with any emotional reactions that may occur.

Follow-up

When should the therapist offer follow-up contacts, designed to obtain information about a family's progress? It can be tempting, when a family's case is being closed, to offer an appointment or a telephone contact a few weeks or months ahead in order to check on whether progress is being maintained. While it may help families to feel that the therapist is still available to them, there is a danger of giving the message that further problems are likely. The family should not leave feeling that the therapist expects it to fall apart again! After you have expressed a positive view of the family's competence, the message should not be weakened by any implication of doubt about the longer-term outcome.

A case can be made for saying that therapy is finished. You do not expect that further treatment will be needed. The family now has the resources to cope with any challenges it may meet. It may be permissible to add, 'I (or we) will always be here if you need me (or us), of course, but I (or the team) really don't believe you will.'

The problem with the above approach is that it deprives the therapist of follow-up information. Yet it is important for us to know whether changes in families that occur during treatment are maintained. Fortunately there is a way of resolving this dilemma, at least in part. This is for the therapist to make it a policy to follow up every family at certain pre-determined intervals, perhaps at 4 or 6 months, or at both 6 and 12 months. If we do this we can truthfully say to families, at closure, 'You don't need any more treatment, but it is my policy (or perhaps the policy of the agency or clinic), with all the families I see, to contact them after 6 months (or whatever interval or intervals are chosen), because I am interested in knowing how they are getting along, and what further progress they have made.' An alternative is to say that the information is needed 'for research purposes', if the data are indeed to be used for research purposes.

Follow-up contacts may be made by telephone, letter or an appointment at the clinic or office. A face-to-face meeting with the family generally gives the most information and may need to be no longer than half an hour. Some families are willing to respond to a telephone call, but not to pay a visit to the therapist. Some also respond to letters or questionnaires requesting information, but this seems to be the method that yields the least return.

Dealing with treatment interruptions

Sometimes the course of treatment is interrupted by such things as physical illness in the family, illness affecting the therapist, vacations, or a move out of the area by family or therapist. Occasionally these circumstances may lead to the termination of therapy, but more often there are better ways of dealing with them.

As far as possible these issues should be discussed well in advance. If you are expecting to be away from your work for a time during the family's projected course of treatment, the family should be warned of this, and the dates mentioned, before treatment starts. In the same way we should ask the families we see whether, and when, they expect to be away. In either case there should be agreement in advance about how absences will be managed. Sometimes sessions can be scheduled to avoid vacations and other known forthcoming events. Longer breaks than usual can sometimes be used by the family to practise skills they have learned. If you are going to be absent for a long period, however, it may be best to arrange for a colleague to see the family in your absence. In any case, someone should be available to deal with issues which cannot wait until you return.

We have already considered, in Chapter 9, what we can do when some family members fail to attend. If the entire family fails to attend regularly, this is an issue which usually needs to be addressed when the family does come. When this, or other breaches of the contract by the family, become serious problems, a session may be devoted to discussing them, and it may be necessary to renegotiate the contract. If the renegotiated contract is then broken this may be an indication for ending treatment.

Dealing with illnesses in families can present problems. While physical illness can afflict both therapist and family members, it can also be used by family members as an excuse for non-attendance. If you have doubts about whether illnesses reported in family members are genuine, it is usually best to discuss these openly with the family. If therapy seems unlikely to be effective without the 'sick' member, whether the sickness is a 'genuine' physical illness or not, this may be a good reason to suggest suspending therapy until the person concerned has recovered. A new course of treatment, based on a new contract, may be offered when all necessary people can attend.

The absence or sickness of family members may be manifestations of the problems which have brought the family to therapy. It makes little sense to suspend or terminate therapy because of these problems. Discontinuing treatment, or threatening to, is not always the best way of dealing with these difficulties. Through working with those family members who do attend it is sometimes possible to get the absentee members to come, and even to make beneficial changes in the family system without their being present.

Finally, it is important always to remember that we have an ethical responsibility to see families through, once we have accepted them for treatment, as long as they wish us to continue treating them. If we become incapacitated, or move away, we must ensure that they are properly handed over to the care of colleagues. Similarly, if families have to move away from us, we should do everything we can to put them in touch with help in their new locality, if that is their wish.

Summary

Bringing the treatment of a family to an end requires careful preparation. If a time- or session-limited contract has been made the family should be better prepared for termination than when an 'open' contract has existed.

Therapy may end on the initiative of either the therapist or the family. Termination may be indicated either because the agreed goals have been achieved, because the family has acquired the skills to resolve the remaining problems on its own, because treatment has proved ineffective, or because the family does not wish to continue.

When therapy ends, the changes that have occurred should be identified, and long-range goals discussed. The family's progress, strengths and resources should be the focus of closing interviews, and an affirming, optimistic attitude is usually the best one for the therapist to take. Tasks and rituals, which may have metaphorical significance, can keep memories of the therapy, and reframed attitudes, in the minds of the family.

Closure may bring out feelings related to past losses, and the therapist should be alert for these and ready to deal with them. Caution should be exercised in arranging follow-up, lest families interpret the plans to mean that relapse is expected.

Plans to deal with necessary disruptions of a regular schedule of sessions should, whenever possible, be made well in advance. When other disruptions occur, both the stated reasons, and any underlying factors, should be explored. When interruptions are therapist-related, it is the therapist's duty to make suitable arrangements to meet the clients' needs, including referral to colleagues if need be.

Chapter 16
Teaching and Learning Family Therapy

Family therapy is practised by, and therefore taught to, people from various mental health disciplines notably social work, clinical psychology and psychiatry. Professionals from other groups, for example nursing and occupational therapy, are also learning family therapy. There has also emerged a new professional group, those who have not previously trained in another field.

The pioneers of family therapy came from various disciplines, but many were physicians, usually psychiatrists – for example, Midelfort, Ackerman, Bowen, Wynne, Lidz, Whitaker, John E. Bell, Laing, Boszormenyi-Nagy and Minuchin. But there were notable exceptions, such as Haley, Weakland, Satir, Watzlawick and Bateson. Today the proportion of physicians among those practising family therapy is probably lower.

Much family therapy training is structured to meet the needs of students already trained in other professions. Family therapy concepts and skills are also taught as a part of social work, psychiatry, clinical psychology, child care work, nursing and other courses. This does not make graduates of these courses fully trained family therapists, but exactly how much you need to know to set yourself up in practice as a family therapist is not generally agreed. In many jurisdictions anyone can legally do this, so it is wise for those seeking family therapy to check the training and credentials of their prospective therapists. A university degree or diploma in family therapy (and such degrees and diplomas are becoming increasingly available), are indications that the practitioner has received training and has reached an acceptable level of proficiency in the field.

The American Association for Marriage and Family Therapy (AAMFT)[1] sets rigorous membership standards covering specialized academic training and supervised professional experience. It also examines and accredits centres which provide training in marital and family therapy. It requires its members to have a graduate degree in marital and family therapy, or its equivalent. Courses in the following subjects are required for such a degree:

---

[1] 112 South Alfred Street, Alexandria, Virginia 22314-3061, USA

- Human development
- Marital and family studies
- Marital and family therapy
- Professional studies
- Research methodology

Members must also have had:

- 200 hours of supervision in the practice of marital and family therapy, of which no more than 100 hours may be in group supervision.
- 1500 hours of clinical experience of marital and family therapy.
- 2 years' work experience, after the graduate degree and while receiving supervision from an AAMFT-approved supervisor.

Whether family therapy should be a separate discipline, like dentistry or veterinary medicine, or whether it should remain primarily a field of practice in which professionals from other disciplines can choose to specialize, like hypnotherapy, is not agreed. There is a case for it remaining as one of the treatment skills possessed by therapists who are adept also in other approaches. Such therapists can choose which approach to use, according to the needs of their clients. On the other hand there is also a need for expert, specialist family therapists, who will make this their main, or even their only, field of practice. Such experts can act as consultants to other therapists, treat some of the more complex cases themselves, and play major roles in teaching family therapy and advancing the subject through research.

Who learns family therapy?

Family therapy is taught to three main categories of students:

(1) Those training in some other discipline, such as psychiatry, social work, psychology or nursing.
(2) Established practitioners of one of the above disciplines, or a related one.
(3) Students who have not previously trained in another discipline and are not currently doing so.

To become a fully competent family therapist, able to practise independently, a period of full-time instruction is desirable, though part-time training can be effective also. Those with some professional experience in the mental health field often prove better equipped to undertake this training than those who lack such experience, and a range of varied life experiences, as well as emotional maturity and a secure family life, are helpful too.

Figley and Nelson (1989) surveyed members of the American Family Therapy Association and approved supervisors of the AAMFT. Those who participated, a total of 372, 60% male, 40% female and 94% Caucasian, completed a questionnaire which asked for their opinions on the most important skills and personal traits needed by family therapists. It is interesting that about one-half of the top 'generic skills' identified were considered by the authors as 'more appropriately described as "personal traits".' It seems therefore that the presence of certain traits may be important factors to be taken into account in the selection of family therapy trainees.

Part-time training courses are offered in many centres. These will naturally spread the training over a longer period which may be an advantage in that it gives the student a longer time to consolidate his or her skills before leaving formal training. Part-time courses can provide sound training, and many family therapists have trained part-time.

Quite apart from formal training courses in family therapy, there is much to be said for providing an introduction to the field for all who are training in any of the mental health disciplines. This should provide an understanding of what family therapy is, and when it may be useful, without aiming to make each student a family therapist.

The different possible learning experiences

It is helpful to distinguish training, teaching, supervision and consultation. Wendhorf (1984) pointed out that supervision or training are often confused with therapy and consultation. He uses 'training' as a 'general term meaning the transfer of knowledge and skills', while 'supervision' is the 'hierarchical arrangement of training in which a superior "oversees", evaluates, suggests, gives feedback to, pushes or advises a trainee'. 'Consultation' means 'the giving of feedback and suggestions but with no hierarchical training relationship necessarily involved'. 'Teaching' is not differentiated from training by Wendhorf (1984), but the term is perhaps best used in this context to describe the more formal conveying of knowledge, as in lectures and seminars, though it can be used also in a broader sense.

Methods of learning family therapy

The means whereby students learn family therapy probably vary as much as the various schools of therapy vary in their approach to treating families. For example, an issue on which there appear to be diametrically opposed views, is that of whether or not training should include an examination and review of the trainees's own family background and experiences. In some centres these are explored in depth, with role-playing exercises and an examination of the trainee's current feelings towards, and relationships with, his or her own family. In others, nothing of this sort is done.

At the 1980 meeting of the American Orthopsychiatric Association there were several presentations on family therapy training. Views expressed on this issue varied from those of Epstein and Bishop (whose work I have referred to previously), who said that going into trainees' own family experiences was quite unnecessary and an unwarranted intrusion into their private lives, to those of Philip Guerin, of the Centre for Family Learning, New Rochelle, NY, who maintained that it was important to do this, and stressed it strongly in his description of the training programme at New Rochelle.

The wide divergence of views on this matter was also clear from the review of the literature on family therapy and supervision by Liddle and Halpin (1978). Liddle himself, however, believes that work with the trainee's family is not relevant to the learning of a therapeutic model orientated towards solving presenting problems within a family contract (Liddle, 1980). In this latter paper Liddle contrasts his approach with that of Murray Bowen, who required each of his trainees to complete a 'family voyage' with his or her family of origin.

Keller and Protinsky (1984) described what they called a 'self-management model for supervision' in marriage and family therapy, and adopted a point of view similar to Bowen's. They used 'a model of supervision that places emphasis on increasing self-awareness and the therapeutic management-of-self in the clinical setting'. They find Bowen's 'three-generational emphasis' useful in understanding how family interactional patterns are transmitted, and particularly the patterns of triangulation in which people, including therapists, get involved.

Keller and Protinsky (1984) required each 'supervisee' to present a personal three-generational genogram. The supervisee's family of origin is then carefully examined and probed. That person's videotape therapy material is then presented, and the supervisor and the other 'supervisees' scrutinize it for 'evidences of his/her management-of-self processes'.

Like Bowen, Keller and Protinsky (1984) pay much attention to the process of *triangulation* – the tendency of two people to draw a third person into their relationship, especially when the relationship is in difficulty. Triangles, as Bowen (1978) has repeatedly emphasized in his writings, are commonly found in troubled families. When spouses are in conflict they may involve a child and either, or both, of them may try to use that child as an ally, or in some other way, in their dispute. A parent/child pair, or two children in a family, may similarly triangulate a third family member; or someone in the extended family, or outside it altogether, may be triangulated in by family members. Patterns of triangulation in therapists' families of origin may, Keller and Protinski (1984) believe, be repeated in their interactions with their clients, supervisors and peers. Their paper describes how they assist therapists to be aware of such tendencies, and thus avoid reacting in ways which may not be therapeutically useful.

Coppersmith (1985) reviewed the concept of 'triads', as it is used in family therapy. She pointed out that the ability to 'think in threes', and to analyse complex triads, is a skill required by family therapists. Indeed she stated that teaching triadic theory is 'a crucial aspect of family therapy training'. As an aid to teaching this she developed an exercise, involving a series of role-played simulations, to be enacted and discussed by trainees. These range from 'a simple non-problematic triadic organization to a complex, potentially problematic triadic system' (Coppersmith, 1985, page 62). She found this to be a useful way of teaching both beginners and experienced therapists seeking further training.

It is not difficult to see how self-knowledge, and an understanding of one's family of origin and one's current family, might be of help in dealing with an emotionally challenging family situation. Yet whether such understanding *does* make for better therapy has not been established. Many effective therapists have not undergone an examination of their families of origin. Much may also depend on the style of therapy the therapist will be using. Examining one's own family background may be more important for those who use a 'Bowenian', or extended family systems approach, and perhaps also for those who use experiential methods, than for therapists of other schools.

Family therapy training usually consists of a combination of theoretical instruction and supervised practical experience, whether or not trainees are required or encouraged to examine their own family backgrounds. Theoretical knowledge may be obtained from formal teaching experiences, such as lectures, seminars and tutorial classes. It should be supplemented by reading the relevant literature. There has been an explosion of literature in our field over the course of the last 30 years, so that students, especially when they are first embarking on the study of family therapy, require guidance on what to read. (One of the purposes of this book is to provide such guidance. In addition to the references, a list of relevant journals appears in Appendix A.)

Audiovisual aids

The practical aspects of family therapy are learned by assessing and treating families under supervision. Audiovisual aids are used extensively in this process. I have referred in Chapter 1 to Minuchin's emphasis, in the early days of family therapy, on the importance of the 'live' observation of therapy, as opposed to the acceptance of trainees' reports of what they believed happened during their therapy sessions. It is probably better to supervise all therapy 'live', but it is especially important in family therapy, when there are several people to observe, and a great deal is going on, both between family members and between therapist and family.

The simplest audiovisual aid is the one-way observation screen. This enables observers to watch therapy without themselves being in the therapy room. It is sometimes called a 'one-way mirror', but the 'therapy room' side does not necessarily, nor invariably, have a mirror surface. A sound amplification system enables those viewing the therapy to hear what is happening in the therapy room. This arrangement is the easiest way of conducting live supervision of therapy.

Persaud (1987) raised the interesting question of what effect the one-way mirror has on the process of family therapy. He reviewed several papers that reported comparisons of subjects' behaviour in the presence of a mirror with their behaviour in the absence of one. For example, college students, all of whom had said that cheating was morally wrong, were given a timed IQ test and a chance to work illicitly beyond the time limit. Initially 70% cheated in this way, whereas when a mirror was introduced the rate was reduced to 7% (Diener & Wallbom, 1976). It seems, from this and other articles Persaud (1987) quotes, that the presence of the mirror may affect behaviour. How much, and for how long, and whether the effect fades as subjects get used to the mirror is not clear.

As family therapy has developed, relatively inexpensive closed-circuit television and videotape equipment has become available. Closed-circuit television can serve the same purpose as observation through a one-way screen, especially when a large audience, or one at a distance from the therapy room, is to view the therapy. The therapeutic uses of videotape replay have been outlined in Chapter 11, but videotape equipment is also invaluable as a training device. It can serve a number of purposes:

- Review by therapists of their own work.
- Review by supervisors of the work of their trainees.
- Demonstration of therapy techniques, as when the work of experienced therapists is reviewed by learners. Edited videotapes, some with commentary, are available from many centres.
- Review of the progress of therapist and family, when serial videotapes are made and kept for later use.
- Reviewing, and learning from, role-playing exercises undertaken as part of a training programme.

Kramer and Reitz (1980) described a design for the training of family therapists which used the videotape playback of role-playing exercises to groups of eight to ten students. Trainees were able to see themselves and other members of the group in a series of therapeutic situations, the complexity of which could gradually be increased. This led to sessions in which students learned to increase their 'personal awareness'. By such means students seen as aloof in therapy, or having recurrent difficulties in dealing with certain types of family, can be helped to overcome such problems. Personal relationship problems which may be affecting a therapist's work – as when a therapist has to deal with someone who reminds him of his dominant father, or the sister with whom he feels rivalry – can be rehearsed and explored, for example by setting up a role-played session with a critical supervisor. Students can explore their own appearance on the screen, watching a 'video portrait' of themselves, while being coached in expressing, through their appearance and behaviour, what they want convey to the group and, ultimately, to the families they treat.

Objectives

A teaching programme requires clearly defined objectives. The objectives set in teaching family therapy will depend on the model of family functioning and therapy used in the setting in which the teaching is to be done. There is a need for an explicit theory of how families change (Liddle, 1980). As therapists acquire clinical skills, they can start investigating other models and techniques, and incorporate what they find helpful into their own practice.

Learning family therapy skills

Cleghorn and Levin (1973) defined three types of family therapy skills which must be learned. These are *perceptual*, *conceptual* and *executive* skills. This remains, to this day, a useful model.

Conceptual skills can be taught by various means. The McMaster group used a combination of a 'semi-programmed text', reading materials in which theoretical concepts were explained, and tutorials in which the concepts the trainees had learned were integrated, and problems and issues which remained unclear were resolved. The concepts taught were naturally those upon which the McMaster Model of therapy was based, but this approach could equally well be used to teach any other conceptual scheme.

At each stage it is a good plan to test students' knowledge of what has been taught so far. Conceptual knowledge can be tested using multiple choice methods. If the trainee has not come to a satisfactory understanding of the relevant basic concepts, learning perceptual and executive skills may prove difficult.

Perceptual skills, like conceptual skills, can be learnt without seeing families in therapy. Instead, videotapes of real or simulated families, and role playing, can be used. If, for example, it were the McMaster Model which was being taught, trainees would be asked to rate families on problem-solving, communication, roles, affective responsiveness and involvement, and behaviour control, taking into account the sub-categories of each. Their responses would be discussed in the group and with the teacher. With practice, and appropriate feedback, trainees' skills in perceiving the processes occurring in family groups improve.

Perceptual skills can also be learned by the use of 'scenarios', that is short, one- or two-paragraph summaries of families. After reading each of these, the trainees rate them according to the various categories being used. There must also be categories for no data or insufficient data, since it is important to know when additional information is needed.

Training in *executive skills* should be carried out principally while students work with families, although these skills can be practised initially using simulated families, made up of groups of trainees. The supervisor watches through a one-way screen, or on closed-circuit television, and gives feedback. This may be done in breaks during therapy sessions, by using an intercommunicating phone, or after sessions have ended. Alternatively, videotapes or, less satisfactorily, audiotapes of sessions may subsequently be reviewed. Live supervision has the advantage that the supervisor can, when necessary, intervene during the session. When sessions are being recorded for later review, beginning students may get into difficulties if feedback is not available when things start to go wrong. For students with more experience, review of recordings can be satisfactory. Evaluation of executive skills may be achieved by observing videotapes of students' work, and rating this according to specific criteria.

Liddle and Saba (1982) described a model for teaching family therapy at the introductory level. They drew a parallel between the process of therapy, using Minuchin's (1974) structural model and Haley's (1976) more strategic one, and that of training family therapists. Just as therapy may be viewed in stages (Haley, 1976), so may training. According to Liddle and Saba (1982), three stages characterize both therapy and training: *joining*, *restructuring* and *consolidation*.

Phase I, *joining*, requires the student 'to suspend . . . his existing view of reality', and to adopt, 'at least in experimental spirit, ideas about the etiology and treatment of human problems which are often quite alien to the student's previous training and experience' (Liddle & Saba, 1982, page 65). Joining the training programme is thus seen as analogous to joining a family. This is the first stage of structural therapy, in which the therapist tentatively, but without being engulfed by the family's way of behaving and looking at things, becomes a member of the family group. The content of this phase has much in common with Cleghorn and Levin's (1973) stage of learning conceptual skills.

Phase II is that of *restructuring*. In structural therapy, this is the main change-producing phase of treatment. Similarly, the family therapy student, at this stage, is challenged 'to learn and experiment with new concepts from differing schools'. This has much in common with the learning of executive skills.

In phase III, *consolidation*, 'students are required to take personal and theoretical risks in integrating the various approaches into their professional identities'.

Liddle and Saba (1982) reported that the course, which introduced students to a variety of schools of therapy, had three main areas of impact:

(1)   It sparked student interest in clinical training in family therapy.
(2)   It affected the lives of some of the students, in that it made them more aware of their current families, and their families of origin. Especially after studying the work of Bowen, Boszormenyi-Nagy and Framo, students asked to be allowed to write family autobiographies.
(3)   It affected the students' views of human problems. One student is quoted as saying:

> 'My eyes have been opened to a whole new way of viewing pathology. Clients are no longer isolates to me. I see them in relation to their environment which includes the family as well as myself, the therapist.'

The content of training

Precisely what is taught in any course of training will depend on the orientation of those teaching it. We have seen that there are many schools of family therapy, and it is possible to teach students the theoretical bases of a variety of them. But when actually teaching trainees to work with families it is necessary to use a specific, even if flexible, model. This need not be derived from one particular school of therapy, but may be an eclectic one derived from various sources. An example of such an approach was set out in Chapter 13.

So precisely what is taught will depend on the assessment and therapy model that is being taught. The paper by Figley and Nelson (1989) lists the 'top 100 generic skills' arising out of their survey of teachers of family therapy. Tomm and Wright (1979) were more specific in their listing of the 'functions', 'competencies' and 'skills' needed for each of the four stages of therapy: engagement, problem identification, change facilitation and termination.

Supervision

We have seen that expert supervision, especially live supervision, is a central feature of any good training programme for family therapists. Indeed the would-be student of family therapy might be well advised to avoid any 'training' centre that does not have a good system of supervision. This means that proper audiovisual aids are freely available, with adequate supporting technical staff.

It seems that the term 'live supervision' was coined by Braulio Montalvo (1973). In addition to making some of the points about supervision which we have already discussed, he suggested that the supervisor and the trainee should define in advance the limits within which they will operate, including the situations when it is obligatory for the trainee to do as the supervisor says, and those in which the supervisor's suggestions may be modified; and that the supervisor should not unduly restrict the trainee's freedom to explore and operate within the family, and that if this does happen the trainee should tell the supervisor so. He also recommended that the supervisor should endeavour to use procedures that fit the trainee's style and preferred way of thinking.

Montalvo (1973) also advised that the direction of therapy be worked out before each session, and reviewed after it. The better the advance planning the less likely it is that the therapist and supervisor will have to consult during the session. The intensity of supervision, and the frequency of interventions by the supervisor, may be expected to lessen as the trainee gains experience.

Live supervision is best provided by having the supervisor watch through a one-way observation screen, or on closed-circuit television. Some supervisors like to be able to communicate with their trainees by telephone, but an alternative is the 'bug-in-the-ear', a device which enables the supervisor to talk to the therapist while the latter is interviewing the family, but without the need for the ringing of a telephone. Its drawbacks are that the therapist cannot reply to what the supervisor says, and may face the difficult task of listening to the 'bug' while not appearing discourteous to the family by disregarding it. If either of these methods is used, it has been suggested by both Haley (1976) and Liddle (1980) that only one or two ideas should be communicated to the trainee in the course of one call.

Another arrangement that can work well is for the trainee to leave the room during the session for one or more discussions with the supervisor. It is also possible for the supervisor to tell the therapist when to take a break to discuss progress, by a pre-arranged signal, such as a knock on the door (if there is no telephone intercom system). Whatever the plan, the family should be told about it in advance. Families seldom raise objections to having supervisors watch, and intervene if necessary, especially as they are told that in this type of therapy the input of another therapist, or a team, often enables them to be helped more effectively and quickly. When the situation is properly explained, most families are pleased to learn that more than one person is involved in helping them.

The process of supervision differs from that of therapy in that the supervisor must consider both the family system, and how the family may be helped to resolve its problems, and also the therapist/family system. It is this latter aspect that is the essence of family therapy supervision. A real danger that all family therapists face is that of getting involved emotionally with the families they treat. This can impede therapy or even make it ineffective. Expert supervision can help avoid this danger.

Quinn et al. (1985) offered an interesting model for the group supervision of advanced trainees. They call it the 'stuck-case' model. These authors established a special 'stuck-case clinic', for advanced trainees to bring families to when little or no progress was being made. They found it a useful way of bringing new thinking to difficult or 'stuck' families.

Ungar (2006) discusses the special challenges that supervision presents when post-modern methods are used, and describes how he approaches his work as a 'postmodern supervisor'.

Learning to supervise

The importance of the supervision of family therapy is such that considerable attention has been paid to the process in the literature. Liddle et al. (1984, page 139), however, commented that:

> 'Although the literature on supervision is impressive, it lacks the vital component specifying how supervisors best acquire this knowledge. Considerable clinical experience does not automatically qualify one to be a supervisor, but rather, just as the skills of family therapy can be taught, so also a separate and definable set of supervisory skills can and should be taught systematically to therapists who wish to be competent supervisors.'

Liddle et al. (1984), in the paper from which the above is quoted, describe the 'supervisor extern program' (SEP) at the Family Systems program of the Institute for Juvenile Research in Chicago. The SEP comprises the following components:

- Live observation of supervision.
- A theory seminar.
- Opportunity for supervisors to receive feedback on their supervisory skills and styles (through videotape supervision, and case discussions with trainees).
- Learning and support from peers.
- The practice of the supervisory role and skills at their primary place of work.

Liddle and his co-authors point out that the above list might be suited to any therapist training programme. There are, moreover, many principles common to therapy and supervision. For example the need to set goals, think in stages, be sensitive to contextual cues, establish rapport (called joining by these authors) and challenge realities, all apply to both. Yet there are specific supervisory skills also, and the training system itself, and its components, require that the supervisor has available an adequate conceptual map of the system.

Heath and Storm (1985) described a four-stage course in marriage and family therapy supervision. This is adapted from the scheme described by Liddle and his colleagues (1984). It had four objectives:

(1) To encourage student supervisors to adapt and use their therapy theories as supervision theories.
(2) To facilitate the development of live supervision skills.
(3) To have student supervisors become expert in supervising student therapists with a variety of theoretical orientations.
(4) To provide student supervisors and student therapists with close and consistent supervision.

The course has two components, a seminar and a practicum. The seminar took up 2 hours per week, and aimed to develop the supervisors' conceptual skills. The practicum comprised four stages:

(1) *Stage one*: during this stage the supervisors, as a group, watched the live supervision of a student therapist by one of the authors of the article. The other instructor was with the trainee supervisors, and helped them begin to think as supervisors, rather than as therapists.
(2) *Stage two*: this was the stage of 'individual participation'. The students watched the authors while they supervised family therapy, asking questions and discussing the rationale of what was done. Each was also assigned three therapists to supervise in the next stage.
(3) *Stage three*: during this stage the supervisors received live supervision of their supervision.
(4) *Stage four*: this was the stage of independent supervision.

These two related schemes for training supervisors, though expensive in the time of the instructors, seem to offer the prospect of improving what has in the past been something of a hit-or-miss process.

Consultation

Consultation is another means whereby therapists may both improve their skills, and receive help in treating families. It differs from supervision in two ways. There is no hierarchical distinction between therapist and consultant and consultation is usually an occasional, rather than a regular event; though there is no fundamental reason why a therapist should not seek consultation, or a consultant offer it, on a regular basis.

Bullock and Kobayashi (1978) described a number of situations in which 'live consultation' may be helpful. These are:

(1) Conflict between therapist and patient. The therapist may not be aware of this and the consultant may be able to intervene before the conflict escalates in a therapeutically unhelpful way.
(2) When the therapist becomes 'regulated' by the family, and starts to behave in ways similar to the dysfunctional behaviour of the family.

(3) When the therapist is drifting from the task. Therapists sometimes inadvertently stray from the course necessary to meet the goals and strategies which have been set out.

(4) The 'eureka' effect. This term is used to describe a situation in which the consultant becomes aware of a therapeutic move which would better help the family towards its goals, than the strategy currently being used by the therapist.

(5) When it appears that it may be helpful to create a therapeutic coalition. Thus the consultant may intervene to bring about an alignment of two parties against a third, when this seems likely to increase family members' motivation.

(6) When there is a misreading by the therapist of the family situation or the significance of members' statements.

The above circumstances might also be reasons for intervention by a supervisor if one were involved. In most of them the therapist would probably be unaware of just what had gone wrong with the therapy. Consultation is usually sought when unduly slow progress is being made. The consultant's task is to help discover what has gone wrong or, preferably, find a better approach than that used hitherto.

The responsibility to seek consultation when this is indicated is one of our ethical responsibilities. It is not an admission of failure or inadequacy, for no therapist can expect to succeed, unaided, with every family. On the contrary, it is a sign of a mature and well-trained professional who realizes that he or she has limitations, and that good practice involves having consultants available and using them when necessary. The 'stuck-case clinic' (Quinn et al., 1985) is an example of how these situations may be tackled.

Max van Trommel (1984) suggests that there are three levels at which consultation can occur:

(1) Expanding the field of the therapist but focusing on the family. Consultation initially places emphasis on the family with whom the therapist has reached a deadlock. This may be sufficient to free up the therapeutic process.

(2) Expanding the field of the family. The progress of therapy may be impeded because of the relationship of the family with other systems. These may be the family of origin, a friend, a couple with whom the family is friendly, a school, a neighbourhood, an employer, a welfare system or the referring person or agency.

(3) Expanding the field into a 'metadomain' to focus on the therapist/family system. The system with which the family has become 'inextricably entangled' need not, van Trommel (1984) points out, be another person or organization but may be none other than the family therapist who is working with the family. The therapist/family system may therefore need to be addressed in consultation. If steps 1 and 2 do not lead to satisfactory progress, this area should be explored.

As therapists we have the difficult tasks of both observing and partici-pating in the systems of which we become part. van Trommel (1984) quoted Keeney (1982) who pointed out that 'there is no such thing as an observer-free description of a situation'. A system can only be analysed as a mutual interactional process between the system and some other 'functioning unity . . . for instance, the therapist himself' (van Trommel, 1984, page 471).

van Trommel describes a way of providing consultation to the 'family-plus-therapist'. This comprises the following stages:

- A pre-session discussion. The therapist provides basic information about the family, such as names, ages, who lives in the household, the aims of therapy and the strategies the therapist has used. Data about the content of the problem are not provided, since the consultation team (and this type of consultation is usually provided by a team) is concerned with a higher level of abstraction than that of the family processes themselves. For the second part of the pre-session discussion, the therapist is absent, and the team draws up hypotheses about what has gone wrong with the therapist/family system.
- A consultation session. The interviewer, a member of the team, inter-views the therapist-plus-family, using circular questions (Palazzoli et al., 1980; Penn, 1982). The questions are designed primarily to elicit information about the functioning of the system under investigation. Questions are asked equally of therapist and family. The team may telephone-in advice or comments, and the interviewer may ask the team for advice.
- An intersession break. The therapist stays with the family. This empha-sizes that it is the therapist/family system that is being investigated. Meanwhile the interviewer and the rest of the team discuss the infor-mation obtained. An intervention is then formulated.
- An intervention. During this short session, the family and therapist are informed of the intervention.
- A post-session discussion, with team and therapist present. The content of the intervention is not discussed, and this stage consists simply of a brief, general summing-up to conclude the procedure.

van Trommel (1984) includes two examples of the above process, and also a discussion of it. Those considering using the approach he recom-mends should study his paper first.

Summary

Family therapy is taught to a wide variety of students, not all of whom aim to become specialists in this field. Increasing attention is being paid to defining what should be taught to students at different levels, and to the setting of professional standards for marital and family therapists. Formal

teaching, supervised clinical work, role playing and watching other therapists, live or on videotape, are all valuable components of training programmes. Modern training makes much use of the 'live' viewing of therapy,
and for this adequate audiovisual aids are essential. How necessary it is for
therapists to explore their families of origin, and their current families,
remains unclear. It may depend on the model of therapy to be used.

Well-defined objectives are necessary in training therapists, as they are in
therapy. Means of assessing students' progress in meeting the objectives
should be built into programmes. The content of training depends on the
theoretical model to be taught, but it should cover all phases of therapy,
from joining and assessment to termination and follow-up.

It is important for teachers to learn the specific skills of supervision. These
are not the same as therapy skills. Therapists should also be trained to use
consultation when it is needed. Marital and family therapies are complex
undertakings and when progress is unsatisfactory, the seeking of consultation is one of our ethical responsibilities.

Chapter 17
Research in Family Therapy

Early work in the field of family therapy was mainly descriptive. The pioneers examined families from various points of view and described what they perceived to be going on in them. They also formulated ideas about how families' ways of functioning might help cause and/or maintain symptoms in individual family members. This led them to devise ways of intervening in families. Sometimes their interventions seemed effective but their initial studies were inevitably tentative and exploratory. Putting the field on to a scientific footing has been a challenge family therapy has faced ever since.

Originally, family research and family therapy were carried out by the same people (Wynne, 1983). Indeed research came first and therapy was initially a secondary activity. During the 1960s therapists and researchers diverged. Haley (1978) pointed out that originally therapist and researcher were 'of the same species (although the therapist had a more second-class status)'. By the time Haley was writing this, however, it seemed to him that, 'the research stance and the posture of the therapist [were] quite opposite'.

We have seen that many of the early family researchers and therapists studied the families of patients with schizophrenia. Various processes occurring in such families were identified, including the double-bind, schism and skew, pseudomutuality, pseudohostility and mystification. These discoveries led to further questions. Did these processes in the families *cause* the symptoms of schizophrenia in the afflicted family members? Or could they be the *result* of the schizophrenic disorder in the individual (a less often asked question)? Does the resolution or modification of the supposedly pathological family processes lead to resolution or modification of the symptoms of schizophrenia? Are similar processes found in families in which no one is schizophrenic?

It proved harder to answer questions like the foregoing ones than it was to describe what was happening in the families, except for the last question, to which it soon became clear that the answer was yes. Most of the earlier authors who wrote about 'schizophrenic' families acknowledged that the processes they described could be observed in other families. The double-bind, for example, seemed to be widespread, but it was suggested by some that its use was more frequent and intense in the families of individuals with schizophrenia than in other families.

Much of the early research into schizophrenia was unproductive, insofar as finding a cure for schizophrenia was concerned. Psychopharmacological approaches to treatment gained more acceptance than family therapy ones during the ensuing years. This early work did, however, draw the attention of many therapists to families and family systems. It also raised questions about the relationship between the disorders of individuals and the characteristics of the families of which they were members.

As the field advanced, therapists started trying new techniques that aimed to produce changes in family systems, rather than working with individuals. Many found they could produce changes more quickly than they had been able to do using traditional psychotherapy techniques, sometimes dramatically so. They concluded that the progress of many of those they had treated as individuals had been held back as a result of the characteristics of the family systems of which they had been part.

Unfortunately this new-found enthusiasm sometimes became uncritical. A period was entered upon when a belief in a 'systems approach' to human problems became an article of faith among many, rather than a belief based upon consideration of research data. Research assumed a lower profile than it had done, and was increasingly left to 'family researchers', while the therapists got on with the 'real' work.

The need for family therapy research

Gurman (1983) suggested that research findings are needed by five categories of 'consumer'. These are:

(1) Practising clinicians and students of family therapy who need, and want, to know about the factors that affect clinical outcomes, as a guide to their clinical practice.
(2) 'Theoretician/clinicians' who want to understand the mechanisms of change common to different treatment methods, as well as learning of findings of immediate application.
(3) Practising clinicians, and students and teachers of psychotherapy, 'who are presently outside the family therapy circle'. Gurman expressed the hope that this group may be open to 'the paradigmatic shift that is family therapy'.
(4) The families, that is our potential patients or clients, who want to know how best they may be helped with their problems.
(5) Public policy makers and third-party providers of therapists' fees.

The need for clear thinking

Much that has been written about family therapy in its journals is obscure. It is as if the employment of 'new epistemologies' has been taken to mean that a new jargon is also needed. The very use of the word 'epistemology' perhaps sets the scene for writing which is often as circular as the processes in families are said to be. For example:

'Evolutionary feedback is the idea suggested by (Prigogine et al.): that random oscillations in self-regulating systems can go beyond the limits of self-correction and suddenly and unpredictably become part of deviation-amplifying process, radically restructuring the system and creating increased (less probable) complexity in the system. It could be argued that this is still a cybernetic model, utilizing the basic assumptions of a cybernetic epistemology, e.g. information-guided, circular, mutual causal loops as a basic aspect of psychosocial reality. An evolutionary epistemology makes explicit the levels of organization that are already implicit in a cybernetic one.' (Schwartzman, 1984, pages 231–232).

The above could surely have been stated more simply and clearly. The use of 'utilizing' for 'using' is symptomatic of a wider problem.

Another characteristic of the family therapy literature has been the substitution of polemic for data. As we have seen, one Gerald Erickson (1988) dared to question the value of one of family therapy's most sacred cows, systems theory. Predictably, the response was an outcry. The champions of systems theory hastily put pen to paper – or sat down at their computers – to respond. The resulting articles had titles like, 'Furniture for firewood – blaming the systems paradigm' (Constantine, 1989), which attributed the problem to the use by Erickson of 'bad systems theory'; 'Muddied Batesonian waters' (Morris, 1989), which attributed the problem to a misunderstanding of Bateson's writings; and 'Wrong map, wrong territory' (de Shazer, 1989). The last named author included some dialogue in the style of Doctor Watson describing a conversation with Sherlock Holmes. This is quite entertaining.

'Holmes had some journals strewn about on his table. He spoke first:
"See what you make of this first article, friend Watson." He tossed a journal across to me, and returned to his silence, the rest of the journals spread out before him.
   I looked at the essay before me and started reading, and although it appeared to be in English, I found myself quite unable to discern its meaning.
"Holmes, what is this? It looks like a learned article but it seems absurd."
"But, even if it is a learned article, Watson, what do you make of it?"
"Holmes, it is certainly obscure."
"Obscure enough, Watson."
"Perhaps it is a cypher, then. Well, what do you make of it, Holmes?"
"It does seem to be a cypher, Watson. I am fairly familiar with all forms of secret writings, and am, myself, the author of a trifling monograph upon the subject, in which I analyse one hundred and sixty cyphers; but, I confess, this is entirely new to me . . ."'

Entertaining this may be, but it hardly advances the scientific understanding of our field. Indeed none of the articles referred to, Erickson's included, contains much in the way of scientific data.

Approaches to family therapy research

In *The State of the Art in Family Therapy Research* (Wynne, 1988) 17 'leading family clinicians and researchers discuss the premises and design of optimal family therapy research, given present-day concepts, methods, and practical constraints'. This quotation, from the publishers' back cover 'blurb', does justice to the book, a valuable source of information for anyone considering entering the difficult field of family therapy research.

The early research in the family field was 'primitive' (Wynne, 1983). It mostly lacked controls. The disturbed families were not usually matched with comparable undisturbed families studied in the same way. Tests, self-report measures and rating-scales for use along with therapy had not been developed. 'Even worse,' Wynne (1983, page 114) says, 'We had very small samples of families.' Reports of the treatment of single families, or small series, were indeed common, as they are to this day.

Wynne (1983) may be unduly hard on himself and his colleagues from the early days, because the study of small groups and individual cases is probably an essential part of the development of new concepts and treatment methods. If a treatment method does not show signs of being effective in a small, uncontrolled study, there is little point in comparing it with other treatments, or with no treatment. But if it does appear effective when first tried, this may be an indication for investigating its value in a more rigorous way. Two questions then need to be asked. The first is whether the treatment is better than doing nothing, which is similar to asking whether the problem may be expected to clear up if untreated. The second is, how does it compare with other available treatments for the same condition? The comparison should consider effectiveness, the speed with which improvement occurs, cost, acceptability to those being treated, unwanted side effects, and whether any improvement achieved is maintained in the long term.

Wynne (1988) reviewed areas that family therapy research should address. First he raised the question of how family therapy should be defined. The conference on which the book he edited was based favoured the following definition:

'Family therapy is a psychotherapeutic approach that focuses on altering interactions between a couple, within a nuclear family or extended family, or between a family and other interpersonal systems, with the goal of alleviating problems initially presented by individual family members, family subsystems, the family as a whole, or other referral sources.' (Wynne, 1988, pages 250–252)

Wynne (1988) also pointed out the importance of theoretical studies. We need to know not only that family therapy works (when it does) but also how it works. He goes on to discuss the following important issues:

- The criteria for therapeutic change
- The specification of the model of intervention used
- The relative importance of research into the therapeutic process, as distinct from outcome research
- The selection of measures of family system functioning
- Data analysis

The desire of many workers to improve the scientific status of family therapy research has led to the gradual adoption of more rigorous methods. In research into the social and family aspects of schizophrenia, for example, the work of the Medical Research Council's Social Psychiatry Unit (described in *Expressed Emotion in Families*, by Leff & Vaughn, 1985, and discussed earlier) set a high standard.

Assessing and classifying families

Models for the assessment of families were discussed in Chapter 5. Assessment and classification are closely related. When assessing a family, with a view to placing it in some pre-determined classification, it is necessary to examine those aspects of family functioning used in the classification system being considered.

Fisher (1977), on the basis of a review of the literature, suggested that schemes for the classification of families fell into five groups, according to the parameters used. These schemes were based on, respectively:

- Style of adaptation
- Developmental family stage
- The initial problem or diagnosis of the identified patient
- Family theme or dimension
- Type of marital relationship

This list, derived from a review of various methods of classifying families, could in theory be the basis for the construction of a 'multiaxial' classification, in that it lists a number of separate, and presumably to some extent independent, features of families, as does the triaxial scheme outlined in Chapter 5.

Ideally families should be classified, for clinical purposes, according to whether or not they are disturbed and, if they are, on the basis of the type of disorder present. Attempts have indeed been made to do this, for example by Richter (1974). He distinguished 'family symptom neuroses', and 'family character neuroses', the latter group being divided into 'anxiety-neurotic families', 'paranoid families' and 'hysterical families'.

This method of classifying family disorders has not been adopted by family therapists, probably because it consists only of the application to families of labels devised for use with individuals. Moreover it is not based on research data. Examples of other attempts to categorize family disorders are the concept of Minuchin and his colleagues (1978) of 'psychosomatic families'; and the Milan group's 'families in schizophrenic transaction' (Palazzoli et al., 1978a). These also have not been generally adopted, and the reality of the concept of the 'psychosomatic family' has been challenged by, among others, Coyne and Anderson (1989), who pointed out that data promised when the original work was published in 1978 never appeared.

Although there are a number of ways of looking at families, including those in Fisher's (1977) list, we will here confine ourselves to two:

(1) Considering the family's developmental stage.
(2) Considering the family's way of functioning, the essence of which is how the members relate to, and interact with, each other.

Categorizing families by developmental stage

Categorizing families by developmental stage is a relatively straightforward undertaking. There are two points to be considered: the stage the family should have reached (based on the ages of the children, whether they have left home, and so on), and the stage it *has* reached. When these differ, it probably means the family is having difficulty negotiating one of the family developmental hurdles we have considered earlier.

Categorizing families by family functioning

Categorizing families on the basis of the nature of family interaction is more difficult. An early review of family interaction research appeared in the book *Research in Family Interaction: Readings and Commentary* (Winter & Ferriera, 1969). Another review, by Jules Riskin and Elaine Faunce, appeared in 1972. Riskin and Faunce were concerned with studies which examined the interaction of family members directly, rather than by means of questionnaires, individual interviews or clinical material. Their excellent paper makes it clear that the subject is highly complex, and the methodological problems considerable.

These authors also found that investigators and groups of investigators worked in relative isolation from other workers, interdisciplinary cooperation was generally poor and replication studies, in which a worker or group attempts to confirm findings reported by others, unsatisfactorily few. They discovered many contradictory findings. Nevertheless they found some encouraging signs of progress over the 20 years' history of research in family interaction. They also found some agreement in major areas, notably about the importance of certain variables in family interaction. These were 'humour', 'agreement–disagreement', 'support', 'positive affect', 'acknowledgment–commitment' and 'clarity of communication'. All these seemed, from the research reviewed, to be important factors in the study of family functioning.

Other considerations

There is more to family functioning than how family members interact. We have seen that many other aspects are addressed in the McMaster Model of Family Functioning (Epstein et al., 1978). This model is but one of many that have been proposed and an illustration of the complexity of the subject was provided by Fisher (1976), who reviewed research into family assessment. The studies reviewed concentrated on clinical assessment rather than on theories of family functioning. Twenty-nine schemes for assessing family functioning were reviewed, and there were big differences in the concepts used in them. Fisher managed to bring some sort of order into the data by dividing the assessment strategies used into four groups:

(1)   Single concept notions
(2)   Theoretical notions
(3)   Broadly based clinical lists
(4)   Empirically based approaches

Single concept notions emphasize either a limited range of assessment parameters, or redefine a range of dimensions as variants of a single concept. The single concepts Fisher identified were power, conflict and conflict resolution. These seemed to make sense insofar as these issues, especially conflict and its resolution, often bring families to therapy.

Theoretical orientation has been used as the basis for assessment procedures by such groups as that at the Philadelphia Child Guidance Clinic (Minuchin, 1974), which focused on the 'structural' aspects of the family; and the behaviourists (Hammerlynck et al., 1973) who concentrated on specific interactional behaviours, and assessed families according to the behaviours observed; treatment is then based on the assessment.

By *clinical lists* Fisher (1976) means lists of dimensions which have been found useful in clinical practice, although no great effort is made by those using them to tie the dimensions to an underlying theory. The Family Categories Schema, the predecessor of the McMaster Model of Family Functioning, is an example of this approach. It was considered by Fisher to be the one in which 'perhaps the best balance' had been achieved. The Process Model of Family Functioning (Steinhauer et al., 1984) is another example.

Empirically devised methods are usually based on the administration of scales, either to the family itself, or to observers who either watch the family perform certain tasks or observe them during therapy. The results may then be subject to factor analysis or other statistical procedures. One study (Otto, 1962) focused on family strengths, an unusual approach. Some marital couples were asked to list their strengths, and then met together as a group to discuss these strengths with a view to using them more effectively. The sessions were tape recorded and their content was used, together with material from a questionnaire previously administered, to identify 12 areas of family strengths.

Research on the process of family therapy

Defining the treatment given is probably the least difficult of the three research areas we are considering. Much of the family therapy literature consists of descriptions of therapy methods. It is important, though, to ensure that the therapy methods that are supposed to have been employed actually have been. Much of the family therapy research that has been reported in the literature seems to overlook this. An exception is a study reported by Crowe (1978). This compared three approaches to marital therapy. Forty-two couples were randomly allocated to one of three treatment groups. They were given either 'directive', 'interpretative' or 'supportive' therapy. All sessions were tape recorded. A sample of 40 statements by the therapist from each of four tapes randomly selected from each couple's therapy was analysed by 'blind' raters, that is raters who did not know which therapy method was supposed to be represented on each tape.

The raters correctly assigned 91.4% of the 'directive' tapes, 74.4% of the 'interpretative' tapes and 72.0% of the 'supportive' tapes. Their overall accuracy was 78.2%. While this result is better than chance and represents a significant degree of accuracy, it is nevertheless, as the author points out, less than ideal. It showed an overlapping of technique among the three approaches. It provides an example of the kind of checks which are necessary in well-designed research.

Not only do few research reports indicate that checks were made to discover whether the treatments being investigated were properly applied, but many reports do not even provide adequate descriptions of the intended treatment. To quote but one example, Slipp and Kressel (1978), reporting an attempt to compare 'insight' and 'problem-solving' approaches, give little information about the latter. They state only that it 'consisted of concrete problem-solving advice and emotional support', and that no interpretations were made and no material outside the subjects' conscious awareness was brought to their attention. 'Emotional support' was not defined, and the above description seems a generally inadequate one, especially when it is compared with the several pages spent discussing the results. There was also no attempt to rate what actually did happen during the therapy sessions, as opposed to what was intended. (These authors were, however, aware that there were methodological problems in their study, and commented upon some of them.)

It is not surprising that, with new therapy methods coming into use based on innovative ways of looking at human behaviour, some have questioned the appropriateness of applying traditional methods of research to them. Gurman (1983), however, advocated the employment of 'standard research methods'. He pointed out that such methods 'have already provided data of practical relevance to clinicians, patients and public policy makers', and considered that they should not be abandoned in haste.

Established research methods probably should not be abandoned at all, despite assertions by those whom Gurman termed 'the new epistemologists' (for example Colapinto (1979) and Sheehan et al. (1982)). The latter seem to feel that traditional research concepts are unsuited to the investigation of the newer therapy approaches they favour. But these 'ecosystemic epistemologists' seem at times to let their enthusiasm for new ideas get the better of their scientific objectivity. To quote Keeney and Sprenkle (1982, page 16):

> 'From the level of aesthetics, the therapist's participation in therapy has more to do with being alive than with creating specific outcomes. The immediate implication for therapy is that efforts to make therapeutic problem-solving conscious (e.g. creating packaged cookbook cures) may result in manipulative techniques that are not adequately coupled to the ecology of which they are part.'

Therapy must surely be concerned with specific outcomes. People come to us with particular problems, and ask that we assist them in making changes, whether it be in their family relationships, their ways of communicating with others, their instrumental functioning in various situations, their emotional states, their control over their children, or any one of a myriad of other issues. Certainly it is not necessary for our clients' problem-solving to occur at the conscious level. Yet if there is no describable and replicable therapeutic method, it is hard to see how any teachable body of knowledge can emerge. Nor would outcome research make any sense. For it to do so we must be able to define the process of which we are studying the outcome. Ambiguous and unclear statements, clang associations, alliterations, even poetic language, may have their place in therapy – perhaps because they are meaningful to the right cerebral hemisphere (see Watzlawick, 1978; Barker 1985, pages 21–22) – but they should not be used in the scientific reporting of our work.

Outcome research

The State of the Art in Family Therapy Research (Wynne, 1988) has three chapters on the design of outcome research. Epstein (1988) emphasized the importance of using 'highly specific, operationalized, manualized, and clinically sound interventions'. He recommends the development and use of treatment manuals and suggests that 'the most experienced, best trained therapist be used whenever possible'.

Gurman (1988) discussed 'criteria for assessing amenability of family therapy models to efficacy research'. He suggests the following 'major criteria':

- The degree of technical specificity, replicability and, hence, learnability.
- The relative amount and quality of existing research on outcome evaluation and/or testing of basic propositions (for example, pathological interaction processes).
- The apparent extent of influence on the family therapy field, gauged partly by estimates of the number of its practitioners.
- Other considerations such as the historical significance of the methods (for example, psychodynamic family therapy) and their pervasive influences on practices in the field (Gurman, 1988, page 132).

Jacobson (1988) offered 'guidelines for the design of family therapy outcome research'. He pointed out that studies need to have clinical relevance and that 'statistical significance bears no necessary relationship to clinical significance'. He goes on to discuss the place and value of comparative outcome studies. While such studies seem at first consideration highly desirable, the pitfalls awaiting those who embark on them are, as he points out, many:

> '. . . the experimenter is looking for general, overall differences between two multifaceted treatments typically sharing a number of overlapping features, differences that are sufficiently robust to manifest themselves across a population of heterogeneous clients and therapists, and relatively small sample sizes. In psychological experiments, main effects are seldom found unless other sources of variance can be kept to a minimum.' (Jacobson, 1988, page 145)

Keeping sources of variance to a minimum is hard in family therapy research because families and therapists differ so much and standardizing the therapy presents such a problem. Even if it could be done, Jacobson (1988) pointed out, 'one would end up with a study of highly questionable generalizability'. While not completely disqualifying comparative studies using different treatment models, Jacobson sees 'within-model comparisons' as likely to be more helpful because, 'in clinical practice the technical overlap between models of therapy is extensive'. Comparisons of models thus involve relatively 'weak' manipulations.

'Internal validity' is considered next by Jacobson (1988). During the early stages of research, the random assignment of families to the different treatment conditions is considered essential. Without it, group differences cannot be interpreted. The group with which the treatment is compared may be a no-treatment or a waiting list group. Later, random assignment may not be needed, for example when it is desired to discover whether outcome can be improved by modifying the treatment plan to meet the particular needs of specific families.

An alternative possibility, during the early stages of research, is to compare the treatment being investigated with a standard, established treatment. Unfortunately few of the latter are available in the family therapy field. Possibilities that Jacobson (1988) suggests are parent-training approaches with pre-adolescent boys (Patterson, 1974) and behavioural marital therapy (Jacobson & Margolin, 1979), on both of which there are data from controlled trails.

Finally, Jacobson (1988) suggests that resolution of the presenting problem should be the 'primary criterion for success'. He points out that:

> 'Changes in family interaction are often the hypothesized means whereby a family therapist proposes to solve the problems that brought the family in. But this is only a hypothesis. The vindication of a model bent on changing family interaction is whether or not such change leads to elimination of the presenting problem(s).' (Jacobson, 1988, page 153).

A much quoted outcome study is that of Langsley and colleagues (Langsley et al., 1968, 1969). One hundred and fifty families requesting admission to hospital for treatment of severe emotional disturbance in one of their members were treated by short-term crisis-orientated family therapy. These families were compared with a matched group of 150 families in which a member was admitted to hospital for conventional treatment. The second paper describes the methods by which the results were assessed. 'Family crisis therapy', as the authors called their method, proved just as effective as inpatient treatment. Six months later the patients treated by family therapy were functioning just as well as those who had been admitted, and were less likely to have spent some part of the 6 months in hospital. The cost of family treatment was about one-sixth that of inpatient care. Although the methods used in this study have been criticized (Gurman & Kniskern, 1978), this remains a powerful piece of evidence of the value of family therapy.

Gurman and Kniskern (1978) examined and reviewed over 200 research studies. They found evidence of improvement in the quality of the research, compared with earlier reviews. They also devised a 'points system' for rating the quality of research designs. Fourteen criteria were used. Some, such as controlled assignment to treatment conditions and the use of pre- and post-treatment measurement of change, rated five points, while others, for example 3 months or more of follow-up, and outcome assessment allowing for positive or negative change, rated only one each. A score of 26 was possible. Zero to 10 was considered a poor rating, $10\frac{1}{2}$ to 15 fair, $15\frac{1}{2}$ to 20 good, and over 20 very good.

Overall improvement rates for non-behavioural family therapy were found to be in the range 65–75%, except when the identified patient was a daypatient, when it was 57%. All the day hospital studies were of families in which the identified patient was an adult and day hospitals tend to contain mainly chronic and intractable patients, which may account for the lower improvement rates in this group.

Non-behavioural marital therapy was associated with improvement in about 66% of cases when treatment was either conjoint (both partners treated by one therapist), conjoint group (in which groups of marital couples are treated) or collaborative–concurrent (in which spouses are treated by different therapists who communicate with each other); but when individual treatment was used for marital problems, there was improvement in only 48% of cases. The overall improvement rates, derived as they are from a very mixed group of studies, can at best give only a very general idea of the results obtained.

Gurman and Kniskern (1978) also reviewed both comparative and controlled studies of marital/family therapy. Conjoint marital therapy and conjoint group marital therapy were found to be superior to alternative treatments in 70% of the comparisons, and inferior in only 5%. In all six studies that compared these two types of therapy with each other, no differences were found. There were few comparative studies which included concurrent and collaborative marital therapy. In these studies also, the results of individual marital therapy were found to be strikingly inferior to those of conjoint or conjoint group therapy. In only 10% of the comparisons was individual therapy found to be superior to other therapies, and in only 5% was it superior to conjoint or conjoint group therapy.

The publication of the book *Research Methods in Family Therapy* (Sprenkle & Moon, 1996) was an important milestone in the progress of research into our subject. A total of 40 contributors described and discussed many of the current approaches to research. It is clear that by the mid-1990s, research into family therapy had made significant strides.

After an introductory chapter by the editors, the book has sections on:

- Qualitative methods
- Quantitative methods
- Mixed methods

Further progress in the development of methods for studying family therapy is evident in the second edition of this book (Sprenkle & Piercy, 2005). This again covers a wide range of research methods and in addition to the three sections mentioned above, there is an additional one on 'advanced quantitative methods'. The book shows how extensive were the advances in family research that occurred in the 9 years between the two editions.

Nevertheless Sprenkle and Piercy (2005) suggest that 'the growth of the field has depended more on its intuitive appeal than on solid research evidence for its efficacy' (page 3). They go on to quote Crane et al. (2002, page 76):

> 'The culture (of Marriage and Family Therapy) does not support research. Ours remains a field where it is still possible for a highly charis-matic individual to create a model of family therapy, become successful on the workshop circuit, and get lucrative book contracts to promulgate the model, without offering evidence for its efficacy beyond personal testimonies.'

A major goal of *Research Methods in Family Therapy* (Sprenkle & Piercy, 2005, page 4) is 'to contribute to narrowing the divide between researchers and clinicians. Although the book is about research, we insisted that the chapter authors expend considerable effort demonstrating how the methods they describe are connected to the world of practice.' Sprenkle and Piercy (2005, page 4) assert that the 'researcher–clinician gap' has deleterious consequences. These include the following:

- Research often gets dismissed as irrelevant, incomprehensible, or both. So it does not inform practice and clinicians do not refine their practice. They keep on doing what they've been doing.
- A false dichotomy between clinical judgement and the scientific method is perpetuated whereas both are to be valued and questioned.
- It challenges the status of marital and family therapy as an ethical profession. How can we advance the welfare of our clients if we have insufficient evidence regarding which of our interventions are effective?
- It diminishes our credibility to 'outside stakeholders' such as policy makers and health care providers.
- It has contributed to the 'outsourcing' of marital and family therapy research to those whose primary professional identity is something other than marital and family therapy.

These issues seem to become even more critical when we consider some of the 'post-modern' approaches. Here the therapist may do little more than engage in a conversation with the family, with the expectation that solutions to the family's problems will emerge. Thus Harlene Anderson in *Conversation, Language, and Possibilities: A Postmodern Approach to Therapy* (1997) describes 'a therapist-assumed *philosophical stance* [Anderson's italics] that invites a collaborative relationship and process' (page 4). Defining such a process in a way that might be accessible to scientific study presents a challenge.

In *Effectiveness Research in Marriage & Family Therapy* (2002) the editor, Douglas Sprenkle, brought together 26 authors who, between them, reviewed the current status of research into the effectiveness of family therapy in the treatment of conduct disorder and delinquency; substance abuse; childhood behavioural and emotional disorders; alcohol abuse; marital problems; relationship enhancement; domestic violence; severe mental illness; affective disorders; and physical disorders. The final chapter (Shadish & Baldwin, 2002) is devoted to a 'meta-analysis of marital and family therapy interventions'. It includes descriptions of 20 meta-analyses that had already been done on the effects of both therapy and enrichment interventions with couples and families.

It is not possible here to go further into this book's findings, but it is recommended to those who seek more information about the effectiveness of marital and family therapy. Sprenkle (2002), in his introduction, provides 'a fairly positive assessment of the "state of the art" of marital and family therapy research' (page 23). But he also refers to the need to address the 'disastrous gap between researchers and clinicians that continues to plague the field'. He concluded his introduction (also on page 23) with the observation that 'marital and family therapy is an extraordinarily complex operation that defies simple description. We need the wisdom of both art and science to grasp it.'

Enrichment programmes

A limited number of studies have explored how family functioning may be enhanced. These are interesting as they represent attempts to do preventive work in the family field, whereas the great bulk of family therapy research has dealt with established disorders. Programmes such as Marriage Encounter and the Minnesota Couples Communication Program are widely used, and have been thought to help promote better communication and improved relationships.

Giblin et al. (1985) reviewed and analyzed 85 studies of premarital, marital and family enrichment projects, involving 3886 couples or families. An examination of the results, using meta-analysis, indicated that the average participant was better off than 67% of those who did not participate. Yet many studies do not find evidence of significant benefit from these programmes. Giblin and his colleagues found that the studies which did produce significant findings tended to be those that were better designed, used behavioural measures, examined relationship skill areas, and used longer programmes, with less well educated subjects. Studies in which there were more 'distressed subjects' also seemed to be those in which greater effects were seen, perhaps because there was more scope for improvement.

Evidence-based marriage and family therapy

The concept of *evidence-based practice* (EBP) was developed by a team in the Department of Clinical Epidemiology and Biostatistics at McMaster University. In an article published in 1993, Oxman et al. describe how evidence-based practice aims to ensure that patients can be given care based on the best currently available evidence. EBP was originally developed with the whole field of medicine in mind, not specifically for mental health services.

EBP is about using information that has been obtained by research, rather than carrying out research. Since its introduction in the 1990s its use has become widespread through medicine generally, although marriage and family therapists were initially a little slow to incorporate it into their practice.

Sackett et al. (2000) described five steps in the evidence-based process:

(1) The clinician seeking evidence to assist him or her in clinical decision-making must formulate an answerable question.
(2) The clinician tracks down the best empirical evidence relevant to the question being asked. Various computer-based databases are available to assist in this process.
(3) The validity, impact and applicability of the research that has been accessed are appraised.
(4) The clinical research data that have been located are integrated with the clinician's own expertise and the patient's unique characteristics.
(5) Following treatment, the clinician evaluates its effectiveness and usefulness in assisting in the making of treatment decisions.

A fuller account of how the principles of evidence-based practice may be applied in marriage and family therapy is to be found in an article by Patterson et al. (2004). Further information is to be found in the books *Users' Guides to the Medical Literature: A Manual for Evidence-Based Clinical Practice* (Guyatt & Rennie, 2002a) and *Users' Guides to the Medical Literature: Essentials of Evidence-Based Clinical Practice* (Guyatt & Rennie, 2002b).

Integrating research and clinical training

Hodgson et al. (2005) argue that training in marital and family therapy (MFT) has focused on practice at the expense of research. They advocate for training programmes that aim to produce *scientist-practitioners*. They go on:

'Many of the skills necessary for good clinical work are also necessary to be a good researcher. Both must conceptualize ideas within relational problems, decide what questions to ask and how to ask them, and then evaluate the quality of the responses to formulate findings and make determinations for future impact. The processes used are similar and require the professional to apply theory logically, develop hypotheses, determine validity, draw conclusions, and make future plans. As students simultaneously learn the art of practice and research they will gain skills that will be beneficial throughout their careers.'

These authors quote Strickler (1992) who stated that 'the half-life of psychological knowledge' is 10 years, so marital and family therapists who want to maintain an ethical practice based on current knowledge must continue learning throughout their careers. Hodgson and her colleagues (2005) go on to describe how four training sites for marital and family therapists in the USA (The University of Georgia, Auburn University, Texas Tech University and East Carolina University) are endeavouring to integrate research with clinical training.

Williams et al. (2006), in an article entitled 'Panning for gold: a clinician's guide to using research', offer useful guidance for therapists who may have limited time to search the literature, yet need to keep up to date with developments. They point out that the ability of family therapists to integrate research and clinical knowledge is part of Marital and Family Therapy Core Competencies developed by the American Association of Marital and Family Therapy (2004). This is an eminently practical article, which should be of value to all therapists who are not in the habit of routinely looking for evidence on which to base their practice. Among much useful advice are four suggested 'short cuts':

(1) Use electronic articles. This saves the reader the time it takes to visit a library to read articles.
(2) Use reviews of literature and meta-analyses.
(3) Read abstracts.
(4) Use indirect measures of research quality. Several ways of evaluating the quality of research studies are suggested.

Summary

Although family therapy arose out of family research, especially research into the families of patients with schizophrenia, there was subsequently a separation of researchers and therapists, and a change of focus from the families of patients with schizophrenia to a wider range of family problems.

Important areas for family therapy research are the assessment and classification of families; the description and measurement of the process of therapy; and the assessment of outcome. Progress has been made in all these, but much remains to be done. There is a need for further improvement in both the design and the reporting of research projects. It also remains to be established whether or not radically new approaches to research are needed when the newer forms of family therapy are investigated. For the moment it seems important that family therapy, like other forms of treatment, is subjected to scientific scrutiny using established methods.

The field of prevention of family pathology requires further development and evaluation but studies have been carried out to assess the value of 'enrichment' programmes designed to enhance the functioning of marriages and families. There is a need for the further investigation of the effectiveness of specific therapeutic techniques, such as those that have examined the results of paradoxical injunctions.

The last 10–15 years have seen a marked increase in both the amount of research into marriage and family therapy and its quality. There is now evidence that it is of significant value in a wider range of disorders. Marital and family therapy are also becoming more evidence-based, as research findings become increasingly applied in clinical practice. Also apparent has been the need to integrate training in research with clinical training in marital and family therapy.

Chapter 18
Ethics and Family Therapy

Figley and Nelson (1989), when they conducted a survey of family therapy trainers, found that being well informed on ethical issues was among the 'skills' most mentioned as being needed by trainees. This may be because family therapy is liable to confront therapists with certain complex ethical dilemmas peculiar to the field.

One of the difficult issues peculiar to family therapy is the question of who the client is. When one is treating an individual adult, the answer is simple. One's client/patient is the person who comes for treatment. When one is treating a family the answer is not so simple. On many occasions, it is not the family that presents for treatment but an individual member of it. The family members may be unaware that they have a problem as a family, yet the therapist may see the symptoms of the 'identified patient' as being embedded in the functioning of the family system. Change in the family system is seen as necessary for relief or elimination of the presenting symptoms. The needed changes in the family system may however have a variety of effects, not necessarily sought by the family, on the other members of the family.

In 1985, Wendorf and Wendorf reviewed the pre-existing literature on family therapy ethics. They found that the authors whose work they surveyed had identified a number of problem areas. They also found 'that the area of ethics (had not) kept abreast of the rest of the field in its appreciation for and utilization of systems principles as a conceptual base'. Among the possible problems the Wendorfs found in the literature they reviewed were:

- The potentially harmful effects of disclosure of extremely negative affect within the family.
- The possible undermining of authority as parental failings are brought out in therapy.
- The disclosure of personal sexual data.
- Divorce as a result of treating only one partner in a troubled marriage.
- Deciding who is the patient.
- Subordinating children's needs and goals 'to those of the more powerful adults in therapy'.
- When and to whom a therapist may reveal secrets told to the therapist in the course of treatment.

- The intrusion of the therapist's values into the assessment and treatment process without these being clarified for both therapist and patients.
- Whether, or when, it is justifiable to refuse treatment if all family members do not attend.
- Whether multigenerational aspects of each family's situation must always be considered.

Wendorf and Wendorf (1985) described their own 'ethical base', which they believed was 'more systemic than that of previous orientations'. This was as follows:

'We believe that the therapist's task is to help people become more competent in solving their problems as individuals and as systems. This problem-solving should always include the presenting problem but should also consider the problem in its broader patterns, or isomorphic transactions. In addition, this problem-solving should maintain a regard for the short- and long-term needs, growth, and welfare of the other individuals and subsystems that are involved in this mutually recursive system of influence. To be considered are the effects of actions both on and by the therapist and on and by the society in the system of family–therapist–society that forms the context in which family therapy occurs.' (Wendorf & Wendorf, 1985, page 447)

These authors suggested that family therapists tended to view particular problems non-systemically, addressing only the symptomatic behaviour interactions and overlooking the broader context of the behaviours; that they are non-systemic when they neglect to consider the extended family and other generations; and that they are non-systemic when they ignore the recursive effects of the therapy on the therapist and when they do not think systemically about the therapy context.

Wendorf and Wendorf (1985) proceeded to set out how they dealt with issues of family secrets; 'therapist deceptiveness' (the use of 'manipulations' such as paradoxical injunctions and reframings); and advocacy of particular values (for example, feminist ones). Their contribution remains useful and their article a resource well worth consulting, but achieving the admittedly desirable aims set out in the quotation above is not a simple matter.

Informed consent

Ensuring that all concerned have given their informed consent to what is to happen is the best way of dealing with the ethical dilemmas mentioned above. Informed consent can only be given once objectives have been agreed, the proposed treatment has been explained, and the risks, and possible side effects and complications, have been properly discussed with the family members.

According to Jensen et al. (1989) informed consent is 'more than just an ethical or legal obligation: inherent in the process of informed consent is the potential for the enhancement of the clinical work'. Informed consent, these authors believe,

> '. . . is particularly necessary where treatment can be hazardous, where it could have both negative and positive effects, where one treatment is not necessarily superior to another, and where full patient cooperation is necessary for the treatment success. All of these conditions are frequently met in the use of psychotherapy.' (Jensen et al., 1989, page 379)

These authors point out that clarity in the therapist's mind as to who is the patient and in whose 'best interest' the therapist is acting is essential. What is in one person's best interests may be opposed to the best interests of other family members. Furthermore, the judgement of 'best interest' depends on the value systems of the family members and of the therapist. It is also difficult, in many cases, to predict the effects, positive or negative, of family treatment.

These considerations underline the importance of discussing and agreeing the goals of therapy, as set out in Chapter 7. Without clearly established objectives, it is probably unethical even to start therapy. The objective-setting process is a good opportunity for the therapist to raise the questions of who is the patient, and in whose interests the therapy is to be undertaken. Possible side effects, including adverse ones, can also be discussed. Once all these issues have been put on the table and have been discussed and accepted, it is appropriate to start therapy.

Therapists' values

Values are 'enduring beliefs that specific modes of conduct or end-states of existence are personally or socially preferable to opposite modes of conduct or end-states of existence' (Rokeach, 1973). No form of psychotherapy can be value-free. We each have our ideas about how individuals, parents, children, adolescents, family groups, grandparents, employers and a myriad of others should behave and the roles they should play. To pretend otherwise is to deceive ourselves; so is pretending that we can keep our values totally separate from our therapy work. These values may assume more importance when we deal with families than when we are treating individuals.

In much of the literature on family therapy, therapists' values are downplayed. There are some exceptions, though. Kirschner and Kirschner (1986) made quite explicit their view of 'optimal family functioning' and Haley (1980) has long emphasized the importance of a proper hierarchy in the family. These issues were also addressed in *Normal Family Processes* (Walsh, 1993) and *Ethnicity and Family Therapy* (McGoldrick et al., 2005).

There is a substantial literature on the 'feminist' approach to family therapy. Feminist therapy aims 'to free both male and female clients from destructive and unnecessary limitations derived from outmoded sex role constraints and an oppressive social system' (Chaney & Piercy, 1988, quoting Libow et al., 1982). Chaney and Piercy (1988, page 306) suggest that:

'Feminist ideology may be useful in addressing some of the blind spots of more traditional therapies. For example, traditional family therapy may inadvertently give priority to the good of the family or relationship over the needs of the individuals, often the women.'

What seems to be important is that we do our best to communicate our values to our clients as part of the contract- and objective-setting process. It should probably be regarded as unethical to start treatment with any hidden agendas, whether these be 'traditional', feminist or any other views of how families should function.

Confidentiality

It is unethical to reveal client confidences in all forms of therapy. The only exceptions are when the law requires us to do so or when revealing information is necessary to protect someone from harm, as when we learn of a person's intent to commit suicide or homicide. This rule applies as much in family therapy as in other forms of psychotherapy.

It seems that breaches of confidentiality are more common than might be supposed. According to Baker and Patterson (1990), based on their review of the literature, 'sharing clients' confidential information with family or friends is a serious ethical problem'. Engelberg and Symansky (1989) reported that, in the USA, violations of confidentiality and dual relationships are the commonest causes of professional liability claims against family therapists.

Baker and Patterson (1990) quote two examples of breaches of confidentiality:

'*Case 1*. A family therapist comes home from work unusually depressed. When her husband inquires about the reason for her mood, she says that some clients, who are also family friends, have recently discovered that the wife has breast cancer. The therapist is upset and feels the need to process her own feelings of loss.

Case 2. Dr Goodrich gets a phone call in the middle of the night. His wife awakens to hear him talking with a neighbour's teenage son who is suicidal. She wonders whether she should call the neighbour the next morning to see if she can help.' (Baker & Patterson, 1990, pages 296–297)

These authors consider that such breaches of confidentiality are associated with 'overlapping and sometimes inappropriately diffuse boundaries in the therapist's roles as professional and family member' (Baker & Patterson, 1990, page 299). The danger of such information being unethically disclosed seems to be greater in small communities and where there is limited availability of therapists. It is generally undesirable for us to treat families who are known to us socially but this may be inevitable in small communities or, in the USA, when Health Maintenance Organizations mandate that clients are treated by particular therapists.

The limits of confidentiality that apply should be spelled out early in the contact between therapist and family. The circumstances in which outside persons or agencies would need to be given information, mentioned above, should be explained. A suitable time to do this is when the objectives of therapy are being discussed and a therapeutic contract is being developed.

This is also a good point at which to address another aspect of confidentiality: the question of what information may be shared within the family group. This is not usually a problem when all family members are seen together, but it may be when subsystems of the family, or individual members, are seen separately. Here we are dealing with therapeutic as well as ethical issues. The main *ethical* need is to ensure that all appropriate people know what the policies are and accept them. The *clinical* issues are another matter.

My own policy is to tell children that what they tell me in individual sessions is confidential and will not be divulged to their parents, or to anyone else, without their consent, with certain exceptions. The exceptions are when I learn that a child (whether the one being interviewed or another) has been, or may have been, abused; and when I learn of something so serious, such as a child's intention to commit suicide, that I must divulge it. I do however promise to tell the child when I feel obliged to break a confidence and to advocate for him or her, as appropriate. This policy is also communicated to the parents to whom I explain that it is hard for children to speak freely if they feel that anything they say may be passed on to others, including their parents.

When parents are seen apart from their children, the situation is a little different. I undertake not to discuss the children in their absence without feeling free to share the content of the conversation with the children when this seems appropriate. On the other hand I acknowledge that there are some matters which are private issues concerning the parents and their relationship with each other. If an interview is to deal with marital or sexual concerns, I make it clear to the children that these are private matters on which they do not have a right to be informed. Whether they are told anything about them is their parents' decision. This is a way of defining, or strengthening, the boundary between the parental and child subsystems; in other words, a structural intervention.

It is not possible to be categorical about how to deal with other 'secrets' which may be revealed to the therapist by particular family members. These are clinical decisions. Sometimes it is appropriate for them to be 'kept' but in many cases they are features of dysfunctional systems. I therefore make it clear that I can give no guarantee that unsolicited 'secret' material will be kept confidential.

Ethical decision making

Zygmond and Boorhem (1989) described a process of 'ethical decision making' based on a model described by Kitchener (1984, 1985, 1986). These authors pointed out that:

> 'Clinical decisions emerge from the interweaving of a complex set of circumstances consisting of the therapist's theoretical orientation, the idiosyncratic circumstances of the family, the personal values of the therapist that are often beyond awareness, the relationship between the therapist and the family, and the element of timing. These various factors cannot be reduced to a simple process of "If A, then B".' (Zygmond & Boorhem, 1989, page 271)

Which decision is ethically correct may depend on the circumstances of the case. Kitchener's model provides guidelines which therapists may use to evaluate their clinical decisions from an ethical standpoint. It proposes two levels of ethical reasoning:

(1) The intuitive level.
(2) The critical–evaluative level.

The *intuitive level* consists of a firm set of ethical beliefs concerning what is right or wrong, good or bad. Kitchener (1984) calls this 'ordinary moral sense'. Our ordinary moral sense depends on our experiences, ethical knowledge and level of ethical development. It is not a fixed, static set of beliefs but can change over time as we acquire new knowledge and have new experiences. It is a good day-to-day guide and individuals are more likely to act unethically if they ignore their moral sense than if they follow it. But it is not infallible, and it may not give us a clear signal as to what course of action to take in unique or complex clinical situations. A further, important reason for not relying solely on intuition is that doing so does not provide us with a means of evaluating critically the decisions we make.

The *critical–evaluative level* is divided into three hierarchical, mutually exclusive levels of ethical reasoning:

(1) Ethical rules. These are prescribed standards of behaviour. Zygmond and Boorhem (1989) cite as examples the Code of Ethical Principles

of the American Association for Marital and Family Therapy (AAMFT) and the Ten Commandments. Unfortunately these codes tend to consist of general principles and do not give guidance as to how to apply these in practice. The AAMFT code says that family therapists 'are dedicated to advancing the welfare of families and individuals' but is silent on what we are to do when the needs of different family members are in conflict.

(2) Ethical principles. The five that Kitchener (1984, 1985, 1986) stresses are:
- Autonomy. This is the principle that individuals have the right to freedom of action, choice and thought as long as this does not compromise the rights of others. Even if we disagree with an individual's choice we must respect it if it causes no harm.
- Nonmaleficence. This is doing no harm. Kitchener (1984) defined harm as engaging in activities with a high probability of hurting others; infringing upon the rights of others; and intentionally inflicting physical and psychological pain on others.
- Beneficence. This is the concept of contributing to the health and welfare of others.
- Fidelity. This is the principle of being faithful, keeping promises, being loyal and respecting others' rights. It is essential to all voluntary relationships such as therapeutic ones. Without it, it is not possible to establish meaningful relational bonds.
- Justice. This is the principle that people should be treated equally, unless there is difference, or inequality, which is relevant to the issue in question. Thus the abused child and the abuser are different to an extent that fully justifies different treatment.

Ethical principles take precedence over personal and group values. An ethical principle must be upheld unless it is in conflict with other ethical principles. For example, if a person indicates suicidal intent the principle of nonmaleficence takes precedence over the principles of autonomy and fidelity – that is, the right to privacy.

(3) Ethical theory. This is required when ethical principles are in conflict. Kitchener's (1984) two ethical theories are 'universalizability' and 'the balancing principle'. *Universalizability*, not a happy term, means that an act is ethical if 'it can be unambiguously applied to all similar cases' (Kitchener, 1984). Zigmond and Boorhem (1989) explain that this implies asking these questions:
- 'If I were in a similar situation, would I want my therapist to make this decision?'
- 'If my family were in a similar situation would I want my therapist to make this decision?'
- 'If other people were in a similar situation, would I want their therapist to make this decision?'

The *balancing principle* states that when ethical principles are in conflict, an ethical decision is one that produces the least amount of *avoidable* harm to all concerned, even if it limits the possible benefits.

Zygmond and Boorhem (1989) recommend the use of this model both in clinical situations and in classroom teaching and supervision.

Keeping informed and up to date

As we saw in the preceding chapter, therapists, and indeed the members of all the helping professions, have an ethical obligation to keep themselves informed about advances in their field. Just as a person with diabetes would not want to be treated by a physician who was unaware of recent advances in the treatment of that condition, or a person with arthritis of the hip would not desire to be operated on by a surgeon who does not know of the latest and most effective procedure for hip replacement, so those seeking family therapy will expect their treatment to be carried out by a therapist who is up to date and can offer them the benefit of the latest research in the area.

This is a difficult area. Reliable information about which treatment is likely to be most helpful for particular family problems is scarce, despite the increasing amount of research data that are becoming available. Keeping up to date involves more than reading about the latest research findings. An ever-increasing variety of families and family problems are presenting to therapists. This means that a variety of treatment approaches are needed. Discussing 'the new practice of family therapy', Carlson et al. (2005, page 11) suggest that the contemporary family therapist should possess:

- A solid grounding across diverse theoretical approaches
- A broad repertoire of intervention approaches
- The skill needed to carry out a comprehensive assessment of the family system
- The ability to choose intervention strategies tailored to the individual family

It is perhaps unfortunate that, even in the middle of the first decade of the twenty-first century and when family therapy now has a history of 50-plus years, there is much to be learned about which approach is best for which family problem or situation. Also unfortunate is the continuing relative lack of attention given to ethical issues in the family therapy literature.

Evidence-based clinical practice (Guyatt & Rennie, 2002a; 2002b; Patterson et al., 2004) is probably nowadays an ethical imperative. The principles of evidence-based practice have been outlined in the previous chapter. Related to this is the 'research-practice gap' that has for long existed in marital and family therapy. This, Sprenkle (2003, page 88) points out, 'challenges our status as an ethical profession'. We are required to advance the welfare of our clients, but how, Sprenkle (2003) asks, 'can we do that if most practitioners have insufficient information [on] which of our treatments are effective, which do little good, and which may cause harm?'

Ethical issues in family therapy research

Research in marital and family therapy presents additional ethical issues. Regular clinical practice has the sole aim of providing help to the families that present for therapy. In many research projects, however, there is an additional aim, that of achieving one or more specific research goals. These may be in conflict with the therapy process. It is therefore imperative that all research proposals are reviewed by the appropriate ethics committee. Universities, hospitals and other institutions in which research is carried out have such committees, which may approve or reject research proposals or, often, suggest modifications after which they are again reviewed.

Some of the ethical issues that may arise in relation to research studies are discussed by Lyness et al. (2005, pages 307–309); Dahl & Boss (2005, pages 76–78); and Mancini et al. (2005, pages 289–290).

Summary

Family therapy presents a number of special and ethical challenges. Deciding who the patient is, and whose best interests the therapist should be concerned with can present major problems. Other issues are the choice of therapeutic approach; whether treatment should be contingent on all family members attending; and whether it should be mandatory to consider the extended family system and larger social systems.

The many imponderables make it particularly important that the therapist obtain informed consent. In doing so, the objectives of therapy should be agreed, the treatment approach explained and possible adverse effects discussed.

Therapists need to be as aware as possible of the values they bring to the therapy situation and they should share these with the family. The limits of confidentiality should be explained and carefully observed.

A scheme for ethical decision, proposed by Zygmond and Boorhem (1989) has been outlined. An ethical imperative is that we must keep up to date in our field, so that we can offer our clients the best currently available treatment.

References

Ackerman, N.W. (1956) Interlocking pathology in family relationships. In: *Changing Concepts of Psychoanalytic Medicine* (eds S. Rado & G. Daniels). Grune & Stratton, New York. (Reprinted 1982 in *The Strength of Family Therapy* (eds D. Bloch & R. Simon) Brunner/Mazel, New York.)

Ackerman, N.W. (1958) *The Psychodynamics of Family Life.* Norton, New York.

Ackerman, N.W. (1961) A dynamic frame for the clinical approach to family conflict. In: *Exploring the Base for Family Therapy* (eds N.W. Ackerman, F.L. Beatman & S.N. Sherman). Family Services Association of America, New York.

Ackerman, N.W. (1966) *Treating the Troubled Family.* Basic Books, New York.

Ackerman, N.W. (1970a) Family interviewing: the study process. In: *Family Therapy in Transition* (ed. N.W. Ackerman). Little Brown, Boston.

Ackerman, N.W. (1970b) Child participation in family therapy. *Family Process,* **9**, 403–410.

Ackerman, N.W. (1970c) Family psychotherapy today. *Family Process,* **9**, 123–126.

Alexander, J. & Barton, C. (1976) Behavioural systems therapy for families. In: *Treating Relationships* (ed. D.H.L. Olson). Graphic, Lake Mills, Iowa.

Alexander, J.F. & Parsons, B.V. (1973) Short-term behavioral intervention with delinquent families: impact on family process and recidivism. *Journal of Abnormal Psychology,* **81**, 219–225.

Alger, I. (1969) Therapeutic use of videotape playback. *Journal of Nervous and Mental Disease,* **148**, 430–436.

Alger, I. (1973) Audio-visual techniques in family therapy. In: *Techniques of Family Psychotherapy* (ed. D.A. Bloch). Grune & Stratton, New York.

Allman, L.R. (1982) The aesthetic preference: overcoming the pragmatic error. *Family Process,* **21**, 43–56.

Andersen, T. (1987) The reflecting team. *Family Process,* **26**, 415–428.

Andersen, T. (ed.) (1991) *The Reflecting Team: Dialogues and Dialogues about the Dialogues.* Norton, New York.

Anderson, H. (1997) *Conversation, Language, and Possibilities.* Basic Books, New York.

Anderson, H. & Goolishian, H. (1988) Human systems as linguistic systems: evolving ideas about the implications for theory and practice. *Family Process,* **27**, 371–393.

Andolfi, M. (1979) *Family Therapy: An Interactional Approach.* Plenum, New York.

Angelo, C. (1981) The use of the metaphoric object in family therapy. *American Journal of Family Therapy,* **9** (1), 69–78.

Anonymous (1972) On the differentiation of self. In: *Family Interaction: A Dialogue Between Family Therapists and Family Researchers* (ed. J. Framo). New

York: Springer. (Reprinted 1978 in *Family Therapy in Clinical Practice* (ed. M. Bowen). Jason Aronson, New York.)

Aponte, H. (1976) The family-school interview: an eco-structural approach. *Family Process*, **15**, 303–311.

Atwood, J.D. (1997) Social construction theory and therapy. In: *Challenging Family Therapy Situations: Perspectives in Social Construction* (ed. J.D. Atwood). Springer, New York.

Auerswald, E.H. (1968) Interdisciplinary versus ecological approach. *Family Process*, **7**, 202–215. (Reprinted 1972 in *Progress in Group and Family Therapy* (eds C.J. Sager & H.S. Singer) Brunner/Mazel, New York.)

Baker, L.C. & Patterson, J.E. (1990) The first to know: a systemic analysis of confidentiality and the therapist's family. *American Journal of Family Therapy*, **18**, 295–300.

Bandler, R. (1984) *Magic in Action*. Meta Publications, Cupertino, California.

Bandler, R. & Grinder, J. (1975) *The Structure of Magic*, Vol. 1. Science and Behaviour Books, Palo Alto, California.

Bandler, R. & Grinder, J. (1979) *Frogs into Princes*. Real People Press, Moab, Utah.

Bandler, R., Grinder, J. & Satir, V. (1976) *Changing with Families*. Science & Behaviour Books, Palo Alto, California.

Barker, P. (1981a) *Basic Family Therapy*. Granada, London.

Barker, P. (1981b) Paradoxical techniques in psychotherapy. In: *Treating Families with Special Needs* (eds D.S. Freeman & B. Trute). Alberta and Canadian Associations of Social Workers, Ottawa.

Barker, P. (1985) *Using Metaphors in Psychotherapy*. Brunner/Mazel, New York.

Barker, P. (1986) *Basic Family Therapy*, 2nd edn. Blackwell, Oxford.

Barker, P. (1994) Re-framing: the essence of psychotherapy? In: *Ericksonian Methods: The Essence of the Story* (ed. J.K. Zeig). Brunner/Mazel, New York.

Barker, P. (1996) *Psychotherapeutic Metaphors: A Guide to Theory & Practice.* Brunner/Mazel, New York.

Barker, P. (2004) *Basic Child Psychiatry*, 7th edn. Blackwell, Oxford.

Barnhill, L.H. & Longo, D. (1978) Fixation and regression in the family life cycle. *Family Process*, **17**, 469–478.

Barton, C. & Alexander, J.F. (1981) Functional family therapy. In: *Handbook of Family Therapy* (eds A.S. Gurman & D.P. Kniskern). Brunner/Mazel, New York.

Bateson, G. (1980) *Mind and Nature: A Necessary Unity*. Dutton, New York.

Bateson, G., Jackson, D.D., Haley, J. & Weakland, J. (1956) Toward a theory of schizophrenia. *Behavioural Science*, **1**, 251–264. (Reprinted 1968 in *Theory and Practice of Family Psychiatry* (ed. J.G. Howells). Oliver & Boyd, Edinburgh; and 1978 in *Beyond the Double Bind* (ed. M.M. Berger). Brunner/Mazel, New York.)

Baucom, D., Shoham, V., Mueser, K., Daiuto, A. & Stickle, T. (1998) Empirically supported couple and family interventions for marital distress and adult mental health problems. *Journal of Consulting & Clinical Psychology*, **66**, 53–88.

Beal, E.W. (1976) Current trends in the training of family therapists. *American Journal of Psychiatry*, **133**, 137–141.

Beavers, W.R. (1982) Healthy, midrange, and severely dysfunctional families. In: *Normal Family Processes* (ed. F. Walsh). Guilford, New York.

Beavers, W.R. & Hampson, R.B. (1990) *Successful Families: Assessment & Intervention*. Norton, New York.

Beavers, W.R. & Voeller, M.N. (1983) Family models: comparing and contrasting the Olson circumplex model with the Beavers systems model. *Family Process*, **22**, 85–98.

Beckett, J.A. (1973) General systems theory, psychiatry and psychotherapy. *International Journal of Group Psychotherapy*, **23**, 292–305.

Bell, J.E. (1961) *Family Group Therapy*. Public Health Monograph, No. 64. U.S. Government Printing Office, Washington, DC.

Bell, J.E. (1962) Recent advances in family group therapy. *Journal of Child Psychology & Psychiatry*, **3**, 1–15.

Bell, J.E. (1975) *Family Therapy*. Jason Aronson, New York.

Benningfield, A.B. (1980) Multiple family therapy systems. *Journal of Marriage & Family Counselling*, **4** (2), 25–34. (Reprinted in *Advances in Family Psychiatry*, vol. II, (ed J.G. Howells). International Universities Press, New York.)

Berger, P.L. & Luckman, T. (1966) *The Social Construction of Reality*. Doubleday, New York.

Bogolub, E.B. (1995) *Helping Families Through Divorce: An Eclectic Approach*. Springer, New York.

Boscolo, L., Cecchin, G., Hoffman, L. & Penn, P. (1987) *Milan Systemic Family Therapy*. Basic Books, New York.

Boszormenyi-Nagy, I. & Framo, J. (eds) (1965) *Intensive Family Therapy: Theoretical and Practical Aspects*. Harper & Row, New York.

Boszormenyi-Nagy, I. & Spark, G. (1973) *Invisible Loyalties: Reciprocity in Intergenerational Family Therapy*. Harper and Row, Hagerston.

Bowen, M. (1960) A family concept of schizophrenia. In: *The Etiology of Schizophrenia*, (ed. D.D. Jackson). Basic Books, New York.

Bowen, M. (1961) Family psychotherapy. *American Journal of Orthopsychiatry*, **31**, 40–60.

Bowen, M. (1966) The use of family theory in clinical practice. *Comprehensive Psychiatry*, **7**, 345–374. (Reprinted 1971 in *Changing Families* (ed. J. Haley). Grune & Stratton, New York; and 1978 in *Family Therapy in Clinical Practice* (ed. M. Bowen). Jason Aronson, New York.)

Bowen, M. (1976) Theory in the practice of psychotherapy. In: *Family Therapy: Theory & Practice* (ed. P. Guerin). Gardner Press, New York. (Reprinted 1978 in *Family Therapy in Clinical Practice* (ed M. Bowen). Jason Aronson, New York.)

Bowen, M. (ed.) (1978) *Family Therapy in Clinical Practice*. New York: Jason Aronson.

Bruner, J. (1976) *Actual Minds, Possible Worlds*. Harvard University Press, Cambridge, Massachusetts.

Bullock, D. & Kobayashi, K. (1978) The use of live consultation in family therapy. *Family Therapy*, **5**, 245–250.

Byng-Hall, J. (1973) Family myths used as defence in conjoint family therapy. *British Journal of Medical Psychology*, **46**, 239–250.

Canadian Psychiatric Association Working Group (2005) *Clinical Practice Guidelines – Treatment of Schizophrenia*. CPA, Ottawa.

Carlson, J., Sperry, L. & Lewis, J. (2005) *Family Therapy Techniques: Integrating & Tailoring Treatment.* Routledge, New York.

Carter, E.A. & McGoldrick, M. (eds) (1980) *The Family Life Cycle: A Framework for Family Therapy.* Gardner Press, New York.

Cecchin, G. (2003) Constructing therapeutic possibilities. In: *Therapy as Social Construction* (eds S. McNamee & J.K.J. Gergin). Sage, London.

Chaim, G., Armstrong, S., Shenfeld, J., Kelly, C. & Li, S. (2003) *Brief Couples Therapy: Group and Individual Couple Treatment for Addiction and Related Mental Health Concerns.* Center for Addiction and Mental Health, Toronto.

Chaney, S.E. & Piercy, F.P. (1988) A feminist family behaviour therapy checklist. *American Journal of Family Therapy*, **16**, 305–318.

Clarkin, J.F., Frances, A.J. & Moodie, J.L. (1979) Selection criteria for family therapy. *Family Process*, **18**, 391–403.

Cleghorn, J.M. & Levin, S. (1973) Training family therapists by setting learning objectives. *American Journal of Orthopsychiatry*, **43**, 439–446.

Colapinto, J. (1979) The relative value of empirical evidence. *Family Process*, **18**, 427–441.

Coleman, S.B. & Gurman, A.S. (1985) An analysis of family therapy failures. In: *Failures in Family Therapy* (ed. S.B. Coleman). Guilford, New York.

Constantine, L.L. (1989) Furniture for firewood - blaming the systems paradigm. *Journal of Marital & Family Therapy*, **15**, 111–113.

Coogler, O.J. (1978) *Structured Mediation in Divorce Settlements.* Lexington Books, Lexington, Massachusetts.

Coppersmith, E.I. (1980) Expanding use of the telephone in family therapy. *Family Process*, **19**, 411–417.

Coppersmith, E.I. (1981) Developmental reframing. *Journal of Strategic & Systemic Therapies*, **1**, 1–8.

Coppersmith, E.I. (1985) Teaching trainees to think in triads. *Journal of Marital & Family Therapy*, **11**, 61–66.

Coyne, J.C. (1985) Toward a theory of frames and reframing: the social nature of frames. *Journal of Marital & Family Therapy*, **11**, 337–344.

Coyne, J.C. & Anderson, B.J. (1989) The 'psychosomatic family' reconsidered II: Recalling a defective model and looking ahead. *Journal of Marital & Family Therapy*, **15**, 139–148.

Coyne, J.C., Denner, B. & Ransom, D.C. (1982) Undressing the fashionable mind. *Family Process*, **21**, 391–396.

Crafoord, C. (1980) Put the booze on the table: some thoughts about family therapy and alcoholism. *Journal of Family Therapy*, **2**, 71–81.

Crane, D.R., Wampler, K.S., Sprenkle, D.H., Sandberg, J.G. & Hovestadt, A.J. (2002) The scientist-practitioner model in marriage and family therapy doctoral programs. *Journal of Marital & Family Therapy*, **28**, 75–83.

Crowe, M. (1978) Conjoint marital therapy: a controlled outcome study. *Psychological Medicine*, **8**, 623–636.

Dahl, C.M. & Boss, P. (2005) The use of phenomenology for family therapy research. In: *Research Methods in Family Therapy*, 2nd edn (eds D.H. Sprenkle & F.P. Piercy). Guilford, New York.

Dare, C. & Lindsay, C. (1979) Children in family therapy. *Journal of Family Therapy*, **1**, 253–269.

Dattilio, F.M. (2005) The restructuring of family schemas: a cognitive-behavioral perspective. *Journal of Marital & Family Therapy*, **31**, 15–30.

Dattilio, F.M. & Epstein, N.B. (2005) The role of cognitive-behavioral interventions in couple and family therapy. *Journal of Marital & Family Therapy*, **31,** 7–13.

Dell, P.F. (1982) Beyond homeostasis: toward a concept of coherence. *Family Process*, **21**, 21–41.

de Shazer, S. (1982) *Patterns of Brief Family Therapy: An Ecosystemic Approach*. Guilford, New York.

de Shazer, S. (1989) Wrong map, wrong territory. *Journal of Marital & Family Therapy*, **15**, 117–121.

Dicks, H. (1963) Object relations theory and marital studies. *British Journal of Medical Psychology*, **36**, 125–129.

Dicks, H. (1967) *Marital Tensions*. Routledge & Kegan Paul, London.

Diener, E. & Wallbom, M. (1976) Effects of self awareness and attitudes toward punishment. *Journal of Experimental Social Psychology*, **11**, 976–987.

Dilts, R., Grinder, J., Bandler, R., Bandler, L.C. & DeLozier, J. (1980) *Neuro-linguistic Programming*: Vol I. Meta Publications, Cupertino, California.

Dishion, D.J. & Kavanagh, K. (2003) *Intervening in Adolescent Problem Behavior: A Family Centered Approach*. Guilford, New York.

Donovan, J.M. (ed.) (1999) *Short-Term Couple Therapy*. Guilford, New York.

Duhl, F.J., Kantor, D. & Duhl, B.S. (1973) Learning, space and action in family therapy; a primer of sculpture. In: *Techniques of Family Psychotherapy* (ed. D.A. Bloch). Grune & Stratton, New York.

Duvall, E.M. & Miller, B.C. (1985) *Marriage & Family Development*, 6th edn. Harper & Row, New York.

Ellis, E.M. (2000) *Divorce Wars: Interventions with Families in Conflict*. American Psychological Association, Washington, DC.

Engelberg, S. & Symansky, J. (1989) Ethics and the law. *Family Therapy Networker*, **13**, 30–31.

Epstein, N.B. (1988) Dilemmas and choices in the design of family therapy research. In: *The State of the Art in Family Therapy Research* (ed. L.C. Wynne). Family Process Press, New York.

Epstein, N.B. & Bishop, D.S. (1981) Problem centered systems therapy of the family. *Journal of Marital & Family Therapy*, **7**, 23–31.

Epstein, N.B., Bishop, D.S. & Levin, S. (1978) The McMaster model of family functioning. *Journal of Marriage & Family Counselling*, **4**, 19–31.

Epstein, N.B., Rakoff, V. & Sigal, J.J. (1968) *Family Categories Schema*. Monograph prepared in the Family Research Group of the Department of Psychiatry, Jewish General Hospital, Montreal, in collaboration with McGill University Human Development Study.

Epstein, N., Schlesinger, S.E. & Dryden, W. (1988) *Cognitive-Behavioural Therapy with Families*. Brunner/Mazel, New York.

Erickson, G.D. (1988) Against the grain: decentering family therapy. *Journal of Marital & Family Therapy*, **14**, 225–236.

Erickson, M.H. (1980a) *The Nature of Hypnosis & Suggestion* (Collected papers, vol. I, ed. E.L. Rossi). Irvington, New York.

Erickson, M.H. (1980b) *Hypnotic Alteration of Sensory, Perceptual & Psychological Processes* (Collected papers, vol. II, ed. E.L. Rossi). Irvington, New York.

Erickson, M.H. (1980c) *Hypnotic Investigation of Psychodynamic Processes* (Collected papers, vol. III, ed. E.L. Rossi). Irvington, New York.

Erickson, M.H. (1980d) *Innovative Psychotherapy*. (Collected papers, vol. IV, ed. E.L. Rossi). Irvington, New York.

Erickson, M.H. (1980e) *A Teaching Seminar with Milton H. Erickson, M.D.* (ed. J.K. Zeig). Brunner/Mazel, New York.

Erickson, M.H. (1982) *My Voice Will Go With You: The Teaching Tales of Milton H. Erickson, M.D.* (ed. S. Rosen). Norton, New York.

Erickson, M.H., Hershman, S. & Sector, I.I. (1961) *The Practical Application of Medical and Dental Hypnosis*. Seminars on Hypnosis Publishing Co, Chicago.

Erikson, E. (1965) *Childhood and Society*. Hogarth Press, London; & Penguin, London.

Falloon, I.R.H., Boyd, J.L. & McGill, C.W. (1984) *Family Care of Schizophrenia: A Problem-solving Approach to the Treatment of Mental Illness*. Guilford, New York.

Fenell, D.L. & Weinhold, B.K. (1989) *Counseling Families: An Introduction to Marriage & Family Therapy*. Love Publishing, Denver, Colorado.

Figley, C.R. & Nelson, T.S. (1989) Basic family therapy skills, I: Conceptualization and initial findings. *Journal of Marital & Family Therapy*, **15**, 349–365.

Fisch, R., Weakland, J. & Segal, S. (1982) *The Tactics of Change: Doing Therapy Briefly*. Jossey-Bass, San Francisco.

Fish, L.S. & Harvey, R.G. (2005) *Nurturing Queer Youth: Family Therapy Transformed*. Norton, New York.

Fisher, L. (1976) Dimensions of family assessment: a critical review. *Journal of Marriage & Family Counselling*, **2**, 367–382.

Fisher, L. (1977) On the classification of families. *Archives of General Psychiatry*, **34**, 424–433.

Fleck, S. (1980) Family functioning and family pathology. *Psychiatric Annals*, **10**, 46–54.

Frankl, V. (1960) Paradoxical intention: a logotherapeutic technique. *American Journal of Psychotherapy*, **40**, 520–535.

Friedman, H., Rohrbaugh, M. & Krakauer, S. (1988) The time-line genogram: highlighting temporal aspects of family relationships. *Family Process*, **27**, 293–303.

Gatti, F. & Coleman, C. (1976) Community network therapy: an approach to aiding families with troubled children. *American Journal of Orthopsychiatry*, **46**, 608–617.

Giblin, P., Sprenkle, D.H. & Sheehan, R. (1985) Enrichment outcome research: a meta-analysis of pre-marital, marital and family interventions. *Journal of Marital & Family Therapy*, **11**, 257–271.

Gleick, J. (1988) *Chaos: Making a New Science*. Penguin, New York.

Glenn, M.L. (1984) *On Diagnosis: A Systemic Approach*. Brunner/Mazel, New York.

Glick, L.D. & Kessler, D.R. (1974) *Marital & Family Therapy*. Grune & Stratton, New York.

Goldstein, M.J. & Rodnick, E.J. (1975) The family's contribution to the etiology of schizophrenia: current status. *Schizophrenia Bulletin*, **14**, 48–73.

Goolishian, H. (1990) Therapy as a linguistic system: hermeneutics, narrative and meaning. *The Family Psychologist*, **6**, 44–45.

Goolishian, H. & Anderson, H. (1990) Understanding the therapeutic process: from individuals and families to systems in language. In: *Voices in Family Psychology* (ed. F. Laslow). Sage, Newbury Park.

Gordon, D. (1978) *Therapeutic Metaphors*. Meta Publications, Cupertino, California.

Gordon, S.B. & Davidson, N. (1981) Behavioural parent training. In: *Handbook of Family Therapy* (eds A.S. Gurman & D.P. Kniskern). Brunner/Mazel, New York.

Gorell Barnes, G. (2004) *Family Therapy in Changing Times*, 2nd edn. Palgrave-Macmillan, Basingstoke, Hampshire.

Green, R.G., Harris, R.N., Forte, J.A. & Robinson, M. (1991) Evaluating FACES III and the Circumplex Model: 2,440 families. *Family Process*, **30**, 55–73.

Grinder, J. & Bandler, R. (1976) *The Structure of Magic*, vol 2. Science and Behaviour Books, Palo Alto, California.

Gross, G. (1979) The family angel – the scapegoat's counterpart. *Family Therapy*, **6**, 133–136.

Group for the Advancement of Psychiatry (1970) *The Field of Family Therapy*. Report No. 78. G.A.P., New York.

Guerin, P.J. (ed.) (1976) *Family Therapy: Theory & Practice*. Gardner Press, New York.

Guerin, P.J. & Pendagast, E.G. (1976) Evaluation of family system and genogram. In: *Family Therapy* (ed. P.J. Guerin). Gardner Press, New York.

Gurman, A.S. (1983) Family therapy research and the 'new epistemology'. *Journal of Marital & Family Therapy*, **9**, 227–234.

Gurman, A.S. (1988) Issues in the specification of family therapy interventions. In: *The State of the Art in Family Therapy Research* (ed. L.C. Wynne). Family Process Press, New York.

Gurman, A.S. & Kniskern, D.P. (1978) Research on marital and family therapy: progress, perspective and prospect. In: *Handbook of Psychotherapy & Behavior Change*, 2nd edn (eds S.L. Garfiel & A.E. Bergin). Wiley, New York.

Gurman, A.S. & Kniskern, D.P. (1981) Family therapy outcome research: knowns and unknowns. In: *Handbook of Family Therapy* (eds A. Gurman & D. Kniskern). Brunner/Mazel, New York.

Gurman, A.S. & Kniskern, D.P. (1986) Individual marital therapy – have reports of your death been somewhat exaggerated? *Family Process*, **25**, 51–62.

Guttman, H.A. (1975) The child's participation in conjoint family therapy. *Journal of the American Academy of Child Psychiatry*, **14**, 490–499.

Guyatt, G. & Rennie, D. (eds) (2002a) *Users' Guides to the Medical Literature: A Manual for Evidence-Based Clinical Practice*. American Medical Association.

Guyatt, G. & Rennie, D. (eds) (2002b) *Users' Guides to the Medical Literature: Essentials of Evidence-Based Clinical Practice*. American Medical Association.

Haley, J. (1963) *Strategies of Psychotherapy*. Grune & Stratton, New York.

Haley, J. (1967) Speech sequences of normal and abnormal families with two children present. *Family Process*, **1**, 81–97.

Haley, J. (1973) *Uncommon Therapy: The Psychiatric Techniques of Milton J. Erickson.* Norton, New York.

Haley, J. (1976) *Problem-Solving Therapy.* Jossey-Bass, San Francisco.

Haley, J. (1978) Ideas which handicap therapists. In: *Beyond the Double Bind* (ed. M.M. Berger). Brunner/Mazel, New York.

Haley, J. (1980) *Leaving Home.* McGraw Hill, New York.

Haley, J. (1984) *Ordeal Therapy.* Jossey-Bass, San Francisco.

Haley, J. (1985a) *Conversations with Milton H. Erickson, M.D. Volume 2, Changing Couples.* Triangle Press, New York.

Haley, J. (1985b) *Conversation with Milton H. Erickson, M.D. Volume 3, Changing Children and Families.* Triangle Press, New York.

Hall, A.D. & Fagan, R.E. (1956) Definition of system. *Yearbook for the Advancement of General Systems Theory*, **1**, 18–28.

Hammerlynck, L.A., Handy, L. & Mash, E.S. (1973) *Behavioural Change: Methodology, Concepts & Practice.* Research Press, Champaign, Illinois.

Hammond, C.D. (1984) Myths about Erickson and Ericksonian hypnosis. *American Journal of Clinical Hypnosis*, **26**, 236–245.

Hare-Mustin, R. (1975) Treatment of temper tantrums by a paradoxical intervention. *Family Process*, **14**, 481–485.

Hatfield, A.G. (1983) What families want of family therapists. In: *Family Therapy in Schizophrenia* (ed. W.R. McFarlane). Guilford, New York.

Haynes, J.M. (1981) *Divorce Mediation: A Practical Guide for Therapists & Counselors.* Springer, New York.

Haynes, J.M. (1982) A conceptual model of the process of family mediation: implications for training. *American Journal of Family Therapy*, **10**, 5–16.

Heath, A.W. & Storm, C.L. (1985) From the institute to the ivory tower: the live supervision stage approach for teaching supervision in academic settings. *American Journal of Family Therapy*, **13** (3), 27–36.

Henao, S. & Grose, N.P. (1985) *Principles of Family Systems in Family Medicine.* Brunner/Mazel, New York.

Hodge, D.R. (2005) Spiritual assessment in marital and family therapy. *Journal of Marital & Family Therapy*, **31**, 341–356.

Hodgson, J.L., Johnson, L.N., Ketring, S.A., Wampler, R.S. & Lamson, A.L. (2005) Integrating research and clinical training in marriage and family therapy training programs. *Journal of Marital & Family Therapy*, **31**, 75–88.

Hoffman, L. (1981) *Foundations of Family Therapy: A Conceptual Framework for Systems Change.* Basic Books, New York.

Hoffman, L. (2002) *Family Therapy: An Intimate History.* Norton, New York.

Holman, A.M. (1983) *Family Assessment: Tools for Understanding & Intervention.* Sage Publications, Beverly Hills, California.

Howells, J.G. (1968) *Theory & Practice of Family Psychiatry.* Oliver & Boyd, Edinburgh.

Hünler, O.S. & Gençö, Z. (2005) *Contemporary Family Therapy*, **27**, 123–236.

Imber-Black, E. (1988) Ritual themes in families & family therapy. In: *Rituals in Families & Family Therapy* (eds E. Imber-Black, J. Roberts & R. Whiting). Norton, New York.

Imber-Black, E. (ed.) (1993) *Secrets in Families & Family Therapy*. Norton, New York.

Imber-Black, E., Roberts, J. & Whiting, R. (eds) (1988) *Rituals in Families and Family Therapy*. Norton, New York.

Irving, H.H. (1980) *Divorce Mediation: The Rational Alternative*. Universe Books, New York.

Irving, H. (1981) Family mediation: a method for helping families: resolve legal disputes. In: *Treating Families with Special Needs* (ed. D.S. Freeman & B. Trute). Alberta & Canadian Associations of Social Workers, Ottawa.

Jackson, D.D. (1961) Interactional psychotherapy. In: *Contemporary Psychotherapies* (ed. M.T. Stein). Free Press of Glencoe, New York.

Jackson, D.D. (1965) Family rules: the marital quid pro quo. *Archives of General Psychiatry*, **12**, 589–594.

Jackson, D.D. & Weakland, J.H. (1959) Schizophrenic symptoms and family interaction. *Archives of General Psychiatry*, **1**, 618–621.

Jackson, D.D. & Weakland, J.H. (1961) Conjoint family therapy: some considerations on theory, technique and results. *Psychiatry*, **24** (suppl. 2), 30–45.

Jacob, T. (1975) Family interaction in disturbed and normal families: a methodological and substantive review. *Psychological Bulletin*, **82**, 33–65.

Jacobson, N.S. (1984) A component analysis of behavioral marital therapy: the relative effectiveness of behavior exchange and problem solving training. *Journal of Consulting & Clinical Psychology*, **52**, 295–305.

Jacobson, N.S. (1988) Guidelines for the design of family therapy outcome research. In: *The State of the Art in Family Therapy Research* (ed. L.C. Wynne). Family Process Press, New York.

Jacobson, N.S. & Christensen, A. (1996) *Acceptance & Change in Couple Therapy*. Norton, New York.

Jacobson, N.S. & Follette, W.C. (1985) Clinical significance of improvement resulting from two behavioral marital components. *Behavior Therapy*, **16**, 249–262.

Jacobson, N.S. & Margolin, G. (1979) *Marital Therapy: Strategies Based on Social Learning & Behaviour Exchange Principles*. Brunner/Mazel, New York.

Jacobson, N.S., Follette, W.C. & Pagel, M. (1986) Predicting who will benefit from behavioral marital therapy. *Journal of Consulting & Clinical Psychology*, **54**, 518–522.

Jacobson, N.S., Schmaling, K.B. & Holtzworth-Munroe, A. (1987) Component analysis of behavioral marital therapy: two-year follow-up & prediction of relapse. *Journal of Marital & Family Therapy*, **13**, 187–195.

Jensen, P.S., Josephson, A.M. & Frey, J. (1989) Informed consent as a framework for treatment: ethical and therapeutic considerations. *American Journal of Psychotherapy*, **43**, 378–386.

Johnson, S.M. (1999) Emotionally focused couple therapy. In: *Short-Term Couple Therapy* (ed. J.M. Donovan). Guilford, New York.

Johnson, S.M. (2003) The revolution in couple therapy: a practitioner-scientist perspective. *Journal of Marital & Family Therapy*, **29**, 365–384.

Johnson, S. & Lebow, J. (2000) The 'coming of age' of couple therapy: a decade review. *Journal of Marital & Family Therapy*, **26**, 23–38.

Johnson, S.M., Hunsley, J., Greenberg, L. & Schlinder, D. (1999) Emotionally focused couples therapy: status and challenges. *Clinical Psychology: Science & Practice*, **6**, 135–152.

Kagan, R. & Schlosberg, S. (1989) *Families in Perpetual Crisis*. Norton, New York.

Kaplan, H.S. (1974) *The New Sex Therapy*. Brunner/Mazel, New York.

Kaplan, H.S. (1979) *Disorders of Sexual Desire*. Brunner/Mazel, New York.

Karpel, M.A. & Strauss, E.S. (1983) *Family Evaluation*. Gardner Press, New York.

Kaslow, F.W. (1984) Divorce mediation & its emotional impact on the couple and their children. *American Journal of Family Therapy*, **12** (3), 58–66.

Keeney, B.P. (1982) What is an epistemology of family therapy? *Family Process*, **21**, 153–162.

Keeney, B.P. & Sprenkle, D.H. (1982) Ecosystemic epistemology: critical implications for the aesthetics and pragmatics of family therapy. *Family Process*, **21**, 1–19.

Keller, J.F. & Protinsky, H. (1984) A self-management model for supervision. *Journal of Marital & Family Therapy*, **10**, 281–288.

Kirschner, D.A. & Kirschner, S. (1986) *Comprehensive Family Therapy: An Integration of Systemic & Psychodynamic Models*. Brunner/Mazel, New York.

Kitchener, K.S. (1984) Intuition, critical evaluation & ethical principles: the foundation for ethical decisions in counselling psychology. *Counselling Psychology*, **12**, 43–55.

Kitchener, K.S. (1985) Ethical principles & ethical decisions in student affairs. In: *Applied Ethics in Student Services* (eds H.J. Cannon & R.D. Brown). Jossey-Bass, San Francisco.

Kitchener, K.S. (1986) Teaching ethics in counselling education: an integration of philosophical processes & philosophical analysis. *Journal of Counselling Development*, **64**, 306–310.

Kramer, J.R. (1985) *Family Interfaces: Transgenerational Patterns*. Brunner/Mazel, New York.

Kramer, J.R. & Reitz, M. (1980) Using videotape playback to train family therapists. *Family Process*, **19**, 145–150.

Kressel, K., Jaffee, N., Tuchman, B., Watson, C. & Deutsch, M. (1980) A typology of divorcing couples: implications for mediation and the divorce process. *Family Process*, **19**, 101–116.

L'Abate, L. (1986) *Systematic Family Therapy*. Brunner/Mazel, New York.

Laing, R.D. (1965) Mystification, confusion and conflict. In: *Intensive Family Therapy* (eds I. Boszormenyi-Nagy & J. Framo). Harper & Row, New York.

Laing, R.D. & Esterson, A. (1964) *Sanity, Madness and the Family*. Tavistock, London; Penguin, Baltimore. (Republished 1971 by Basic Books, New York.)

Landau, B., Wolfson, L. & Landau, N. (2005) *Family Mediation and Collaborative Practice Handbook*, 4th edn. LexisNexis Canada, Markham, Ontario.

Langsley, D.G., Flomenhaft, K. & Machotka, P. (1969) Follow-up evaluation of family crisis therapy. *American Journal of Orthopsychiatry*, **39**, 753–759.

Langsley, D.G., Pittman, F.S., Machotka, P. & Flomenhaft, K. (1968) Family crisis therapy: results and implications. *Family Process*, **7**, 145–158.

Lankton, S. & Lankton, C. (1983) *The Answer Within*. Brunner/Mazel, New York.

Laqueur, H.P. (1973) Multiple family therapy: questions & answers. In: *Techniques of Family Psychotherapy* (ed. D.S. Bloch). Grune & Stratton, New York.

Laqueur, H.P. (1976) Multiple family therapy. In: *Family Therapy: Theory & Practice* (ed. P. Guerin). Gardner Press, New York.

Laqueur, H.P., Wells, C.F. & Agresti, M. (1979) Multiple family therapy in a state hospital. *Hospital & Community Psychiatry*, **20**, 13–22.

Lebow, J. (1995) Open-ended therapy: termination in marital and family therapy. In: *Integrating Family Therapy: Handbook of Family Psychology and Systems Theory* (eds R.H.Miksell, D. Lusterman & S.H. McDaniel). American Psychological Association, Washington, DC.

Lebow, J.L. (2005) Integrative family therapy for families experiencing high-conflict divorce. In: *Handbook of Clinical Family Therapy* (ed. J.L. Lebow). Wiley, Hoboken, New Jersey.

Lederer, W.J. (1981) *Marital Choices: Forecasting, Assessing, and Improving Relationships*. Norton, New York.

Leff, J.P. & Vaughn, C. (1985) *Expressed Emotion in Families*. Guilford, New York.

Leff, J.F., Kuipers, L. & Berkovitz, R. (1983) Intervention in families of schizophrenics and its effect on relapse rate. In: *Family Therapy in Schizophrenia* (ed. W.R. McFarlane). Guilford, New York.

Leiblum, S.R. & Pervin, L.A. (1989) *Principles and Practice of Sex Therapy*, 2nd edn. Guilford, New York.

Libow, J.A., Raskin, P.A. & Caust, B.L. (1982) Feminist and family systems therapy: Are they irreconcilable? *American Journal of Family Therapy,* **10** (3), 3–12.

Liddle, H.A. (1980) On teaching a contractual or systemic therapy: training content, goals and methods. *American Journal of Family Therapy*, **8** (1), 59–69.

Liddle, H.A. & Halpin, R.J. (1978) Family therapy training and supervision literature: a comparative review. *Journal of Marriage & Family Counselling*, **4**, 77–98.

Liddle, H.A. & Saba, G.W. (1982) Teaching family therapy at the introductory level: a conceptual model emphasizing a pattern which connects training and therapy. *Journal of Marital & Family Therapy*, **8**, 63–72.

Liddle, H.A., Breunlin, D.C., Schwartz, R.C. & Constantine, J.A. (1984) Training family therapy supervisors: issues of content, form and context. *Journal of Marital & Family Therapy*, **10**, 139–150.

Lidz, R.W. & Lidz, T. (1949) The family environment of schizophrenic patients. *American Journal of Psychiatry*, **106**, 332–345.

Lidz, T., Cornelison, A.R., Terry, D. & Fleck, S. (1958) Intrafamilial environment of the schizophrenic patient: VI – the transmission of irrationality. *A.M.A. Archives of Neurology and Psychiatry*, **79**, 305–316.

Lowery, C.R. (1984) Parents and divorce: identifying the support network for decisions about custody. *American Journal of Family Therapy*, **12** (3), 26–32.

Lyness, K.P., Walsh, S.R. & Sprenkle, D.H. (2005) Clinical trials in marriage and family research. In: *Research Methods in Family Therapy*, 2nd edn (eds D.H. Sprenkle & F.P. Piercy). Guilford, New York.

MacGregor, R. (1962) Multiple impact psychotherapy with families. *Family Process*, **1**, 15–29.

MacGregor, R., Ritchie, A.M., Serrano, A.C. & Schuster, F.P. (1964) *Multiple Impact Therapy with Families*. McGraw-Hill, New York.

MacKinnon, L. (1983) Contrasting strategic and Milan therapies. *Family Process*, **22**, 425–438.

Madanes, C. (1981) *Strategic Family Therapy*. Jossey-Bass, San Francisco.

Mancini, J.A., Huebner, A.J., McCollum, E.E. & Marek, L.I. (2005) Program evaluation of science and family therapy. In: *Research Methods in Family Therapy*, 2nd edn (eds D.H. Sprenkle & F.P. Piercy). Guilford, New York.

Marlow, L. (1985a) Divorce mediation: therapists in the legal world. *American Journal of Family Therapy*, **13** (1), 3–21.

Marlow, L. (1985b) Divorce mediation: therapists in their own world. *American Journal of Family Therapy*, **13** (3), 3–10.

Masters, W. & Johnson, V. (1966) *Human Sexual Response*. Little Brown, Boston.

Masters, W. & Johnson, V. (1970) *Human Sexual Inadequacy*. Little Brown, Boston; Churchill, London.

Maturana, H.R. (1978) Biology of language: the epistemology of reality. In: *Psychology and Biology of Language and Thought* (eds G.A. Miller & E. Lenneberg). Academic Press, New York.

McCarthy, B.W. & Bodnar, L.E. (2005) Couple sex therapy: assessment, treatment & relapse prevention. In: *Handbook of Clinical Family Therapy* (ed. J.L. Lebow). Wiley, Hoboken, New Jersey.

McDermott, J.F. & Char, W.F. (1974) The undeclared war between child & family therapy. *Journal of the American Academy of Child Psychiatry*, **13**, 422–436.

McFarland, D.J. (1971) *Feedback Mechanisms in Animal Behaviour*. Academic Press, London.

McFarlane, W.R. (1983a) *Family Therapy in Schizophrenia*. Guilford, New York.

McFarlane, W.R. (1983b) Introduction. In: *Family Therapy in Schizophrenia* (ed. W.R. McFarlane). Guilford, New York.

McFarlane, W.R. (1983c) Systemic family therapy in schizophrenia. In: *Family Therapy in Schizophrenia* (ed. W.R. McFarlane). Guilford, New York.

McGoldrick, M. (1982) Ethnicity and family therapy: an overview. In: *Ethnicity and Family Therapy* (eds M. McGoldrick, J.K. Pearce & J. Giordano). Guilford, New York.

McGoldrick, M. & Carter, E.A. (1982) The family life cycle. In: *Normal Family Processes* (ed. F. Walsh). Guilford, New York.

McGoldrick, M. & Gerson, R. (1985) *Genograms in Family Assessment*. Norton, New York.

McGoldrick, M., Giordano, J. & Garcia-Preto, N. (eds) (2005) *Ethnicity and Family Therapy*, 3rd edn. Guilford, New York.

McGoldrick, M., Pearce, J.K. & Giordano, J. (eds) (1982) *Ethnicity and Family Therapy*. Guilford, New York.

McNamee, S. & Gergin, K.J. (eds) (1992) *Therapy as Social Construction*. Sage, London.

Midelfort, C. (1957) *The Family in Psychotherapy*. McGraw Hill, New York.

Mikesell, R.H., Lusterman, D.-D. & McDaniel, S.H. (1995) *Integrating Family Therapy; Handbook of Family Psychology and Systems Theory*. American Psychological Association, Washington, DC.

Mills, J. & Crowley, R. (1986) *Therapeutic Metaphors for Children and the Child Within*. Brunner/Mazel, New York.

Minuchin, S. (1974) *Families and Family Therapy*. Harvard University Press, Cambridge, Massachusetts.

Minuchin, S. (1984) *Family Kaleidoscope*. Harvard University Press, Cambridge, Massachusetts.

Minuchin, S. & Fishman, H.C. (1981) *Family Therapy Techniques*. Harvard University Press, Cambridge, Massachusetts.

Minuchin, S., Baker, L., Rosman, B.L., Liebman, R., Millman, M. & Todd, T.G. (1975) A conceptual model of psychosomatic illness in children. *Archives of General Psychiatry*, **32**, 1031–1038.

Minuchin, S., Montalvo, B., Guerney, B.G., Rosman, B.L. & Schumer, B.G. (1967) *Families of the Slums*. Basic Books, New York.

Minuchin, S., Rosman, B.L. & Baker, L. (1978) *Psychosomatic Families: Anorexia Nervosa in Context*. Harvard University Press, Cambridge, Massachusetts.

Mirkin, M.P. & Koman, L. (1985) *Handbook of Adolescents & Family Therapy*. Gardner Press, New York.

Montalvo, B. (1973) Aspects of live supervision. *Family Process*, **12**, 343–359.

Morris, J. (1989) Muddied Batesonian waters. *Journal of Marital & Family Therapy*, **15**, 115–116.

Murdoch, D. & Barker, P. (1991). *Basic Behaviour Therapy*. Blackwell, Oxford.

Napier, A.Y. & Whitaker, C.A. (1978) *The Family Crucible*. Harper & Row, New York.

New English Bible (1970) Quotation from Leviticus, Chapter 16, verses 20–22.

Nichols, M.P. (1984) *Family Therapy: Concepts and Methods*. Gardner Press, New York.

Nichols, M.P. (1987) *The Self in the System: Expanding the Limits of Family Therapy*. Brunner/Mazel, New York.

Nichols, W.C. (1996) *Treating People in Families: An Integrative Framework*. Guilford, New York.

O'Hanlon, W.H. & Hexum, A.L. (1990) *An Uncommon Casebook: The Complete Clinical Work of Milton H. Erickson*. Norton, New York.

Oliver, J.E. & Buchanan, A.H. (1979) Generations of maltreated children & multiagency care in one kindred. *British Journal of Psychiatry*, **135**, 289–303.

Olson, D., Portner, J. & Lavee, Y. (1985) FACES III. University of Minnesota, Family Social Sciences, St Paul.

Olson, D.H., Russell, C. & Sprenkle, D.H. (1983) Circumplex model of marital and family systems: VI. Theoretical update. *Family Process*, **22**, 69–83.

Olson, D.H., Sprenkle, D.H. & Russell, C. (1979) Circumplex model of marital and family systems: I. Cohesion and adaptability dimensions, family types and clinical applications. *Family Process*, **18**, 3–28.

Otto, H. (1962) The personal and family resource development programmes: a preliminary report. *International Journal of Social Psychiatry*, **2**, 329–338.

Oxman, A.D., Sackett, D.L. & Guyatt, G.H. (1993) Users guide to the medical literature: I. How to get started. *Journal of the American Medical Association*, **270**, 2093–2095.

Palazzoli, M.S. (1978) *Self-Starvation*. Jason Aronson, New York.

Palazzoli, M.S. (1980) Why a long interval between sessions? The therapeutic control of the family-therapist system. In: *Dimensions of Family Therapy* (eds M. Andolphi & I. Zwerling). Guilford, New York.

Palazzoli, M.S., Boscolo, G., Cecchin, G. & Prata, G. (1978a) *Paradox and Counterparadox*. Jason Aronson, New York.

Palazzoli, M.S., Boscolo, L., Cecchin, G. & Prata, G. (1978b) A ritualized prescription in family therapy: odd days and even days. *Journal of Marriage & Family Counseling*, **4**, 3–9.

Palazzoli, M.S., Boscolo, L., Cecchin, G. & Prata, G. (1980) Hypothesising – circularity – neutrality: three guidelines for the conductor of the session. *Family Process*, **19**, 3–12.

Papp, P. (1977) *Family Therapy: Full Length Case Studies*. Gardner Press, New York.

Papp, P. (1980) The Greek chorus & other techniques of paradoxical therapy. *Family Process*, **19**, 45–57.

Papp, P. (1982) Staging reciprocal metaphors in a couples group. *Family Process*, **21**, 453–467.

Patterson, G.R. (1974) Interventions for boys with conduct disorders: multiple settings, treatments, and criteria. *Journal of Consulting & Clinical Psychology*, **42**, 471–481.

Patterson, G.R., Reid, J.B. & Dishion, T.J. (1992) *A Social Learning Approach: IV. Antisocial Boys*. Castalia, Eugene, Oregon.

Patterson, G.R., Weiss, R.L. & Hops, H. (1976) Training in marital skills: some problems and concepts. In: *Handbook of Behaviour Modification & Behavior Therapy* (ed. H. Leitenberg). Prentice Hall, Englewood Cliffs, New Jersey.

Patterson, J.E., Miller, R.B., Carnes, S. & Wilson, S. (2004) Evidence-based practice for marriage and family therapists. *Journal of Marital & Family Therapy*, **30**, 183–195.

Penn, P. (1982) Circular questioning. *Family Process*, **21**, 267–280.

Persaud, R.D. (1987) Effects of the one-way mirror on family therapy. *Journal of Family Therapy*, **9**, 75–79.

Quinn, W.H., Atkinson, B.J. & Hood, C.J. (1985) The stuck-case clinic as a group supervision model. *Journal of Marital & Family Therapy*, **11**, 67–73.

Richter, H.E. (1974) *The Family as Patient*. Souvenir Press, London.

Riskin, J. & Faunce, E. (1972) An evaluative review of family interaction research. *Family Process*, **11**, 365–455.

Ritterman, M. (1983) *Using Hypnosis in Family Therapy*. Jossey-Bass, San Francisco.

Roffman, A.E. (2005) Function at the junction: revisiting the idea of functionality in family therapy. *Journal of Marital & Family Therapy*, **31**, 259–268.

Rokeach, M. (1973) *The Nature of Human Values*. Macmillan, New York.

Ruesch, J. & Bateson, G. (1968) *Communication: The Social Matrix of Psychiatry*. Norton, New York.

Rueveni, U. (1975) Network intervention with a family in crisis. *Family Process*, **14**, 193–203.

Rutter, M., Maughan, N., Mortimore, P. & Ouston, J. (1979) *Fifteen Thousand Hours*. Open Books, London.

Rutter, M., Tizard, J. & Whitmore, K. (1970) *Education, Health and Behaviour*. Longman, London.

Sackett, D.L., Straus, S., Richardson, S.W., Rosenberg, W. & Haynes, B.R. (2000) *Evidence-Based Medicine: How to Practice and Teach EBM* (2nd edn). Churchill Livingstone, New York.

Satir, V. (1967) *Conjoint Family Therapy*. Science & Behaviour Books, Palo Alto.

Schwartzman, J. (1984) Family theory and the scientific method. *Family Process*, **23**, 223–236.

Schwebel, A.I. & Fine, M.A. (1994) *Understanding & Helping Families: A Cognitive-Behavioral Approach*. Lawrence Erlbaum, Hillsdale, New Jersey.

Searight, H.R. & Merkel, W.T. (1991) Systems theory & its discontents: clinical and ethical issues. *American Journal of Family Therapy*, **19**, 1931.

Shadish, W.R. & Baldwin, S.A. (2002) Meta-analysis of MFT interventions. In: *Effectiveness Research in Marriage and Family Therapy* (ed. D.H. Sprenkle). American Association for Marriage & Family Therapy, Alexandria, Virginia.

Sheehan, R., Storm, C.L. & Sprenkle, D.H. (1982) *Therapy Based on a Cybernetic Epistemology: Problems and Solutions for the Researcher*. Panel presented at the Annual Meeting of the American Association for Marriage & Family Therapy, Dallas, October, 1982.

Sheinberg, M. (1985) The debate: a strategic technique. *Family Process*, **24**, 259–271.

Singer, M.T. & Wynne, L.C. (1965) Thought disorder and family relations in schizophrenia. IV: results and implications. *Archives of General Psychiatry*, **12**, 201–212.

Singer, M.T., Wynne, L.C. & Toohey, M.L. (1978) Communication disorders and the families of schizophrenics. In: *The Nature of Schizophrenia* (eds L.C. Wynne, R.L. Cromwell & S. Matthysse). Wiley, New York.

Skynner, A.C.R. (1969a) Indications and contra-indications for conjoint family therapy. *International Journal of Social Psychiatry*, **15**, 145–149.

Skynner, A.C.R. (1969b) A group-analytic approach to conjoint family therapy. *Journal of Child Psychology & Psychiatry*, **10**, 81–106.

Skynner, A.C.R. (1976) *One Flesh: Separate Persons*. Constable, London. (Published in the USA as *Systems of Family and Marital Psychotherapy*. Brunner/Mazel, New York.)

Slipp, S. & Kressel, K. (1978) Difficulties in family therapy evaluation. *Family Process*, **17**, 409–422.

Speck, R.V. & Attneave, C. (1971) Social network intervention. In: *Changing Families* (ed. J. Haley). Grune & Stratton, New York.

Speck, R.V. & Rueveni, U. (1969) Network therapy: a developing concept. *Family Process*, **8**, 182–191.

Sprenkle, D.H. (ed.) (2002) *Effectiveness Research in Marriage & Family Therapy.* American Association for Marriage and Family Therapy, Alexandria, Virginia.

Sprenkle, D.H. (2003) Effectiveness research in marriage and family therapy. *Journal of Marital & Family Therapy*, **29**, 85–96.

Sprenkle, D.H. & Moon, S.M. (eds) (1996) *Research Methods in Family Therapy.* Guilford, New York.

Sprenkle, D.H. & Piercy, F.P. (eds) (2005) *Research Methods in Family Therapy*, 2nd edn. Guilford, New York.

Steinberg, D. (1983) *The Clinical Psychiatry of Adolescence.* John Wiley, Chichester.

Steinglass, P. (1996) Family Process at 35. *Family Process*, **35**, 1–2.

Steinglass, P., Bennett, L.A., Wolin, S.J. & Reiss, D. (1987) *The Alcoholic Family.* Basic Books, New York.

Steinhauer, P.D., Santa-Barbara, J. & Skinner, H. (1984) The process model of family functioning. *Canadian Journal of Psychiatry*, **29**, 77–88.

Strickler, G. (1992) The relationship of research to clinical practice. *American Psychologist*, **47**, 543–549.

Sutcliffe, P., Lovell, J. & Walters, M. (1985) New directions for family therapy: rubbish removal as a task of choice. *Journal of Family Therapy*, **7**, 175–182.

Tildin, T. & Dattilio, F.M. (2005) Vulnerability schemas of individuals in couples relationships: a cognitive perspective. *Contemporary Family Therapy*, **27**, 137–160.

Tomm, K. (1980) Towards a cybernetic systems approach to family therapy at the University of Calgary. In: *Perspectives on Family Therapy* (ed. D.S. Freeman). Butterworth, Toronto.

Tomm, K. (1981) The Milan approach to family therapy: a tentative report. In: *Treating Families with Special Needs* (eds D.S Freeman & B. Trute). Alberta & Canadian Associations of Social Workers, Ottawa.

Tomm, K. (1984a) One perspective on the Milan approach: Part I. Overview of development, theory and practice. *Journal of Marital & Family Therapy*, **10**, 113–125.

Tomm, K. (1984b) One perspective on the Milan approach: Part II. Description of session format, interviewing style and interventions. *Journal of Marital & Family Therapy*, **10**, 253–271.

Tomm, K. (1987a) Interventive interviewing: I. Strategizing as a fourth guideline for the therapist. *Family Process*, **26**, 3–13.

Tomm, K. (1987b) Interventive interviewing: II. Reflexive questioning as a means to enable self-healing. *Family Process*, **26**, 167–183.

Tomm, K. (1988) Interventive interviewing: III. Intending to ask lineal, circular, strategic or reflexive questions? *Family Process*, **27**, 1–15.

Tomm, K. & Wright, L. (1979) Training in family therapy: perceptual, conceptual and executive skills. *Family Process*, **18**, 227–250.

Treacher, A. (1989) Termination in family therapy – developing a structural approach. *Journal of Family Therapy*, **11**, 135–147.

Tseng, W.S. & McDermott, J.F. (1979) Triaxial family classification. *Journal of the American Academy of Child Psychiatry*, **18**, 22–43.

Ungar, M. (2006) Practicing as a postmodern supervisor. *Journal of Marital & Family Therapy*, **32**, 59–71.

van Trommel, M.J. (1984) A consultation method addressing the therapist–family system. *Family Process*, **23**, 469–480.

van der Hart, O. (1983) *Rituals in Psychotherapy: Transition & Continuity*. Irvington, New York.

Vogel, E.F. & Bell, N.W. (1960) The emotionally disturbed child as the family scapegoat. In: *A Modern Introduction to the Family*, *Revised Edition* (eds N.W. Bell & E. Vogel). Free Press of Glencoe, New York.

von Bertalanffy, L. (1968) *General Systems Theory: Foundations, Development, Application*. Braziller, New York.

Wahler, R.G. (1976) Deviant child behaviour within the family: developmental speculations & behaviour change strategies. In: *Handbook of Behaviour Modification & Behaviour Therapy* (ed. H. Leitenberg). Prentice Hall, Englewood Cliffs, New Jersey.

Wallace, A.F.C. (1966) *Religion: An Anthropological View*. Random House, New York.

Walrond-Skinner, S. (1976) *Family Therapy: The Treatment of Family Systems*. Routledge & Kegan Paul, London.

Walrond-Skinner, S. (1978) Indications and contra-indications for the use of family therapy. *Journal of Child Psychology & Psychiatry*, **19**, 57–62.

Walrond-Skinner, S. (ed.) (1979) *Family & Marital Psychotherapy*. Routledge & Kegan Paul, London.

Walsh, F. (ed.) (1982) *Normal Family Processes*. Guilford, New York.

Walsh, F. (ed.) (1993) *Normal Family Processes*, 2nd edn. Guilford, New York.

Watzlawick, P. (1978) *The Language of Change*. Basic Books, New York.

Watzlawick, P. (1982) Hermetic pragmaesthetics or unkempt thoughts about an issue of Family Process. *Family Process*, **21**, 401–403.

Watzlawick, P. (1983) *The Situation is Hopeless but not Serious*. Norton, New York.

Watzlawick, P., Beavin, J.H. & Jackson, D.D. (1967) *Pragmatics of Human Communication*. Norton, New York.

Watzlawick, P., Weakland, J. & Fisch, R. (1974) *Change: Principles of Problem Formulation and Problem Resolution*. Norton, New York.

Weakland, J. (1977) OK – you've been a bad mother. In: *Family Therapy: Full Length Case Studies* (ed. P. Papp). Gardner Press, New York.

Weakland, J. (1979) The double-bind theory. *Journal of the American Academy of Child Psychiatry*, **18**, 54–66.

Weeks, G.R. & L'Abate, L. (1982) *Paradoxical Psychotherapy: Theory and Practice with Individuals, Couples and Families*. Brunner/Mazel, New York.

Weeks, G.R., Odell, M. & Methven, S. (2005) *If Only I Had Known: Avoiding Common Mistakes in Couple Therapy*. Norton, New York.

Weiner, N. (1948) *Cybernetics, or Control & Communication in the Animal and the Machine*. Technology Press, Cambridge, Massachusetts.

Weiss, R.L., Birchler, G.R. & Vincent, J.P. (1974) Contractual models for negotiation training in marital dyads. *Journal of Marriage & the Family*, **36,** 321–331.

Wells, R.A. & Gianetti, V.J. (1986a) Individual marital therapy: a critical reappraisal. *Family Process*, **25**, 43–51.

Wells, R.A. & Gianetti, V.J. (1986b) Rejoinder: Whither marital therapy? *Family Process*, **25**, 62–65.

Wendorf, D.J. (1984) A model for training practicing professionals in family therapy. *Journal of Marital & Family Therapy*, **10**, 31–41.

Wendorf, D.J. & Wendorf, R.J. (1985) A systemic view of family therapy ethics. *Family Process*, **24**, 443–460.

Whitaker, C.A. (1958) Psychotherapy with couples. *American Journal of Psychotherapy*, **12**, 18–23.

Whitaker, C.A. (1982) Comments on Keeney and Sprenkle's paper. *Family Process*, **21**, 405–406.

White, M. & Epston, D. (1990) *Narrative Means to Therapeutic Ends*. Norton, New York.

Whitehead, A.N. & Russell, B. (1910) *Principia Mathematica*. Cambridge University Press, Cambridge.

Whiting, R.A. (1988) Guidelines to designing therapeutic rituals. In: *Rituals in Families and Family Therapy* (eds E. Imber-Black, J. Roberts & R.A. Whiting). Norton, New York.

Wilder, C. (1982) Muddles and metaphors: a response to Keeney & Sprenkle. *Family Process*, **21**, 397–400.

Wilkinson, I.A. & Stratton, P. (1991) The reliability and validity of a system for family assessment. *Journal of Family Therapy*, **13**, 73–94.

Williams, L.M., Patterson, J.E. & Miller, R.B. (2006) Panning for gold: a clinician's guide to using research. *Journal of Marital & Family Therapy*, **32**, 17–32.

Winnicott, D. (1960) *The Maturational Process and the Facilitating Environment*. Hogarth, London.

Winter, W. & Ferriera, A.J. (eds) (1969) *Research in Family Interaction: Readings & Commentary*. Science & Behavior Books, Palo Alto.

Wolin, S.J. & Bennett, L.A. (1984) Family Rituals. *Family Process*, **23**, 401–420.

Wood, A. (1988) King Tiger and the roaring tummies: a novel way of helping young children and their families change. *Journal of Family Therapy*, **10**, 49–63.

Wright, L.M. & Leahey, M. (1984) *Nurses & Families: A Guide to Family Assessment and Intervention*. F.A. Davis, Philadelphia.

Wright, L.M. & Leahey, M. (2005) *Nurses & Families: A Guide to Family Assessment and Intervention* (4th edn). F.A. Davis, Philadelphia.

Wynne, L.C. (1981) Current concepts about schizophrenics and family relationships. *Journal of Nervous & Mental Disease*, **167**, 144–158.

Wynne, L.C. (1983) Family research and family therapy: a reunion? *Journal of Marital & Family Therapy*, **9**, 113–117.

Wynne, L.C. (ed.) (1988) *The State of the Art in Family Therapy Research*. Family Process Press, New York.

Wynne, L.C., Cromwell, R.L. & Matthysse, S. (1978) *The Nature of Schizophrenia: New Approaches to Research and Treatment*. Wiley, New York.

Wynne, L.C., Ryckoff, I., Day, J. & Hirsch, S. (1958) Pseudomutuality in the family relations of schizophrenics. *Psychiatry*, **21**, 205–220.

Zygmond, M.J. & Boorhem, H. (1989) Ethical decision making in family therapy. *Family Process*, **28**, 269–280.

Appendix A

The following are some of the major family therapy journals, listed in the order in which they were founded. This list is not exhaustive and articles on family therapy topics are published from time to time in psychiatry, psychology, social work and other journals.

Family Process is the longest established and one of the most prestigious family therapy journals. It was founded in 1962, when family therapy was in its infancy, by two of the pioneers in the field, Nathan Ackerman and Don Jackson. For over forty years now it has been a major resource and has remained one of the foremost journals in the field. It appears quarterly and is published by Blackwell Publishing in the USA.

Family Therapy was founded in 1972 by the Family Therapy Institute of Marin. It is now the journal of the California Graduate School of Family Psychology. It publishes 'succinct, well written papers within the broad field of family and marital therapy. Clinical articles devoted to techniques, and richly endowed with illustrative dialogue, are most highly regarded.' It appears three times a year and is published by Libra Publishers in the USA.

The Journal of Marital and Family Therapy is the official journal of the American Association for Marriage and Family Therapy. It was formerly the Journal of Marriage and Family Counseling and was founded in 1975. In its present form it dates from 1979. It appears quarterly. With over 20,000 subscribers it claims to be the best known and most influential family therapy journal in the world.

The Journal of Family Therapy is published in the UK by Blackwell Publishing for the Association for Family Therapy and Systemic Practice. It is the foremost UK family therapy journal and aims to advance the understanding and treatment of human relationships in couples, families, professional networks and wider groups by publishing articles on theory, research, clinical practice and training. It was founded in 1979 and appears quarterly.

The American Journal of Family Therapy is described as 'the incisive, authoritative, independent voice in an ever-changing field'. In addition to its general content, it includes the following regular sections:

- Family measurement techniques
- Family behavioral medicine and health

- Family law issues in family therapy practice
- Continuing education and training
- Book and media reviews
- Journal file
- International department

It is published in the USA by Routledge and appears five times a year. It was founded in 1979.

Contemporary Family Therapy: An International Journal is published by Springer Science and Business Media. It presents the latest developments in theory, research and practice pertaining to family therapy with an emphasis on examining families within the broader socio-economic and ethnic matrices of which families and their members are a part. It is published quarterly and dates from 1979.

The Australian and New Zealand Journal of Family Therapy is published by the Australian and New Zealand Journal of Family Therapy Association, Inc. It is reputed to be 'the most stolen professional journal in Australia' and is read by clinicians as well as by academics. It is 'a lively magazine that keeps its finger on the pulse of family therapy in Australia and New Zealand via local correspondents'. Four foreign correspondents report on developments in the United States and Europe. 'The Journal endeavours to retain the lightness of spirit and optimism that characterized early family therapy in Aotaoroa/New Zealand and Australia.' Publication started in 1985. It was formerly the Australian Journal of Family Therapy.

The Journal of Feminist Family Therapy provides an international forum for the exploration of the relationship between feminist theory and family therapy theory and practice. It is published in the USA by Haworth Press and has appeared quarterly since 1989. It aims to:

- Critique family therapy concepts from a feminist perspective with careful attention to cultural, class, and racial differences;
- Apply a feminist-sensitive perspective to the treatment issues particular to women such as depression, agoraphobia, eating disorders, incest, and domestic abuse;
- Explore the implications of a feminist approach to training and supervision in family therapy;
- Examine the field of family therapy and its organization and institutional structure from a feminist perspective;
- Describe clinical applications of feminist-informed treatment in family therapy.

The Family Journal: Counseling and Therapy for Couples and Families. This is the official journal of the International Association of Marriage and Family Counselors and is published in the USA by Sage Publications. *The*

Family Journal advances the theory, research and practice of counseling with couples and families from a family systems perspective. It provides 'groundbreaking, innovative scholarship for counseling researchers, educators and practitioners.' It appears quarterly and was founded in 1993.

The International Journal of Narrative Therapy and Community Work has been published quarterly since 2002. In each issue, practitioners from a range of different countries discuss the ideas and practices that are inspiring them in their work, the dilemmas they are grappling with, and the issues dearest to their hearts. The first section of each issue revolves around a particular theme, while the second consists of a collection of practice-based papers on various topics. The journal has four issues per year and is published in Australia by Dulwich Centre Publications. It is the successor to the Dulwich Centre Journal.

Index of Authors

Subject Index